Where Spring Never Came

Widnes 1919-1945

Jean M. Morris

Widnes and St. Helens, where are situated the principal works in the alkali industry, are at all times the most dreary of places. Their especial ugliness is, however, never more marked than when the spring is making beautiful every nook and corner of England, for the spring never comes hither. It never comes because, at Widnes nor at St. Helens, is there any place in which it can manifest itself. The foul gases, which belched forth night and day from the many factories, have killed every tree and every blade of grass for miles around .... trees cannot live here but men must.

Robert H. Sherard
"White Slaves of England" (1896)

Published 2007 by arima publishing

www.arimapublishing.com

ISBN 978 1 84549 255 7

Printed and bound in the United Kingdom

Typeset in Palatino Linotype 10/14

arima publishing
ASK House, Northgate Avenue
Bury St Edmunds, Suffolk IP32 6BB
t: (+44) 01284 700321

www.arimapublishing.com

For my grandchildren, Conor and Sean

Acknowledgements

One of the joys of working on this book has been the experience of receiving the generous help of so many different people. The Staff of record offices, various libraries, and other more specialised archives have been generous with their time and assistance. Numerous local people were willing to share their memories, family correspondence, and other memorabilia with me. Industrial companies and organisations allowed me access to their records, while friends and past colleagues near and far shared their knowledge and their time. I wish to thank all those who helped me in any way in the research work that has been the basis of this book.

There are a number of people to whom I owe a special gratitude. Firstly, I would like to thank Lord Ashley of Stoke for his generosity of spirit, and for his continued interest, support and friendship. I thank him particularly for offering, once again, to write the endorsement for my book. I am proud to have his name associated with this work, especially as threads of his own background are inextricably woven into the history of this town.

Dr. William Petrie, as usual, was munificent with his support and advice. Irish Labour historian, Conor McCabe; Virginia Hyvarinen, an archivist from New York; and American writer and historian Dr. Richard Hudelson, were all extremely helpful and amazingly generous with their time, information, and correspondence relating to Jack Carney. I sincerely thank all these people for their help.

Halton Librarian, Jean Bradburn, was enormously helpful and supportive throughout my research. The Staff at Widnes Library also deserve special mention; therefore I would like to thank Nikki Lamb and Joan Taylor for their help and patience during the seemingly endless periods of my research. I would especially like to say thank you to Rosie Parker, whose help, good humour, and infectious enthusiasm gave me an encouraging boost whenever I started to flag.

Paul Meara, of the Catalyst Museum, once again gave me unlimited access to their archives, as well as additional information and answers to queries. Special thanks are also due to Kevin Lucas who kindly read the manuscript for egregious errors – any that remain will be entirely my own. Robert Martindale was able to provide many of the local photographs from his extensive collection. Gordon Gilmour and Robin Faulkner provided information and photographs relating to Widnes Cricket Club. Finally, I would like to say a very special thank you to my friend, Mary Riley, not only for sharing her memories of the war years, but also for the countless interesting and stimulating conversations over the years.

This book is essentially about local people and the events which affected our communities, so without individual recollections and oral history this book would have no real substance. I am fortunate to have received an enormous amount of support and information from local people whose testimony to the past has been invaluable. I would like to thank all those who provided information and who have allowed me to document these facts in this book. It would be almost impossible to name everyone, but they know who they are and I thank them most sincerely.

I would like to state that I am entirely responsible for the contents of this book and I alone am accountable for any errors or omissions that may have inadvertently occurred within these pages.

Contents

Preface

In my previous book, *"Into the Crucible"*, I described the development of Widnes from the inception of the chemical industries in the 1840s up until the time of the First World War. That book was a story of industrial and population growth, of human resourcefulness and determination, and also of the dire social and economic conditions experienced by communities in this town. It seems only natural that I should follow up on this by providing a sequel that will bring our history into the realms of living memory.

Widnes had rapidly developed from almost nothing in the nineteenth century. It had no former nucleus prior to industrialisation. By the 1870s a whole new society had formed to meet the needs of the chemical industry. The early industrial workers who came into Widnes included people from other countries as well as the internal migrants who came from all corners of this island. These new townspeople formed the fabric of our society and the majority of our present day inhabitants descend from these early immigrants.

The rapid and unparalleled population growth in Widnes during the nineteenth century created numerous social problems. These problems arose essentially out of the interactions of masses of human beings living in close proximity to one another. The crowded urban developments of substandard housing and the dreadful working conditions did not provide an opportunity for a pleasant life. In the factories, the outlook of the industrial worker was confined by factory discipline to the dull performance of monotonous repetitive tasks in hazardous and unhealthy surroundings. Away from work, the pub was a more pleasant prospect than the dismal squalor of their overcrowded homes. In consequence, a way of life evolved which was a response to that environment.

Widnes is rich in history yet there are aspects of its history that remain little known, even to lifetime residents. Like everywhere else, personal and social circumstances play a role in creating meaning. In a curious way, the evidence of our history is both visible and invisible, depending on who is telling the story and to whom it is being told. In this book, I would like to touch on subjects and events in this town that have had no previous written emphasis, and bring into focus the names of people who made outstanding contributions to the benefit of our community. Many of our worthy men have had their names perpetuated in street names. However, some real heroes were consigned to history without recognition of their valuable roles in service to the people of this town.

Those of you who read *"Into the Crucible"* will remember that Dr. John O'Keeffe diligently served this town for almost 40 years, part of that time as Medical Officer of Health. He dedicated the greater part of his life to the welfare of the poor of Widnes and endeavoured to improve living conditions within the town. The provision of our Public Library was due to his determined efforts, although there are no formal acknowledgements of this or of his many other important works in the town. Likewise, in later times, there was Councillor Dan Garghan, who led hunger marches and worked hard to ensure that the children of unemployed workers did not starve during periods of economic depression. Another who deserves special mention in these pages is Councillor David Lewis, who was largely involved in the development of the architectural layout of the modern town and its road systems. He served this town for numerous years, not only as a town councillor but also as a prominent member of the Primitive Methodist Church and the Free Church Council. David Lewis was a devout and compassionate man who attempted to improve living standards in the town. He was also a man of vision who made a valuable contribution to our written history by producing a booklet entitled *"Widnes: a review and forecast"* (1910). In a postscript written on 3rd May 1911, David Lewis said that his hope for the future of the town was: *"that her people may be well "towned" and prosperous, and that she may never lack men and women possessing ideals and enthusiasm and willing to serve"*

This book, *"Where Spring never came"*, covers the period from 1919 to 1945. This phase, from the end of one war to the end of another, spans many momentous social and historical events in England and worldwide. The book deals with these events and their impact on the citizens of our town, and the social problems that faced a changed society. As in my previous book, I have included relevant local issues, local personalities, and a general history of the town during these decades. In order to avoid embarrassment to living relatives I have omitted names from many of these reports – however, some names are included in cases where this information is already in the public domain and where I think the content is unlikely to cause offence to any persons living.

In earlier years, the town had received people from other parts of the United Kingdom and from the Baltic regions. The various ethnic groups that populated the town formed the structure of our society as later generations intermarried and became part of mainstream life. However, from 1920 onwards, Official Immigration Authorities were empowered to exclude all foreign nationals who had either not received official permission to enter this country, or who had lacked a completed landing or embarkation card. This *"Aliens Restriction Act"* was a stringent piece of legislation that had been pushed through Parliament in an upsurge of panic following an influx of aliens during the first war. Although this procedure did not apply to British or Commonwealth citizens, it did have an effect on people of other nationalities and numbers coming from Eastern Europe decreased considerably, even though those who genuinely wished to settle here were seldom excluded. Subsequently between 1919 and 1931 only 758 people who were described as "Poles" settled in this country.

Whilst our town had received countless immigrants during the early years of industrialisation, the 20th century provided opportunities for British nationals to try their luck at a new life in other countries. *The Empire Settlement Act of 1922* assisted those people who wished to move to other countries in the Commonwealth. Many Widnesians were attracted by offers of assisted passages to places like Australia; Canada; New Zealand and Southern Rhodesia.

In the period 1919 to 1945 we saw the introduction of many new laws, social reforms, and technological changes. The country also experienced a general strike, a great depression, an abdication crisis and the gathering clouds that heralded the Second World War. In 1939, Widnesians left home in uniform as the country went to war once again with Germany. How these events influenced our local communities, as well as the local events and controversies of those times, are documented here in the second volume of my history of Widnes.

Within these pages I have tried to evoke, fairly, the manifold development and significant features of our society and culture over this period. I have also tried to illuminate the experiences of people who left no illustrious names behind them. The lives of ordinary people are seldom deemed worthy of historical record, but these forgotten men and women are the basic fabric of our social order. Their lives are the threads from which our present society is woven and their weighty effort strengthened the base on which this town was built.

Jean M. Morris
Widnes, 2007

The Aftermath of War

In 1918 Lloyd George promised the electorate that they would have a land fit for heroes to live in. As the country gradually returned to peace many of the returning "heroes" found that they had returned to a housing shortage, high prices, and profiteering as well as large-scale unemployment. Therefore, the start of this new decade was to be greeted with little optimism by the people of Widnes and the general population of the country.

At the start of 1920 Lloyd George was beginning to lose support not only amongst the members of the coalition but also among members of his own party. Some MPs were calling for reforms, which would inevitably lead to an increase in taxes, and national newspapers accused the Government of *"squander mania"*. The aftermath of the war had left the country with a whole new set of problems. The increased cost of living was blamed on the flood of paper money and manufactured credit due to the war. Because increasing the "national debt" had paid for the bulk of the war, there were now problems with repayment.

In the 1918 election, Unionist candidate Colonel William Hall Walker was elected MP for the Widnes division. It was said at the time that this election was the quietest on record. However, the following year, in 1919, Colonel Hall Walker, a member of the Walker brewing family[1], was elevated to the peerage and became Lord Wavertree. The by-election that followed was to be an

---

[1] *The Walker Art Gallery in Liverpool was opened with the generous patronage of this family.*

historic one because the people of Widnes elected Arthur Henderson as their first Labour MP.

In view of our long record of having a Labour representative in Parliament, I suppose Arthur Henderson should take a place in the history of our town as being the first of many. Henderson had previously been MP for Barnard Castle and during that time held a cabinet post. In May 1915 Herbert Asquith invited him to join his Coalition Government. He served as President of the Board of Education and later as Paymaster General. He resigned after Lloyd George and the cabinet voted against his proposals for an International Conference on the war, in Stockholm. Arthur Henderson had numerous disagreements with other politicians, mainly because he believed that Germany was being treated too harshly after the war. As a result of these views, and public opinion in the aftermath of war, he lost his Barnard Castle seat in the 1918 election. He returned to the House of Commons the following year as MP for our town, and became chief whip of the Labour Party before being defeated by Dr. G. C. Clayton in the 1922 General Election. Over the following years, Henderson served as an MP for both Newcastle and Burnley, and became the temporary leader of the Labour Party after the resignation of Ramsey MacDonald in August 1931. Between 1932 and 1935 he chaired the Geneva Disarmament Conference and his work in this area was rewarded when he received *The Nobel Peace Prize* in 1934, he died the following year.

The advent of a new decade here in Widnes, as in many other towns, brought into focus a whole series of social issues relating to housing, industry, and high unemployment. These issues were causing grave concern amongst the populace. The editorial for the final issue of *The Widnes Weekly News* for the year 1919 made the following observations:

"What a vista of possibility the opening of 1919 offered! When we rang out the old year, we had experienced a brief respite from the thunder of the

guns and the interlocking of human beings in deadly strife. Over three hundred and fifty days have since been given in which to reap the fruits of victory, but it has been dead men fruit. During the greater part of five years of war, we sowed the wind, and we are truly reaping the whirlwind. He would be a brave man who would face an intelligent audience in an endeavour to prove that in any one particular the people are satisfied with the results so far ensuing from the most tremendous sacrifice in history".

This then was the opinion of the citizens of Widnes as the fingers of time moved towards a new decade and 1920 made its debut.

The process of commemorating the local war dead had begun in 1919 and during that year a number of memorials were installed in the town. In February, the parishioners of St. Paul's Church, in Victoria Square, attended an unveiling ceremony for a memorial window. In June, a crucifix was unveiled in St. Michael's R.C. Church, Ditton, dedicated to the fallen of the parish. The previous month, May 1919, Colonel Ireland Blackburne and his family announced their intention to erect a War Memorial on Hale village green. In the Civic Chambers, Widnes Town Council set up a committee for the purpose of overseeing plans to erect a War Memorial for all the local men who had lost their lives in that bitter conflict.

The shared experiences of war had forged many friendships and most of the returning soldiers were keen to keep the bonds of comradeship strong. Members of the 14th Battery, R.F.A., otherwise known as *"The Widnes Battery"*, organised a Reunion Ball at The Borough Hall in May 1919. Lieutenant Colonel Stanley Rimmer, of Woolton, attended this event for the purpose of decorating a number of local men. A Corporal Connolly was awarded the *Distinguished Conduct Medal* and the *Military Medal*, while Sergeants Hankinson and Hennigan, and Gunner George Morris, also received the *Military Medal*. Colonel Rimmer spoke of

the gallant way the men of the Widnes Battery had gone to war in
1914.   He said:

*"How pleased he was to be once again among the men who were but a few
of the many who had volunteered at the commencement of the war and
who had set such a fine example. The four men he had the honour of
decorating that evening showed the merit of the Battery. Widnes had
reason to be proud of them and he hoped that they would soon have the
whole lot of the boys home again".*

By that time two thirds of them had returned home.   The stated
record of the Widnes Battery, at that time, was:

Military Cross:	*Major A.W. Gossage*
	Lieut. E.C. Whelpton
	Lieut. W. Roberts
Meritorious Service Medal:	*Sergeant Major B. Hall*
	Sergeant Royden
Distinguished Conduct Medal:	*Sergeant S. Matthews*
	Sergeant J. Royden
	Corporal Connolly
Military Medal:	*Sergeant T. Hankinson*
	Sergeant B. Hennigan
	Bombardier J. Forshaw
	Sergeant S. Harrison
	Gunner G. Morris
	Bombardier E. Dalton
	Corporal W. Lawton
	Corporal W. Connolly
French Military Medal:	*Driver J. Martin*
	Driver B.J. Turton
Croix de Guerre:	*Lieut. E. Gardner*

Over the years, many youthful imaginations have been fired by the exploits of the pioneer aviators. Films depicting the flying aces of the First War, with aerial combat between the legendary "Red Baron" (Manfred von Richthofen) and his British counterparts have been the stuff of cinema history. However, in later times, the young boys of Widnes who watched those films were probably unaware that a local man had been one of the "real" heroes of *The Royal Flying Corps*. This man, Thomas Mottershead, lost his life as a result of the terrible burns he sustained during an act of outstanding bravery. Much has been written about the exploits of the members of *The Royal Flying Corps*[2] during this period. The names of Mick Mannock, Albert Ball, and James McCudden are famous ones, but alongside those there are many references to Thomas Mottershead, all of which emphasise his outstanding courage. One book states: *"Mottershead's fighting spirit was undimmed despite his maturity and his dependants – he was twenty four, with a wife and a baby son"*[3]

The death of Flight-Sergeant Thomas Mottershead, in January 1917, was widely reported locally. Graphic accounts of the incident that resulted in him being posthumously awarded *The Victoria Cross* appeared in the national and local press. Thomas Mottershead, who lived at 12 Market Street, enlisted in August 1914 and became a first-class air pilot with *The Royal Flying Corps*. Prior to the incident for which he gained *The Victoria Cross*, he was awarded *The Distinguished Conduct Medal* in 1916. An extract from the Official War Office Record states that:

"The King has been pleased to award the Victoria Cross to No. 1396 Sergeant Thomas Motterhead, late R.F.C. for the most conspicuous bravery and skill while attacked at an altitude of 9,600 feet. The petrol tank was pierced and the machine set on fire. Enveloped in flames, which his Observer, Lieut. Gower, was unable to subdue, this very gallant

[2] The forerunner to the Royal Air Force
[3] *The Royal Flying Corps"* – Ralph Barker (Constable & Robinson Ltd) 2002

soldier succeeded in bringing his aeroplane back to our lines, and though he made a successful landing the machine collapsed on touching the ground, pinning him beneath the wreckage, from which he was subsequently rescued.   Though suffering extreme torture from burns, Sergeant Mottershead showed the most conspicuous presence of mind in the careful selection of a landing place, and his wonderful endurance and fortitude undoubtedly saved the life of his Observer.   He has since succumbed to his injuries".

The Victoria Cross was presented personally by the King to Thomas Mottershead's widow, Lillian, at an open-air ceremony in Hyde Park on 2nd June 1917[4].

The Peace Treaty was finally signed on the 28th June 1919, and on Saturday, 19th July 1919, "Peace Day Celebrations" were held all over Britain. The celebrations in this Borough were presided over by the Mayor of Widnes, Alderman George Davies.   A souvenir programme of the event included a page entitled *"Service Roll and Roll of Honour"* the text is given below[5]

"The town of Widnes in round figures has supplied some 10,000 men to the British Forces.   This seems a very high proportion – almost 1 in 3 of the total population, but it should be remembered that many workers were attracted to the town during the war through its industries, and were gradually absorbed into the Army through local channels.   Of this ten thousand, roughly 1 in 10, or 1,000 all told, have been killed in action, or died of wounds or disease, or have been reported as missing.   1,400 incapacitated men are on the books of the local War Pensions Committee. Widnes men to the number of 150 have been prisoners of war, either in Germany or the East.   Over 300 naval and military distinctions and decorations have been gained by sailors and soldiers from the town and its immediate district".

---

[4] Thomas Mottershead was interred at Bailleul Cemetery in France. His funeral was conducted with full military honours on 13th January 1917.

[5] *Celebration Programme* – kindly loaned to author by Mr. M. Freeman

The same booklet gives a view of industrial Widnes and its contribution to the war effort.

"Just as Widnes through its intimate associations with the renowned 29th, 55th, and 57th Divisions earned its full share of military and martial glory, so in the Army generally, the Air Force, the Navy, and the Mercantile Marine, the Widnes man was ever to the fore. The town was represented, and worthily represented, in every arm and in every theatre of war.

At home, in the Munitions industry, the part played by Widnes was of paramount importance. In heavy chemicals, in bases for high explosives, in poison gases, smoke screens, antiseptics, sanitation agents, in kegs, drums and cases, trench covers, dugout roofs, stoves, castings of all sorts, copper, iron, brass – in endless supplies of manufactured materials for use overseas, soaps, glycerines, chloroforms, disinfectants, paints, oils, extracts, colours – the name of Widnes was a name to conjure with. The output of the chemical and metal trades, in short, enters in so many ways into the general composition of wartime trade and commerce that towns of the Widnes type – and they are not many – enjoyed a special and unusual prominence."[6]

There was a natural and understandable revulsion against war in the 1920s. The war had affected not only those who had participated in the combat but also their families at home. Most people held a conviction that another war should be fought only as a last resort, and this helped to produce a pacifist movement in the following decades. In the years immediately following the end of the war, there was concern about the welfare of ex-servicemen and women. For this reason, *The British Legion* was founded in May 1921 to provide care and support.

The Widnes War Memorial was finally unveiled in September 1921. The reports of the unveiling ceremony and the events preceding it are very moving. The official party of civic

---

[6] *Peace Celebration Programme* – courtesy of Mr. M. Freeman

dignitaries had assembled in Victoria Square, along with Lord Derby, who was to perform the unveiling ceremony at Victoria Park. Shortly before 3 o'clock, the dignitaries were conveyed in a procession of cars to the Park, accompanied by Mounted Police and the Band of The Prince of Wales Volunteers. Behind the cars were the relatives and friends of the fallen, demobilised men of military and naval services, and following on, at the rear of the procession, was *Gossages Brass Band*. It was said that a solid chain of townspeople lined the route from the Square to the Park. As the procession moved away from Victoria Square, Lord Derby noticed a young man on crutches who seemed intent on hobbling to Victoria Park. He asked his driver to stop the car and offer the young man a lift. The young man, who had lost a leg in the War, was subsequently conveyed to Victoria Park in the company of Lord Derby and the Mayor and Mayoress of Widnes. This young man was Private Wright, who came from Moss Bank.

The scenes at the Memorial, as one can imagine, were those of extreme sadness and grief. Lord Derby himself was overcome with emotion and broke down when the Mayor expressed his thanks on behalf of the townspeople. Among the densely packed crowd around the memorial were Mrs. Mottershead, the widow of *The Victoria Cross* recipient, and her small son. She carried a small bouquet of garden flowers as a personal tribute. Corporal J. Kerr, of *The Irish Guards*, who had himself been wounded at the first Battle of Ypres, laid a wreath on behalf of the British Legion. The Mayor made a very moving speech of which the following is an extract:

"We have here a Memorial intended to commemorate the sacrifice made by men who prior to the outbreak of the great and devastating war, now happily concluded, lived and moved amongst us and who in so many cases were our friends and associates. These men surrendered their lives in what we believe and know to have been a righteous cause. With all other brave and patriotic sailors and soldiers serving their King and Country, they saved us from invasion by a cruel and remorseless enemy,

and our glorious Empire from devastation. Their places can never be replaced in the memories of those dear ones they left behind. At the cost of reopening old wounds and reawakening sad memories, it is to us who survive a pleasing if melancholy duty to tender to all those relations and friends of these valiant men our most sincere and deepest sympathy, and we ask them to regard this memorial as an expression of determination on our part that their great and noble deeds shall never be obliterated from our memories, whilst future generations will regard with pride this memento of the sacrifices and bravery of those who delivered their beloved country from the oppressor. This column has been provided out of funds munificently subscribed by our townsmen and it will in the future be the proud duty of the Town Council to preserve it. This duty will be considered by them in the light of a privilege and will be faithfully executed".

For the families, and the townspeople of Widnes, the names of obscure places in France, Belgium, and Turkey had suddenly acquired a sinister fame and familiarity. Ypres and Loos, the Somme and Passchendaele, Vimy, Gallipolli and the Dardenelles, were all scenes of terrible carnage. The number of names on our War Memorial bears witness to the loss experienced by numerous families throughout the Borough. The silent victims of this war were the bereaved. It is easy to forget that as a result of the war the town inherited a large number of widows and fatherless children. With the loss of the breadwinner, some families were left in dire economic circumstances because, at that time, widows with children to support were given no State aid.

Apart from the dreadful loss of human life, many men returned home with permanent physical disabilities. There were also men suffering from "shell-shock" who had been so traumatised by their experiences in the trenches that they were left with severe and lasting mental disabilities. The nightmare of trench warfare scarred a whole generation of men. The soldiers had lived for months amid squalor. They were unable to wash properly or change their clothes for days on end and living underground left them filthy and riddled with lice. Rain turned the trenches into quagmires and the mud and slime meant that many soldiers succumbed to crippling "trench foot". Decomposing human remains lying unburied attracted maggots and flies, as well as rats and mice. Naturally, this meant that disease was rife in these unwholesome conditions.[7] The soldiers also lived in constant fear of death as they were often under heavy bombardment. Along with the fear that the next huge shell would kill them, and the constant threat of snipers, there was the terrible prospect of the clouds of poison gas.

When we consider these dreadful conditions, we should also remember that two Widnes men were shot by firing squad – and their dependants denied the right to any pension. These two men were in the same regiment and were shot within days of each other in February 1917, in Mesopotamia. In those days, the term "post traumatic stress disorder" was unheard of, but there is little doubt that many of the 306 men who were shot for "desertion or cowardice" during this terrible war were indeed suffering from this condition. In the case of one of those Widnes men, his crime was to fall asleep on duty. He was 22 years old. At the time of writing, the Government has just gained Parliamentary approval for a group pardon for all 306 soldiers who were executed during the First World War. This seems fitting, as all these men were victims of war who paid the ultimate cost of this terrible conflict.

---

[7] *Daily Mail Correspondent - 1917*

The 1920s

The 1920s was a period of re-adjustment.   Initially, people were more concerned with things like peace negotiations, demobilisation, and a great desire to punish Germany, than they were with the economic and social state of the nation.   However, by 1920, concern about the actual conduct of the war, and the failure of the great sacrifices made to bring about "a brave new world", left many disillusioned. Most families had been seriously affected by the events of the war.   Some had been bereaved, while others had husbands, brothers, and sons returning with serious disabilities.   As unemployment grew, this concern began to manifest itself. Numerous writers and journalists of the time have documented these feelings far more expressively than I am able or qualified to do.[8] The unemployment problem was to remain a chronic feature throughout this decade and strikes were to become an expression of social as well as economic conflict.

Today, we find it hard to accept the fact that thousands of young men who died fighting for their country had at that time been considered unworthy of the vote. In the early years of the century, the registered electorate was only 60% of all British men and those who were left out were mainly working-class.   In 1918, *The Representation of the People Act* brought some change, enfranchising nearly all men and most women over 30 years of age.   There is no doubt that the war had been pivotal in accelerating this franchise reform.   In 1920 women under 30 still had no vote although there had now been a great deal of advancement in breaking down the barriers of inequality. I think it

---

[8] Suggested reading: " *England After the War*" (Charles Masterman)

is also worth mentioning that at that time there was still a system of "dual voting" for certain businessmen and university graduates, so whilst some people were not entitled to vote, others had dual voting rights. This dual system did not end entirely until 1948.

At the beginning of 1920 Lady Nancy Astor became the first woman to take a seat in the House of Commons[9] – her maiden speech concerned the evils of drink. Later, our local MP, Dr. G. C. Clayton, was asked by the Widnes Wesleyans to give support to Lady Astor's "Bill" which would prohibit the sale of alcohol to anyone under 18 years of age. In Widnes also, women were entering public life and adapting to new roles in society. In March 1920, the first list of appointments of women to be Justices of the County Palatine included two Widnes women, Mrs. Squires and Mrs. Swales. Both these women were closely associated with charitable work in the town and both were members of the Widnes Queens Nurses Association and the Red Cross. Tragically, Mrs. Squires was killed in a car crash in June 1927. Her husband Councillor Squires, was badly injured, he died later that year.

At this time, many of the townspeople were immigrants or the descendants of earlier immigrants. In the early days, immigrants into Widnes had suffered status disadvantages and racial discriminations. The process of assimilation had been gradual, particularly for the Lithuanians and Poles who, because of major language and cultural differences, were always going to find it more difficult to integrate. It was much easier for the Irish who shared the same language as the native population, were British citizens by an *Act of Union,* and also because they had been here longer, some having come into the town with the opening of the

---

[9] *Lady Astor was the first woman to take her seat in the House of Commons, although she was not the first elected woman M.P. Irish activist, Lady Constance Markiewicz, was the first woman elected, although she never took her seat in Parliament.*

first chemical factories. By the 1920s a large proportion of the Widnes Irish community were second or even third generation.

Among the legacies of the war were a reinforced xenophobia and a fear that immigrants would take jobs from the native population. Restrictions on immigration were strictly imposed and the entry and employment of "aliens" was rigorously controlled, almost to the point of total exclusion. Because of this, Eastern European immigration into England virtually stopped in the inter-war period, so practically no new immigrants from those countries joined the existing Widnes communities during this time. However, these long-distance migrants continued to use a network of family connections. This meant that there was still movement of Lithuanians and Poles to and from Widnes, from other places, or to other places, in Britain. On the other hand, the Irish were classed as British subjects and there were no restrictions on their entry into this country.

Because of the multicultural make-up of our local society, it meant that world events were closely followed here in Widnes. Numerically, the Irish were by far the largest of these groups and consequently there was a great deal of interest in what was happening across the Irish Sea. During the war years the troubles in Ireland had persisted, culminating in a "Rising" in Dublin, at Easter, 1916. Shortly afterwards the leaders of this uprising were executed. Prior to these executions there had been little popular support in Ireland for the rebels. In fact, at that time many Irish had members of their family serving in the British army in France. However, there was a dramatic change in attitude and a marked escalation in violence in direct response to these executions.

Home Rule, which had been promised to Ireland years before, was postponed because of the war. In December 1920 Parliament passed the *Government of Ireland Act,* which gave Southern Ireland (26 counties) and Northern Ireland (6 counties) their own Parliaments. However, Westminster would still have control of key policy areas and retain ultimate sovereignty. This situation was far from satisfactory to the Irish who were, naturally, seeking independence. The violence continued, with some dreadful atrocities being committed, and by January 1921 British policy in Ireland was being criticised not only here but also internationally. The League of Nations put pressure on the Government for a change of policy, and there was much discontent in Parliament at the way the Irish situation was being handled. Herbert Asquith said: *"Things are being done in Ireland which would disgrace the blackest annals of the lowest despotism in Europe"*[10]. On 11th July a truce was called.

In January 1922 the Dāil of the Irish Free State and the British Parliament ratified the *British-Irish Treaty* and a Governor General was appointed. Much controversy still surrounds Lloyd George's part in bringing about this treaty. Some commentators believed he deliberately misled the Irish negotiators by promising a "Boundary Commission", which would make "Ulster" unviable. The signing of *"The Treaty"* was expected to end the troubles in Ireland, but this was not to be the case. In June, anti-treaty republicans seized the Chief of Staff of the Irish army and held him hostage in The Four Courts building in Dublin. There was a huge split in the Irish Republican Army (IRA) and a group who opposed the provisos of the treaty rose in arms against the pro-treaty section. This was followed by a period of heavy fighting in Dublin. The British Government threatened that their troops would again be used in Dublin unless the Free State acted. This statement was the trigger that began a bitter period of civil war in Ireland. This civil war lasted until May 1923. In Widnes, with its large Irish population, these events were of great interest and were being closely monitored. Meetings were organised throughout the town to discuss these terrible developments. There was much discussion and considerable disagreement between the various sections of Widnes Irish, as some were pro-treaty and others anti-treaty.

[10] Contemporary Britain 1914-1979 – *Robert Pearce (Longman History)*

Sadly, the Irish conflict was cruelly felt nearer to home as some Widnes soldiers, serving in the British army, lost their lives in Ireland during this troubled period.

The Lithuanian and Polish members of our local society were also closely watching events in their own homelands in Eastern Europe. The Russian Revolution in 1917 was of considerable interest to them as they had experienced at first hand the effects of the Tsarist regime in their native lands. Indeed, the entire world knew of the sufferings Lithuania and Poland had experienced in the autocratic grip of Russia. To Widnes immigrants, the uprising and overturning of this established system would have impacted greatly upon friends and relatives back in their homelands. Other earlier and later events in their native lands would also have caused concern. In 1915 the Germans had occupied Lithuania and in 1917 they allowed the Lithuanians to form an assembly called *"The Taryba"*. On 16th February 1918 *The Taryba* declared Lithuania independent. Following this, in December 1919 the country was again witnessing aggression as the revolutionary "Bolshevik" forces invaded the eastern borderlands of the Lithuanian Republic. In October 1920, there was a further unpleasant development as the Poles occupied Vilnius and hung onto the city. For Lithuanians living in Widnes all these events had been a cause of great unease as many of them still had parents and other relatives back home. The Polish occupation of Vilnius created considerable tension between local Lithuanians and Poles. The Catholic churches in Widnes said special prayers at this time for the people of Lithuania[11]. In 1920 the situation with Russia resolved itself as Russia finally recognised Lithuanian independence. Although Lithuania had now freed itself politically from Russia, the British authorities persisted in classifying all Lithuanians (and Poles) as "Russians" or "Russian Poles".

---

[11] St. Marie's Parish archives

The 1920s was a period of some social improvement for most people – except the unemployed. In 1925 *The Pensions Act* finally made some provisions for widows and orphans, and payments of 10s.0d. to widows and 7s.6d[12] to orphans was made. Previously the only recourse in difficulty had been the dreaded Poor Law. In theory, the Poor Law system was meant to prevent destitution and starvation. Even with all its cruelties and humiliations, it was a genuine attempt to see that no one starved. In 1928 the State Pension scheme became more comprehensive with the provision of contributory pensions.

In 1928 *The Equal Franchise Act,* which saw the voting age for women in Britain reduced from 30 to 21, came into being. The main implications of this Act were that the proportion of women voters in the electorate was increased to approximately 53 per cent. The size of the country's total electorate also increased from 21.7 million to 28.9 million. In the following year, 1929, the first elections were held under universal adult suffrage. Labour won that election although, in hindsight, political observers have said that this was an unlucky win. Four months after they took office the "Wall Street Crash" triggered the worst depression the world had known. Few Governments around the world were able to survive this and the Labour Government was no exception.

By the mid 1920s countless homes had acquired a gramophone and the "wireless set" had been given pride of place in many Widnes households. *The Widnes Weekly News,* keeping abreast of current trends, was now running feature articles on gramophone recordings and wireless programme information. The men who worked at Widnes Foundry probably felt a special connection with the new "wireless" as many of them had been employed on the production and testing of Marconi's first steel masts. The influence of this new media on public mood became an important

---

[12] Pre-decimal currency conversion: 20 shilling (s) = £1. 12 pence (d) = 1 shilling.

feature of this, and the following decades. As the "wireless" gained in popularity throughout the country, there were concerns in Government about the control of this media. In 1926 it was decided that it was to be run by a Crown appointed chairman and governors, and would be funded by a licence fee. The new concern came into force in January 1927 and was subsequently called the *British Broadcasting Corporation* (BBC).

As the wireless arrived on the scene, other new entertainment "facilities" were also being unveiled. On 28th April 1923, 200,000 football fans saw the F.A. Cup Final held at newly opened Wembley Stadium for the first time. Bolton Wanderers beat West Ham 2-0. Here in Widnes, in that same year, another institution was founded when supporters of the hometown team started *The Widnes Supporters Club*. In the first season of this new decade, the Widnes team made a momentous start to their post war performance by winning The Lancashire Cup in 1920.

During this decade Victoria Road was still a prime shopping area. Here we would have found Unsworth's, competing for business with J. Phillips, Natco, and Frank Johnson in the realms of tailoring. A lady called Mrs. Corke offered millinery and dresses, while Calvert's continued to provide general drapery and quality wear for all the family. Stationers seemed to be plentiful in this road, so if you required writing materials Thomas Swale or Wilkinson's could supply a wide selection. R.J. Gow and Mather's sold newspapers and tobacco, whilst Dawson's provided the townspeople with gramophones and records. For those setting up home, all types of furnishings for the modern house were available from J. Harris & Sons or Barkla's.[13]

---

[13] See Notes

Industry and Employment

During the previous decade the industrial face of Widnes had continued to change. A number of new non-Leblanc companies had come to the town. W. J. Bush set up a works in the Marsh region in 1916 specialising in the manufacture of flavouring essences. Three years later Peter Spence & Sons established a works in Moorfield Road, manufacturing alum and other chemicals. The Gossage's Soap Works, which had been acquired by the Brunner Mond Company in 1911, was subsequently sold to Lever Brothers in 1920.

By 1920 the old Leblanc process of manufacture was coming to an end and many of the chemical companies of the early days had closed down. Soda was no longer made locally, although a new electrolytic process was now producing caustic soda and chlorine. The Mort-Liddell Works finally closed its doors in this first year of the new decade. The United Alkali Company was also drawing to the end of its days, before it would be absorbed into the new chemical amalgamation that was to be known as Imperial Chemical Industries.

Nationally, 1920 had started with good trade prospects but by the autumn the industrial boom was clearly over and unemployment was widespread throughout the country. Labour Party posters of the time show illustrations of returning soldiers and their destitute families, the captions read: *"Yesterday, the trenches - Today, unemployment"*.

In Widnes, by the end of the year, there were stoppages in many of the major works in the town. In December 1920 the

United Alkali Company closed all their works for 10 days – "laying off" in the region of 3000 men for that period. This meant that these men would have no income for the 3 weeks after Christmas. The company made provisions for bona-fide employees to have a loan of £1, which was to be repaid at the rate of 3 shillings a week when normal working was resumed. It was the first time in the history of the company that there had been such a long stoppage. A spokesman for the company said *"that it was unprecedented for vitriol plants to be stopped"* he blamed the state of the chemical trade in general and lack of orders in particular. The Birmingham Corrugated Iron Co. Ltd. also closed down that same weekend, saying that the works would be closed for *"an indefinite period"*. This shutdown was rendered necessary due to shortage of trade and the high price of steel. Widnes Foundry also gave their workers a "long" Christmas holiday, as did Gossages Soap Works; The Mersey Copper & Sulphate Company; Thos. Bolton & Sons; Peter Spence & Sons; and Orr's Zinc White Ltd. All these manufacturers claimed that business had not been too brisk for some time, so the Christmas period seemed a good time to have an extended break.

The war undoubtedly had an effect on the role and status of women. Because of the war, there were changes in the sort of work women were perceived as being capable of undertaking. Consequently, a vast influx of women into jobs previously occupied by men was in progress. It has been said that some employers seized the opportunity to use women as cheap labour, and so undermined the levels of wages and conditions for which the unions had previously won recognition. In Widnes, women had never been employed in the chemical industry until the war. However, prior to the war, women and children *had* worked in industries such as the textile trade and the coalmines in other parts of Lancashire. It should be said that, at that time, in almost every occupation women were paid less than men for doing the same work – even in the civil service and teaching.

After the demobilisation process, some women were forced to cede their jobs to returning soldiers. A number of Ex-Servicemen corresponded at length with the editor of *The Widnes Weekly News* on the subject of women in the workplace. It appears that the sight of female clerical staff employed by the Council had caused considerable anger

"I think the Corporation should lead the way in the matter of getting rid of female labour. So far as I can see all the old servants have come back, but still one can see lady clerks flitting about the Town Hall. What they do I am at a loss to understand. So far as I can see from my periodical visits to the Town Hall, each department seems well staffed without the employment of girls. I would suggest to the Council that a committee be formed to go into the whole matter and not leave it to individual heads of departments. While I agree that the Corporation should be a model employer, those in authority ought not at the same time to lose sight of the fact that they have a duty to the ratepayers. It would be interesting to know the amount paid in salaries at the present time compared with 1914".

Other disgruntled readers writing on the same topic aired their views – one correspondent wrote:

"It is high time someone took up the question of the continued employment of female labour. It makes one think that there was more behind the white feather incidents than met the eye. When young ladies presented young men with these emblems of cowardice was it from a spirit of patriotism or one of selfishness that they wanted to take their jobs? In the light of what is happening, it looks as if the latter was the motive. I wonder if some of these young ladies, many of whom can do without work, realise that they are in some cases the means of creating great hardship. It may be that in some instances they are the direct cause of kiddies being in want. I suggest that now is the opportunity for many young ladies to show their gratitude to those men who went out to fight, by giving up their jobs to ex-servicemen and ex-servicemen only".

A "disabled" reader also added his voice to the "outrage" of women being employed by Widnes Corporation.

"Might I be permitted to say a few words in your valuable paper with reference to the various letters published last week on the subject "Unemployment of Ex-servicemen" to commence with, I am quite in accordance with the remark that Widnes Corporation should "lead the way" by combing out female staff. Obviously, as another writer suggests, each case should be determined on its own merits, but I would like to know firstly, if the lady municipal clerks are necessary, and secondly, whether they are dependant on their remuneration for a living or does it go to satisfy a craving for the latest in crepe-de-chine blouses and rainbow hued stockings. By the way, imagine the ordinary male clerk arriving at the office in a frock coat and tall hat! The fact still remains that there is a large number of unemployed in Widnes. It is immaterial whether the Labour Exchange classes them as ex-servicemen or civilians".

The references to "fashions" may indicate the obvious changes in women's attitude to work and dress. The effects of the war meant that women were becoming more self-determining and financially independent. This was reflected in shorter skirts and hairstyles, and the wearing of "slacks", which had previously been unheard of. For married women, working outside the home was a new concept and for the first time they were being incorporated into the formal economy of the household.

The role of older children also changed between the war years and in its aftermath. "The little wage earner" was often a child of fourteen, or sometimes much younger. The fact that *The Fisher Education Act of 1902* had raised the school leaving age did not mean that industrial obligations on a child had ceased. Statistics show that the number of children of fourteen, or under, at work had quadrupled since 1918[14]. Sometimes children worked illegally. In many cases, because of economic hardship there were pressures

---

[14] *A Social History of England* – Asa Briggs (Penguin Books 1985)

to add to the family income as soon as possible, so this employment was considered a necessity.

In February 1921 the management of The British Asbestilite & Everite Company held their first annual dinner. Incidentally, the Managing Director, Mr. K. Fontana Jucker, was also the Italian Consul to Manchester. At that time, the "Everite Factory" had been in operation for just three and a half years, although the building work on the factory had started almost two years before that. In 1921, although industry in general was going through a bad patch, "The Everite" appeared to be fairly buoyant. The Managing Director told his staff that their products were of "permanent value". Of course, at that time no one was aware of the dangers of asbestos. He continued thus:

"I estimate that well over one million pounds worth of galvanised corrugated sheets rust and fade into thin air every year. This industry of corrugated asbestos cement sheets, on the other hand, produce an article which will eventually mean an enormous saving to this country by replacing material which is subject to decay; and further will release a substantial quantity of steel for more useful purposes. Apart from that, we have opened up an altogether new export market. Especially in the tropical countries, we do not compete with any existing British industry, as these sheets of ours, by virtue of their insulating properties are now used where before the main covering was palm leaves, earwigy materials; galvanised corrugated iron, which would have created an atmosphere like a furnace.

You have seen the latest developments in our work. I refer to the new asbestos cement gutters and rainwater goods department. After extensive experiments we have now put on the market an article which not only competes favourably with cast iron rainwater goods, of which it is well known there is a great shortage, but which has the solid advantage of not being affected by rust".

A 1920s Trade advertisement for Everite products said that:

There are many advantages to be derived from the use of Everite pipes and fittings. In the first place, the materials themselves, Asbestos and Cement, cannot corrode, and under normal conditions the fittings will last forever, becoming actually stronger with age. They also have an important advantage over the usual sheet metal in that they have insulative and heat resisting properties that eliminate condensation troubles.

The conditions under which a large majority of Widnes workers had to toil had improved only slightly in the years since Robert H. Sherard had shocked the country with his account of the Alkali Trade in Widnes. His *"White Slaves of England"* articles, written in 1896, gave graphic descriptions of actual incidents in Widnes chemical factories and cited individual cases:

A mere walk through a yard is dangerous, for the tanks leak here and there, and corrosive fluids drop and drop. One hears of a man who was slowly eaten to death in a vitriol-tank into which he had fallen, and in which he was caught fast. A priest tried to reach him to anoint him, but failed. Hundreds, powerless to help, were looking on. He joked at them between his screams. "Were they all out on strike to be idling there?" In Whiston Workhouse is a legless man, with whom an armless man keeps company. They were both alkali workers.

One wonders how the workers can clothe themselves. They must wear wool, for the gas rots cotton in forty-eight hours. Men are seen going home with their breeches roped around their legs, because their garments were sewn with cotton, and the seams have given; or in a network of woollen woof, the cotton warp having disappeared. I saw one man clothed mainly with an old nitre-bag.

The men work with a thick oakum gag or "muzzle" in their mouths, in a cloud of white particles. In the summer, the heat is quite intolerable. When they have done their work, they wash themselves with oil or tallow, and dry themselves on wisps of brown paper. This is all the toilet that they know. The use of water would flay them alive. [15].

Although some improvements had come about through various Government *Health and Safety Acts* there were still numerous accidents and deaths in the workplaces of Widnes. An Act of Parliament passed in 1897 meant that workmen would be compensated for accidents, but often these payments were little more than an insult. In 1921, no less than eight Widnes men met their deaths in their place of work that year. In January, a man was killed at Muspratt's Works[16]. In February, a man from Farnworth was killed at Sutton Manor Colliery. In March, four men were killed at the United Alkali Company. In August, a man was killed by a falling wall at the U.A.C's Liver Works, and in October a man fell to his death at the Widnes Gas Works. Throughout this decade there were numerous other industrial fatalities. Amongst them were the following incidents:

In February 1923 a man was crushed to death whilst unloading sand at Widnes Dock, in the same month a man died after falling from a ladder at the United Alkali Company. Two months later, a Widnes man was killed at Clock Face Colliery and in the same week, another miner was killed at Sutton Manor. In May 1924, a man was burned to death at J.H. Dennis & Co. when a chamber collapsed. In July 1925, a process worker in the employment of Messrs. Orr's Zinc White Ltd. died as a result of inhaling gas which was impregnated with arsenic. In March 1928, a man met his death by falling into a vat of caustic at Gossages works.

This is by no means a complete list of industrial accidents and fatalities during this decade. There were also numerous serious accidents, although thankfully, these did not all result in death.

---

[15] Robert.W.Sherard *"The White Slaves of England"*
(Pearson`s Magazine 1896)
[16] This man came to Widnes in 1874 from Banff and had lived in the town 47 years.

The deaths of the four young men at the United Alkali Company, in March 1921, left the people of West Bank shocked and saddened as three of these men were local residents. The accident happened at the electric power station belonging to the United Alkali Company. It appears that two of the men entered a cylinder (60 ft. high and 20 ft in diameter) to clear a blockage. After what seemed an unusually long absence, two other men followed to see what was happening. When none of the men returned the alarm was raised, but by this time, all four men had been fatally gassed. There were many volunteers and numerous attempts were made to go down into the cylinder to bring the men up. Two of the rescuers were also affected by the gas and were hospitalised. As the news of the accident spread around West Bank people started to congregate in small silent groups in the vicinity of the arches at Church Street and Parsonage Road. Then came the awful reality as the men were brought out on their journey to the mortuary. Three of the young men were in their twenties and the other was just 19 years old. To add to the awful loss experienced by their families, one family was experiencing double tragedy as two of these young men were brothers-in-law, being married to two sisters.

The fact that the plant where this accident happened was, at that time, considered one of the most modern and advanced in the country also added to the feeling of disbelief that spread through the district. Before the war, there had been no great demand for power in the chemical industry and a number of works had small power stations, which were adequate for their needs. However, during the war there had been an increase in power requirements at the Pilkington Sullivan Works because of the expansion of the electrolytic production of chlorine. In 1920, the United Alkali Company found it necessary to establish a central power station for its Widnes factories. This new power station was sited at West Bank Dock because this location was convenient for obtaining fuel and water for the turbine condensers.

As a note of interest, in later years I.C.I. found the need to greatly increase the capacity of the West Bank power station in order to meet the increased demands for the factories within the group. A high voltage transmission supplied the sub-stations at various works and many miles of 6000 and 11000-volt cables were laid beneath the streets of Widnes. Two power stations, at West Bank and Weston Point, were linked in an electrical grid, which served all the company's factories in the Widnes and Runcorn area.[17]

In January 1921 the Town Council put a committee in place to deal with the distribution of *Government Unemployment Grants*. The Government had provided these funds for the purpose of assisting Local Authorities to carry out work on which the unemployed could be engaged. By September of that year, a schedule of work was inaugurated for the relief of the unemployed. This public utility work included the widening and improvement of some of the roads in the Borough and some work in the Gas and Water Departments. The road improvement scheme included Liverpool Road from Stewards Lane to Hough Green Station; Hale Road from Chestnut Lodge to Ditton Bridge; Chapel Lane and Prescot Road; Norlands Lane and Cronton Lane. Earlier that year there had also been formal sanctions from the Ministry of Health for the construction of Leigh Avenue and improvements to Lowerhouse Lane and Frederick Street.

In March 1921 The United Alkali Company announced that they intended to reduce their workmen's' wages:

"In view of the deplorable conditions of industry and likelihood of a decrease to the cost of living a reduction in wages of our processmen, labourers and others is imperative. Notice has therefore been given to Trade Union Representatives and those workers whose wages have

---

[17] *A History of the Chemical Industry in Widnes*: D.W.F. Hardie (I.C.I. 1950)

hitherto followed the chemical trade awards will be reduced on or after 31ˢᵗ March 1921. The Industrial Court Award of 4ᵗʰ January 1921 will be reversed. All men 21 and over who are employed on time work and are in receipt of twelve and a half percent bonus on earnings shall have deducted from their wages 3s.6d. per week being at the rate of 7d per day or shift for each day or shift worked. Boys and youths 18 years of age or over, but under 21, shall have deducted 2s.6d per week being the rate of 6d per day or shift worked".

An official of The Ministry of Labour intervened in this matter and it was decided to postpone the reductions until the end of April, in order to give the union representatives time to organise meetings of their members to explain these actions. It is worth noting that the United Alkali Company's profits for the years 1921 and 1922 were £1,003.377. Their profits had been increasing steadily since 1913. In 1923 they declared a dividend of 10% on the ordinary shares and also gave their shareholders a free gift of 308,000 bonus shares.

A short while after the United Alkali Company announced that they would reduce wages, "The Everite" also made cuts to their rates of pay. The firm stated that they generally followed the movement of wages in the chemical trade but that the economic circumstances of the business also necessitated this reduction. You will remember, not long before this, their Managing Director was telling his staff that they had opened up a successful export market for their products, where *"they did not compete with any other British Company"*. The proposed reduction prompted *The General Workers Union* to take the matter to an Industrial Court, to decide whether the rate paid to piece workers was sufficient. The men concerned were employed in handling crates, asbestos sheets, and bags of cement. Payment was made on a tonnage basis. The original rate, fixed when the factory opened, was stated to have been 2 shillings a ton. Afterwards it was reduced to 1s.6d. It was further reduced to 1 shilling a ton. In addition to these reductions, a bonus payment of 10d a day had also been discontinued. The

Industrial Court decided that the company were not under any obligation to pay more, but after consultation with them, they had agreed to increase the payment by a halfpenny a ton.

By the summer of 1921 there were over 2,000,000 unemployed people in England and strikes were on the increase.[18]   The unemployed were depressed and frustrated. In May, the windows of The Widnes Labour Exchange were smashed. There was widespread suffering and deprivation. Household fuel was an expensive necessity; subsequently there were numerous convictions for stealing coal. On one occasion 17 men were fined for trespassing on the L. & N. W. Railway – they were looking for coal on the siding behind Mathieson's Works. The same week, a youth was fined for stealing 50 lbs of coke from the United Alkali Company. The waste heaps also attracted people searching for coal and it was not uncommon to see crowds of people scavenging there. The removal of coal from these tips did not appear to carry any legal penalties because it was "waste" material. *The Widnes Weekly News* editorial of that time made reference to this practice in their article on *"The Widnes Coal Field"*:

"The prevailing industrial inertia in Widnes has one striking contrast, the Widnes "coal field" having come into its own.   Not one of the badly paying "coal fields" of South Lancashire could compare for difficulty of working with the coal places that have been opened on waste heaps in the centre of the chemical town.   No complaint is heard because the coal does not appear in four or five feet seams, or because a lot of dirt has to be removed before the precious mineral is found. No, the "colliers" are glad if they come across four or five inch pieces, not seams, and if a good place is discovered there is aroused a feeling akin to that of the prospector who finds traces of gold.

---

[18]*In fact, there had been dramatic waves of strikes even before this time, during 1919 and 1920 even the police went on strike.*

There is one industrious family, or rather a succession of industrious families engaged in exploiting the Widnes "coal field". Father and mother, the grown up son and daughter, and even the babies are to be seen among the little pits. There are all manner of contrivances for the conveyance of the fuel - including barrows, handcarts, boxes-on-wheels, perambulators, and go chairs. Those fortunate enough to "win" coal from the Widnes "coal field" claim that its value far exceeds the best household coal that was ever brought into Widnes, a remarkable claim when it is remembered that it is the refuse from the industrial ash heap, and that any virtue it ever possessed must in the ordinary course of events have departed years ago".

The beach at West Bank was also a popular place for collecting coal, which had presumably been washed up from boats. In July 1921 three men were preparing to go to the beach for coal, but in order to do so they needed to repair the bucket they used for this purpose. In those days, prior to our modern "throw away" society, it was usual for pots, pans, and buckets to be repaired, not discarded when they had holes in them. On this occasion, the occupier of a house in Beaumont Street and his two grown-up sons received a huge shock and a number of injuries when mending their bucket. In order to do the necessary repair it was decided to use a copper bolt which measured about one and a half inches long with the diameter of an ordinary bolt. Some time previously this "bolt" had been picked up on the beach, and in this period of waste not want not, it was put aside until some useful purpose presented itself. The father was looking on as his sons attempted to cut the "bolt". Directly on striking the "bolt", there was a terrific explosion and the three men were thrown to the other side of the yard, all received injuries and had to be taken to the nearby Accident Hospital. The explosion created a good deal of noise and shocked nearby residents. It was discovered that the "copper bolt" was in fact an electric detonator of the sort used in mines. How it came to be on the beach at West Bank was not known.

During this time, and in later years of this decade, there were also numerous prosecutions for stealing potatoes from outlying farms in the district. Almost all of these cases involved young children who were stealing potatoes to put food on the table. In one case, the Widnes Police Court missioner *(sic)* stated that: *"I was in that boy's home yesterday when they were trying to scrape a dinner together for the family. They are in very poor circumstances".* The child was sent to a Borstal Institution for the crime.

By September 1921 the unemployment situation in the town was causing great hardship. The scale of benefits paid to those in need was inadequate. In response to this situation, local councillor, Dan Garghan, organised a march to Whiston Institute[19] to make a personal appeal to The Guardians. On 15th September almost one thousand men marched from Widnes to Whiston, where the Board of Guardians were holding a special meeting to consider the scale of pay for the unemployed. Just before noon on that day, the men, led by Councillor Dan Garghan, accompanied by a group of local men including Messrs. J. Tague, J. Grimes, F. Hulme and B. Pitt, as well as representatives from St. Helens and Woolton, assembled in Victoria Square. It was a fine day and the men set out in orderly fashion on their five-mile walk. When they reached Rainhill they met up with a contingent from St. Helens, who had just attended a meeting in the market square. By this time the combined number of marchers was in excess of two thousand men. On reaching Whiston Institute, a deputation of representatives consisting of, Dan Garghan from Widnes, Mr. Charnock from St. Helens and Mr. J. Tipton from Woolton, were received by the Board. The unemployed men stood en masse in the roadway outside the building for several hours while the representatives placed their appeals before the Guardians. In his personal appeal to the Board of Guardians, Councillor Garghan said:

---

[19] *This was the Workhouse, later it was to form part of Whiston Hospital*

"As a worker, brought up among workers he knew of the suffering that Widnes was enduring. For 27 or 28 weeks, the chemical trade had been stagnant, and the men bore it bravely until a fortnight ago, when they could stand it no longer. There had been subscriptions from the masters and the workers and from other sources, and Widnes had not asked that Board to grant anything. Unfortunately, they had now been driven to desperation and had combined to ask for subsistence. The conditions in Widnes were improving slightly. The Town Council had decided to start a scheme that would employ 300 or 400, mainly married men. The chemical trade was slightly reviving, and he did not think if the Guardians granted the relief, that they would trespass long upon their goodness. They were living in expectation of better days. Their appeal at the moment was to save life. Children were hungry, and men were looking for work. They wanted work and not doles".

The Guardians were informed that at that time there were 3,700 on the unemployment register in Widnes. After due consideration the Board of Guardians set out a new scale of benefits. Although not as generous as the deputation had hoped for, it was more than they had been receiving prior to the march. The following scale was agreed upon.[20]

Man and wife	*25s.0d.*
First child	*6s.6d.*
Second child	*5s.6d.*
Third child	*4s.6d.*
Fourth child	*3s.6d.*
All other children	*2s.6d.*
Single men	*12s.6d.*
Single men (16 to 20)	*10s.0d.*
Single women	*10s.6d.*
Single women (16 to 20)	*8s.6d.*

---

[20] Currency Conversation for today - *£1 would equal 20 shillings in pre-decimal terms. 12 pennies was equal to 1 shilling. (s)shilling. (d)penny.*

In November 1921 a semi-private meeting was held to discuss the possibility of organising a Chamber of Commerce in the town. Later that month *The Widnes Weekly News* editorial made the following comments regarding the prospect of us having such an organisation:

"That Widnes has never been given its position in national life is a truism which none will question. The town has been derided for its odours and condemned on account of the bad conditions under which its people work and live – blots which have been or are being removed – but it has seldom if ever been commended for its contribution to national welfare in raw materials for medicine and drugs and for industry generally, not to mention its provision of soap to make possible the cleanliness which is next to godliness. One remembers also the great national and international institutions, for example the Society of Chemical Industry, have had their birth here. The point of it all is that Widnes folk are too modest in regard to their own achievements and too silent when outsiders exaggerate our bad points.

It is therefore with a distinct sense of gratification that one welcomes the first steps towards the formation of a Chamber of Trade and Commerce for Widnes. May it have the progress and the success that its sponsors have visualised. The functions of such a body may be all embracing. Certainly, Widnes offers scope for much real spadework. Many grievances under which the industries, and even small traders, suffer will never be remedied until united and persistent representation is made to those in authority in London. From an administrative point of view, one has just to imagine a visitor coming to Widnes and enquiring for the Post Office, only to find it in practically a stable, with an entrance through a back door in a side street. In local government, similar disregard to legitimate claims has often been noted. From a transport standpoint, the railway facilities are a standing joke.

Widnes cannot hope to take its rightful place until by its very importunity it compels recognition from the powers that be. The

Chamber of Trade and Commerce will therefore have great work before it".

The Widnes Chamber of Trade and Commerce was inaugurated in January 1922.

Naturally, working conditions and processes in the Widnes chemical industry had improved since the inception of the chemical industry in the mid nineteenth century. However, some of the techniques in operation in the 1920s were still hazardous and gruelling. The J. H. Dennis Cornubia Copper Works, founded in 1883 by James Hawke Dennis, was one such firm where men worked under harsh and demanding conditions. The company produced bars of copper and copper sulphate. One man described the jobs of the men working by the blast furnace, which was used to concentrate low-grade copper[21].

"Although the furnace was built of heavy magnesite bricks, sometimes it collapsed into heaps of rubble, which had to be cleared by the workmen at great risk to themselves. Occasionally, the furnace would become blocked. To free it, the men would need to use a sledgehammer near to the exit from which the molten copper flowed out, making sure to dodge the flow once the blockage had been cleared. The base of the blast furnace was also liable to cracking and when this happened the molten copper would break out and flow across the floor of the works. From the blast furnace, the copper ran into a round converter, which was subjected to blasts of air to purify the copper. A man using a rod systematically prodded a line of holes along the side of this converter. Sometimes the pressure could cause the rod to bounce back and seriously injure the man."

The blast furnace was only one of numerous unpleasant processes in this works. In fact, any chemical worker of those times could tell you a thousand similar stories of bad working conditions and practices in almost all of our factories. In 1925 a

[21] Interview : Catalyst Museum Archives Ref: MP/1/82/2

new copper sulphate plant was built at J. H. Dennis's Widnes Works. It was said at the time to be the most modern plant in Widnes. It had an electric powered monorail, which carried skips to transport material to the shot towers.

In October 1925 industry throughout the country was in a bad condition. The Chemical Employers' Federation decided the remedy for this was to be a reduction in wages. The Federation put forward a proposal to reduce workers wages by 2s.6d. a week. In Widnes, The Transport and General Workers Union organised a mass meeting at the Borough Hall. The audience were informed that the Joint Industrial Council had received a proposal from employers to nullify an industrial award of 2s.6d that had been granted to them in June 1924. Although the United Alkali Company, one of the town's main employers, was not at that time a member of the Chemical Employers' Federation, it was expected that they would soon follow suit and look for a reduction in wages as they had done in the past. The meeting, at the Borough Hall, was presided over by Councillor Pat Hanley and among the speakers were various representatives of The Transport and General Workers Union. One of these, Mr. H. Brown, said:

"The employers were asking for a reduction of 2s.6d. and if this came off for other chemical workers they feared it would also apply to the workers at Widnes as the United Alkali Company had not a reputation of paying higher wages than those obtained in other chemical yards "rather the reverse" could be argued. The people of Widnes had sitting as their member in The House of Commons a director of The United Alkali Company. When Dr. Clayton came before them at the last election, he did not tell them that in less than twelve months time the chemical workers of this country would be faced with a reduction of probably 2s.6d.

He thought it was a disgrace that a man who did not understand their conditions, who looked upon them as a machine to produce wealth, should represent them in The House of Commons. The electors however had their pick and they had selected him. He hoped the lesson would not be forgotten".

Wage reductions, and strikes connected with them, were to be a feature of the 1920s. Just a year prior to this, on 9th October 1924, Parliament had been dissolved following the defeat of Labour on the question of prosecuting J. R. Campbell, who was the editor of *"Workers' Weekly"*. Campbell was said to be inciting soldiers to mutiny rather than be used to break strikes.

By the beginning of 1926 the hardship caused by unemployment was highlighted by the existence of various relief funds. At a meeting of the members of *"The Mayor's Hot Pot Fund"* Councillor Dan Garghan said that he had investigated the Wards where the distress and suffering was most acute. He named these as the Victoria, Waterloo and Halton Wards. He therefore proposed to set up soup kitchens in these areas to help feed the children. Another fund, *"The Widnes Unemployment Distress Fund"*, endeavoured to bridge the gap locally between the end of the boom period and the organisation of relief measures on a national scale. It was hoped that this fund would soften the first harsh effects of the slump in the chemical trade. This fund was later renamed *"The Widnes Medical Relief and Distress Fund"* – their main form of expenditure appears to have been in providing clogs for needy children, the footwear was distributed by the school attendance officers.

In May 1926 the country experienced its first General Strike. It lasted 9 days, from May 3rd to the 12th. The strike was an unsuccessful attempt by the Trades Union Congress to force the Government to act to prevent wage reductions and worsening conditions for coal miners. There was a long history of poor industrial relations in the mining industry, much of the grievance stemmed from the appalling safety record in the industry. In a two-year period, between 1922 and 1924, over 3500 miners had lost their lives, while over 500,000 had been involved in some form of industrial accident or were suffering from respiratory complaints[22].

The mining industry had suffered economic crisis during this period due to cheaper imports (and free coal from Germany sent as reparations after the war).   There were also losses due to oil fuel replacing coal in steamships, as well as a reduction in demand from overseas markets.   In addition to this, the coal industry was dated in its techniques and organisation.   At this time there were around 2000 mines operated by more than 1000 separate small companies.

In April 1926 the mine owners announced their intention to reduce miners' wages and also to extend their working day.   They told the workers that if they did not accept these new terms and conditions by the first day of May, they would be locked out of the pits.   A conference of the T.U.C was held on 1st May 1926 and afterwards it was announced that a General Strike *"in defence of miners' wages and hours"* was to begin two days later.   Although Widnes was not really a mining district, nevertheless there were about two hundred miners and their families resident in the town.[23]   There were four collieries in our neighbouring areas, Sutton Manor, Clock Face, Lea Green and Bold as well as the local one at Cronton[24].

Initially, the strikers were only to be those in key industries such as railway men, transport workers, dockers, printers, builders, iron and steel trades, and chemical and power workers.   Only later would other trade unionists be called out on strike[25].   In view of the fact that Widnes was an important industrial area,

[22] Contemporary Britain 1914-1979 – *Robert Pearce (Longman History)*
[23] See Ref: Widnes Education Committee Report – June 1926
[24] *Cronton Colliery* was originally called *The Hulton Colliery Co.*   It was begun in 1913 and the first coal was raised in April 1915. It closed in 1984.
[25] *British Library of Political & Economic Science: (Coll.Misc.0140).*

there was a great deal of speculation prior to the strike as to what would actually happen here in town. The stoppages in the coalfields were, in themselves, enough to cause severe problems to industrial production in Widnes, and the stoppage of railways and other transport would mean a creeping paralysis on local industry. The United Alkali Works posted 7 days notices to their employees and other local works quickly followed their example.

On the first day of the strike, the railways came to a complete standstill and all local stations were closed. Widnes Corporation buses were seriously affected, although one or two buses did operate on that first day (because of some misunderstanding!) however, the following day the bus service was also at a complete standstill. The Secretary of The Widnes Trades and Labour Branch, writing to the Regional Organiser, on the second day of the strike, complained:[26]

"That our members at the Kastner Kelner's (sic) Works, Runcorn, are still at work. As a matter of fact all artisans at the above works are still working. Can you bring this matter to the notice of the Council of Action so as to bring pressure upon all trades to put into action the definite instruction issued by the T.U.C.".

Although there were no serious incidents in Widnes, rumour of various disturbances did circulate throughout the town, but thankfully, these proved to be just "Chinese whispers". However, in other parts of Lancashire there were numerous serious clashes between workers and police and the situation was tense. In Preston, 5,000 workers tried to storm a police station after a picket had been arrested. After three baton charges, local police had to call for reinforcements from Lancashire Constabulary. In Liverpool, two battalions of infantry landed from a troopship and marched through the city wearing steel helmets and carrying rifles. The battleships *Ramillies* and *Barham* were recalled from the

---

[26] Liverpool Record Office: 331TRA15/7/24

Atlantic Fleet and anchored in the Mersey. The Government had asked for volunteers to man essential services. They managed to raise 7,000 volunteers in the City of Westminster alone, although it is interesting to note that it appears they were unable to recruit many in Manchester or Liverpool[27].

On the 12th May the news that the strike had ended was first heard by wireless. Newspapers had been stopped by the strike, although the Government produced its own official news pamphlet *The British Gazette*, which was also broadcast by the BBC. Winston Churchill, under the orders of Stanley Baldwin, had been assigned the job of producing *The British Gazette*, which he had printed on the machines of *The Morning Post*. In this publication, Churchill demanded *"unconditional surrender by the strikers"* he also referred to the British workman as *"the enemy of the nation"*, a phrase that consequently outraged large sections of the population. *The British Gazette* treated the strike almost as a war, and hinted that failure to quell this strike would result in revolution and the downfall of democratic Government.   Some disquieting phrases from *The British Gazette*, 6th May edition, give us an illustration:[28]

"Constitutional Government is being attacked. ...... Stand behind the Government ......The General Strike is a challenge to Parliament and is the road to anarchy and ruin.........either the country will break the General Strike, or the General Strike will break the country... The authority of Parliamentary Government over any sectional combination must be vindicated".

It was also apparent that some of the statements in this publication were specifically designed to instil panic. Since the Russian Revolution, there was a great deal of interest and admiration within the Labour movement of that time in the new "socialist state" in Russia. Many people were alarmed, and feared

---

[27] Trades Union Congress Archives
[28] Contemporary Britain 1914-1979 – *Robert Pearce (Longman History)*

a rise of "Bolshevism" in England. Their fears seem to have been unfounded, as the Labour Party had repeatedly refused admission to anyone with Communist affiliations. However, the editorial tone of *The British Gazette* encouraged those fears.

In response, here in the northwest, the unions provided their own rival newspaper, *The British Worker*. The Labour politician, Fenner Brockway, produced this paper and published it through the Co-operative Publishing Society in Southport. The editor was very careful to use the phrase "national stoppage" rather than "strike" in order to disassociate them from the idea that the strike was political. They strenuously contradicted rumours voiced in *The British Gazette* and denied the Government interpretation of the strike. The T.U.C. was offered a generous donation for the strike fund from The Communist Trade Unions of Soviet Russia. This donation was immediately refused, as they were keen to distance themselves from any Communist connections.

Within a short time of hearing the news on the wireless, that the strike had ended, people in Widnes flocked into the streets hoping to hear further clarification. The secretaries of the local trades unions soon confirmed the withdrawal of strike action and details of the settlements that had been reached. Contact between the strikers and unions had been maintained throughout the strike through the T.U.C. transport committees, which had mobilised 29 cyclists and 57 motorcyclists to maintain daily contact between every town in Lancashire.

At this point, it was generally supposed by the workers that on presenting themselves at their place of employment they would be automatically reinstated. Most of them resumed work normally, however, when the railwaymen returned to work they were astonished to find that their jobs would be subject to new conditions. Those conditions covered many benefits that had been fought for and won by previous trade union activity. A meeting of railway workers was called and union officials instructed the workers to resume the strike. A number of bricklayers and joiners were also told that there was no work for them when they returned to their jobs after the strike.

A few days after the end of the strike, the Mayor, Councillor Millar, called a special meeting of the Council and the Chamber of Commerce to discuss the industrial and employment consequences of the strike on the town. He made clear that he had no intention of discussing the politics of the matter, nor of the position of the miners and railway men, his intention was to voice the Council's grave concern for the workers of Widnes. Councillor Millar said his concern was for:

"The various tradesmen, who had no grievance with their masters, but who found themselves in the dual position that if they came out on strike they were doing an injustice to their masters and themselves, and if they did not strike they were doing an injustice to their mates and their trade union. He hoped these men would have the consideration of their employers". Extracts of that meeting are outlined below:

Alderman Lewis *asked what was the situation in Widnes. "Were the men getting back to work or were they not? If not, - then why not? Could anything be done to facilitate their getting back?"*

Mr. J. Walwyn White, (Chairman of the Chamber of Commerce) said: *"Perhaps it would be well to consider one or two points. If any of the manufacturers could do anything to assist the situation, they would be only too pleased to do so. There was not a great number out on strike, and a number of men were not working simply because the works had to close down in consequence of transport troubles. He did not see how they could help things until they were over the transport difficulty. The trouble with the railway men, as he was informed, was that they insisted in going back en bloc. If they would give the matter a moment's consideration they would understand that matters were in a state of chaos. They could not stop for 10 or 12 days and then expect to go back as if nothing had happened. It would take weeks and weeks before they* could get going. He thought the men were very ill advised to insist on all going back together. They have made trouble, rightly or wrongly, and they ought to be content to go back as their employers are able to take them back. That applies equally to all workers. Men who were indispensable have gone out. You have replaced them with other men - you were bound to. Is it fair to attack these men who stepped into the breach merely to give these strikers a chance? I think we must first consider the men who were loyal to us, and then if we have any room for sympathy afterwards we will extend it as far as we can. But I do think our sympathy must rest first with the men who stepped late into the breach. Men could not go out at a moment's notice and then insist on going back at a moment's notice. It could not be done it was not an economic proposition"

The Mayor thought that they could not discuss the larger question of the railways but said: "*There is a great deal of discontent amongst the plumbers, joiners, bricksetters and others who were engaged in the works, and who would like to hear a statement on the lines such as Mr. White has indicated, that as soon as required they would be taken back without penalties, such as the taking away of bonuses or losing holidays or anything of that sort. If such a statement were made I believe it would have a good effect*".

Mr. Beech (a member of the Chamber of Commerce), said: "*Is it fair that these men should expect to ask for holidays when they had left their work at a moment's notice and did not care whether the employer had to close or not? It should be left to the master's consideration when they got back*"

Mr. J. H. Smith (another member of the Chamber), said that "*The process men at the United Alkali Company remained loyal and they determined to carry on as long as the circumstances permitted. They had worked a full week but had had to reduce gradually. The position at the moment is that that they will resume full work as soon as it is possible, but as Mr. White had pointed out, they could not shut up as an industry for a fortnight and then get back into their stride again as though nothing* had happened. *Transport was at a standstill and all was being put into stock. Until the miners strike, and more particularly transport, was settled, employment instead of being more, might be reduced".*

At the end of the meeting, Councillor Lewis told them that the unemployment register in Widnes on a pre-war basis was 1,100. This had increased by 1,400 and the register was now 2,500. He had tried to ascertain the number of strikers but could not get anything but a rough estimate of 1,000.

In the weeks following the strike, local churches and charities organised collections for *"The Miners Distress Fund"*. At St. Marie's R.C. Church, in Lugsdale Road, the clergy nominated a number of women parishioners to make weekly collections in Lugsdale and Marrabone, Moss Bank, Halton View, Newtown, Simms Cross, Wareing Street and Moor Lane. The weekly collections averaged between £9 and £10 per week in the first months but reduced to around £5 per week by October. Most of the money was sent to the Nuns at Sutton Manor who used it to feed the children of the miners. The remainder of the money went to a local *"Social Distress Fund"*[29]. In view of the fact that many of these parishioners were themselves feeling the effects of unemployment, or short time working, the few shillings or pence they donated each week would have been a huge sacrifice.

Five months after the strike ended many of the rail workers had still not been allowed to return to work. The miners paid the highest price. They stayed out for six months and were in effect starved back to work having achieved none of their aims, going back for less pay and longer hours. The general feeling of workers throughout the country was that the miners had been let down by the T.U.C. Following on from this, trade union membership declined after the strike. The drain of strike pay and the reduction in membership also depleted union funds. However, the strike

---

[29] St. Marie's RC Church - Parish Archives

had provided an opportunity for the Government to bring in tough measures against trade unions and this led to the passing of the *1927 Trades Disputes Act*, which restricted the ability of workers to strike. Perhaps a fact well worth mentioning here, is that during the 1920s most of the strikes had been *against* wage reductions not *for* wage increases.

When talking about this period in the town's history, it is important to note the outstanding work done for the benefit of our community by individual members of the Council. Councillor Daniel Garghan, who is mentioned many times throughout this book, was always to the fore in fighting for the good of under-privileged members of our society. Another who deserves special mention is Councillor David Lewis, who continually endeavoured to bring about better social conditions in the Borough. During his lifetime he was repeatedly described as *"one of nature's true gentlemen"*.

Councillor David Lewis, later Alderman Lewis, although born in Runcorn, he spent the majority of his life in Widnes where he was a leading member of the Primitive Methodist Church. He was also President of Widnes Free Church Council and a member of the Committee for Methodist Union. During the 1906 "Free Speech" incidents, he was the most prominent of the Free Churchmen who spoke out in defence of the right of the public to free speech in Victoria Square. He attempted to bring some sanity to the situation by introducing proposals at meetings of the Town Council. In another area, he was instrumental in persuading the Council to adopt W. A. Harvey's plan for developing the town, and for the building of the new St. Bede's Road, which we now call Kingsway. His contributions to the life and welfare of this town were numerous and his charitable works countless. He was a devout Christian who had high ideals coupled with sound practical commonsense. Throughout the period of the General Strike and its aftermath, both Daniel Garghan and David Lewis worked hard and selflessly to alleviate the suffering of the local unemployed and their families.

Councillor John Millar should also receive a mention in these pages for his unstinting work at that time for the unemployed of Widnes. John Millar was born in Northern Ireland but lived for over 40 years in Widnes. Apart from his role as a local Councillor, John Millar was a Wesleyan preacher. Before he came to Widnes he travelled the country with *The Blue Ribbon Gospel Army*, and came to this town to take charge of The Blue Ribbon Gospel Mission. This Mission Hall was located in West Bank (on the site that was later occupied by the old Century Cinema). When the Blue Ribbon Hall in West Bank finally closed, he attached himself to the Hartland Church where he became a prominent worker.

The last meeting of the board of the United Alkali Company took place on 29th June 1927. The news that U.A.C. was to combine with Nobel Industries and The British Dyestuffs Corporation, came as something of a shock to the workers of Widnes and Runcorn, as the talks between Sir Alfred Mond, Sir Harry McGowan, and Sir Max Muspratt had been kept secret. Shortly after the announcement of the amalgamation of these industries, *The Widnes Weekly News* editorial made the following observations:

"The secret that negotiations were in progress had been so well kept that Widnes and Runcorn folk were more than mildly surprised when they learned that the largest manufacturing organisations in the British chemical industry were to be combined in one colossal company.

Those who remember the genesis of The United Alkali Company are inclined to regard the present amalgamation with misgiving. They say that the formation of the syndicate was not a good thing, and that, in the old days of highly individualised works, employment, wages, and business were better than they have been since. Be that as it may, it does not necessarily follow that work and wages in the Merseyside chemical industry would have suffered no deterioration had the old order not given place to the new. It is not improbable that the continuation of the industry in un-associated firms would have brought about its own gradual extinction in Widnes and Runcorn.

During the pioneer stages of the industry the world's newly found hunger for chemicals could not be satisfied. Selling problems and the economical organisation of manufacture were not so pressing until the growth of demand had been overtaken by the increase in sources of supply. Then competition from the Continent and America so intensified the competition between firm and firm at home, that in sheer self-preservation, some form of associated control over production and marketing became urgent. The economies and reorganisations consequent upon the formation of the syndicate naturally caused less money to circulate through local channels of retail trade. Shopkeepers, property owners, and others whose incomes were derived from the spending of the chemical workers' wages, regarded the change as disastrous. It was merely a slight hastening of the inevitable, however, for the temporary monopoly enjoyed by the early traders, would have been gradually obliterated by the increasing numbers attracted to share their prosperity, much in the same way as the chemical pioneers suffered the diminution of profit margins when expanding trade brought its concomitant competition".

The new company started business with total assets of £56 million. Among the reasons given for this amalgamation was the fact that research and development were both expensive. The companies thought that by pooling their resources they would be able to expand research and eliminate waste. It is obvious that I.C.I., through their research and development, made impressive scientific progress. This is symbolised by its subsequent development of modern plastics.

In the week that I.C.I. was officially formed, it closed down part of the Weston Works, in Runcorn, with a loss of more than 200 jobs. Those who had voiced their misgivings about this new amalgamation were wondering if their predictions were about to come true. Two years later, reorganisation of I.C.I. local industries brought about the integration of the United Alkali Company, The Castner-Kellner Company, and Chance & Hunt. This merger formed the I.C.I. General Chemicals Group, which was later known as General Chemicals Division.

There was further alarm for employees of I.C.I. in May 1929 when the company announced that they were to close part of the Muspratt Works. This works had previously been producing caustic soda and sulphide. The sulphide side of the business had been improved, by transferring some production to Muspratt's from Birmingham. However, for the caustic process, the primary raw material was soda ash, and as Widnes was unable to pump suitable brine for this process, it was decided to close down that plant. At that time, in Widnes, Imperial Chemical Industries were employing 2,480 men.

Whilst these occurrences were of considerable concern locally, the chairman of I.C.I., Sir Alfred Mond, was involving himself in what was described as *"an attempt to explore means of improving production and increase efficiency in British industry"*. The first suggestions to set up a joint committee, consisting of employers and the general council of the T.U.C., came from Sir Alfred Mond in 1927. These were the first ever proposals for industrial collaboration, and were an attempt by union leaders and employers to find ways of settling common industrial problems. In 1928 Ernest Bevin was also part of this committee, who jointly agreed that higher wages would only come from increased production, not from industrial warfare[30].

In June 1928, the Golding-Davies Works, (producers of chamber vitriol) a section of the Marsh Works of the United Alkali Company, was the scene of a disastrous fire. The vitriol plant at

---

[30] *English History* – A.J.P. Taylor (Oxford University Press 1975)

this works was completely destroyed and hundreds of tons of vitriol (sulphuric acid) were lost, as well as six chambers and a dozen storage tanks. Widnes Fire Brigade was on the scene quite quickly but it soon became apparent that they would be unable to bring the fire under control without assistance. The brigades from Warrington and St. Helens answered the call and all three teams, aware of the dangers of the fire spreading to other nearby works, fought for over five hours before the fire was brought under control. As the fire had progressed, huge quantities of vitriol escaped and became mixed with the floods of water from the hoses. Some of the fire-fighters had their boots and clothing damaged by acid. Huge volumes of choking black smoke drifted over a large area and lingered long after the last flames had been quenched. The United Alkali Company estimated the damage to be in the region of £30,000. Thankfully, there were no dead or seriously injured workers, as the fire had started in the early hours before the majority of workers had arrived for their shifts.

Throughout 1928 rumours circulated that Widnes might be the possible site for a new silk factory. A "Silk Company" from Arnhem, in Holland, had looked at Widnes early in the year. In September, it was rumoured that a German company were also considering opening a silk factory, at Halebank, with a possible 2000 new jobs being created. Unfortunately, neither of these considerations came to fruition. The Dutch later chose Nottingham as a more suitable location. This was another disappointment to those who wished to see new industries established in the town. The previous year "The Sankey Sugar Company" had been seeking a site for a refinery. Widnes and Earlestown were both considered, but later in the year the company completely abandoned their plans to establish a new processing plant.

The prosperity of Widnes depended greatly upon the industrial climate and as this decade drew to a close the effects of unemployment had been felt by a large majority of the population. All the principal industries of the town had been affected in some way during this decade. The United Alkali Company was now incorporated into the Imperial Chemical Industries and William Gossage & Sons Ltd. had been taken over by the UniLever group. At this time, these two companies were the chief mainstays of the Borough.   Among the other major employers were: Thomas Bolton & Sons Ltd.; J. H. Dennis & Co. Ltd.; The Widnes Foundry Co. Ltd.; Orr's Zinc White Co. Ltd.; High Speed Steel Alloys; Birmingham Corrugated Iron Co.; T. Davies Iron Works Ltd.; Richard White & Sons Ltd.; Peter Spence & Sons; McKechnie Brothers; The Mersey Copper & Sulphate Co.; The Calder & Mersey Extract Co. Ltd.; and Bell's Poilite & Everite Co. Ltd. There were also numerous other smaller concerns within the town and its environs, each employing varying numbers of workmen.

Housing and building development

In January 1920 the housing shortage in the country was to the fore in many minds, and caused more discontent than any other problem of that year. The price of building materials rose sharply and an article in *The Daily Express*, on 27th April, claimed that prices of materials were being kept artificially high by a secret combine of suppliers. It seemed to some that a new invention, in the form of prefabricated houses, would be the answer to their prayers. This new system of building would be both economical and fast. It was estimated that it would take just two weeks to erect a house. An additional benefit was that no "skilled labour" would be required to complete this work. The patent for these buildings was to be granted to Public Authorities only, so that there would be no exploitation by speculative builders. However, although this new fast and economical way of providing accommodation was being championed in 1920, it was not until some decades later that Widnes Corporation introduced "prefabs" into the town.

In the autumn of 1919 the MP for Garston and Woolton, Colonel Nathan Raw, gave an address to the Royal Institute of Public Health, in London. In his speech, he highlighted the close relationship between tuberculosis and bad housing. He said that unsanitary houses in overcrowded areas were a prolific cause of this disease, and that the building delay owing to the war had resulted in a marked increase in the spread of this horrible disease. Locally, the housing shortage and bad housing conditions were a cause for considerable concern. To the returning soldiers of Widnes, it would probably have seemed that Lloyd George's promises of reconstruction and homes for heroes were now just a faded mockery.

Even from the inception of the chemical industry in Widnes in the previous century, there had been a recognition that the houses provided for the workforce had been of an extremely poor standard. Because of the rapid growth of industry and population these houses had been erected quickly and cheaply with little thought or concern for the social consequences. In those days, labour markets were constrained by walking distances, and so housing was provided unhealthily close to the factories. Tightly packed streets of cheap houses became home to families whose origins and patterns of life were still rural. The streets were badly lit, and most properties had inadequate sanitary provisions, which meant they were a breeding ground for diseases such as typhoid and cholera. By the 1920s people were still living in these same streets and conditions had improved only slightly. As few people owned houses most of these properties were rented. Although the landlords, in theory, were expected to set aside a proportion of this rent for repairs, few improvements or repairs ever took place.

In 1919 *The Addison Act* brought in Government subsidies for council house building. This Act laid on the Local Authorities the duty of surveying the housing needs of their area and submitting plans for building houses. These houses were to be subsidised from Government funds[31]. In February 1919, at a meeting of the Widnes Town Council, a special sub-committee of the General Purposes Committee was formed to deal with this responsibility. It was agreed that urgent steps should be taken to deal with the issue of town planning, and of providing a sufficient number of houses to accommodate an increased population. Following on from this, an architect and surveyor, Mr. W. A. Harvey, from Birmingham, was engaged to advise on the suitability of the land available and the types and numbers of dwellings to be erected. Mr. Harvey submitted a number of reports and suggestions for consideration. A limit was fixed on the number of dwellings per

---

[31] *The Act* also gave subsidies to private builders to build "reasonably priced" houses.

acre and open spaces were to be reserved for recreational purposes. It was also agreed that factory and residential areas be separate and confined to situations most suitable to their respective needs. In addition, it was recognised that as there had been a rapid increase in road transport during the war years, it would now be necessary to make provisions for much wider roads than people had been accustomed to. These new roads would need to provide for local industry as well as the increased use of buses and charabancs. It was also suggested that old-fashioned type roads should eventually disappear and be replaced with new "boulevard" type thoroughfares.

Mr. Harvey's report was, at that time, one of the most important ever submitted to the Widnes Town Council. The scheme encompassed industrial development, residential requirements, and civic needs. It was to be the blueprint for the development of the town as we now know it. It proposed not only the building of 1000 new houses but also the development of the vacant land surrounding the existing civic buildings. Kingsway was to be the backbone of this new layout, and it was also decided that it would be advantageous to have an entrance to Victoria Road from the side of the Library and Technical schools. Various possibilities for the grouping of proposed new buildings in this area were also suggested. The importance of Kingsway in these plans was emphasised, and it was agreed that this new road should be completed on broad and generous lines and on a scale proportioned by the importance it would ultimately attain.

Councillor David Lewis was instrumental in urging the acceptance of Mr. Harvey's proposals for a new town plan. In submitting and recommending the report to the Council, Councillor Lewis said that:

"The scheme would take advantage of the uplands and sunny slopes of the Borough, favourable to good sanitation and healthy surroundings, the sites were calculated to promote the unity and solidarity of the town's

formation, and would have the important advantage of being convenient to the various centres of employment. The scheme was of course, not likely to be realised all at once, but its scope was sufficiently ample to meet, in its successive stages, the various needs contemplated. Mr. Harvey's report dexterously swept the landscape, omitting no essential feature and laid down a far-reaching programme. What was now proposed was not the end but the beginning. He was glad to be in at the beginning, the inauguration of a scheme big with promise of good to the town and community. It would take time and some of them might not see the reaping of the full harvest, but it was there to be gathered. He trusted the town would not lack gatherers in."

The committee congratulated Councillor Lewis on the report. It was noted that the scheme embodied 130 acres and that if they followed the plan to build 10 houses to the acre that would provide 1300 houses. No scheme that had ever been submitted to the Local Government Board had estimated less than 12 to the acre, and they thought very few had adopted that number. The committee would give the least number per acre because that was what Widnes needed. They realised the importance of this when they considered that the present number in Widnes was something like 40 to 60 per acre. The Chairman of the Bus Committee wanted to develop the bus service and if they went further afield with their houses, they would be increasing another department of the corporate estate. A committee member said that he thought:

"It was most important that industries should be kept in one line, clear and distinct from the operations of living. Some people had remarked that they thought the Park was too far away. They were now reminded it was too near their industries. He had no doubt that the Widnes scheme would be among the best." The same speaker wanted the Corporation to have power of location of industries and *"not allow places where people lived to be made impossible by fumes etc"*. He wanted the

Corporation to have the powers to stop *"the raising of mountains of rubbish right in the centre of where people lived."*[32]

At the end of 1920 the Corporation was in talks with the owner of land in Kingsway. However, the owner of this land was dissatisfied with the price offered to him and the matter went to arbitration. In January 1921 the Town Clerk produced the "Award of the Official Arbitrator" which fixed the price of this land, later to be developed as the Kingsway Estate, at the price of £838.

Towards the end of 1920 the building programme was working at full steam ahead. The Town Clerk had approval from the Housing Commissioner for the acceptance of a tender from Sir Robert McAlpine & Sons for the building of houses off Peelhouse Lane. By September of the following year the first 40 houses on this new "Fairfield Estate" had been allocated. The rents on the first houses were set at 7s.3d per week for a type "A" house, 8s.0d. per week for a type "B" and 10s.6d a week for a type "B4" house. Although this new housing scheme was completed on schedule, it was beset with problems in the form of bricklayers' strikes. Apparently, despite the high levels of unemployment, there was a severe shortage of bricklayers in the town at that time.

The Corporation made good progress with their building schemes and by July 1927 a further two developments, at Kingsway and Halebank, were nearing completion. At the official inspection of these estates, Alderman Wood was presented with a gold key to commemorate the opening of the first door on the Halebank estate. Tenancy of houses on this new estate was given to people who had formerly resided in slum clearance areas of Ditton and Halebank. This clearance included the Johnson Street and Harrison Street areas. These streets were demolished as part of an "Improvement Scheme Order" of 1924, which was

---

[32] *Widnes Council Minutes* - 1919

specifically aimed at what were termed "unhealthy areas". By the autumn of 1928 an additional 284 new houses had been provided, 200 of these were on the Kingsway Estate. The Borough Engineer's Report in September 1928 gave details of the building costs of these new dwellings[33].

Halebank Estate (84 houses)	*total cost £38,669.15s.1d.*
Kingsway Estate (first 100 houses)	*total cost £47,696.5s.6d.*
Kingsway Estate (second 100 houses)	*total cost £46,867.11s.7d.*

The Housing Committee, at that time, drew attention to the growth of Widnes since 1901 when there had been 5,350 inhabited houses in the Borough. Ten years later, the figure had increased to 6,063. In 1921, after the extension of the Borough boundaries, the number rose to 7,148 – then it was estimated that there were over 8,000.

Although much had been accomplished in the ten years since Mr. Harvey had produced his report, outlining plans for the development of the town's civic and residential areas, there was still a great deal more work to be done. In July 1929, Councillor David Lewis, as chairman of the Health Committee, submitted the report of the Medical Officer of Health, Dr. Jones, to the Council. The report said that the provision of further housing in the Borough was a matter of urgency. The census records show that there was still an unacceptable level of overcrowding in houses occupied by single families. There was also a large number of families in the Borough still without separate accommodation, finding it necessary to share a house with another family, or in some dire cases, with two other families.

Giving a few illustrations of how people in the Borough were living, Councillor Lewis said that he did not want to cause a scare

---

[33] *Minutes of Widnes Borough Council - 1928*

but there was sufficient in the report to cause anxiety. He told the
Committee:

*Of the single families occupying houses with **two bedrooms**, there were
146 with 8 persons in each; 95 with 9; 50 with 10; 23 with 11; 2 with 12;
and 3 with 13.*

*In **three bedroom** houses occupied by a single family, there were 60 that
had 9 persons in each; 34 with 10; 19 with 11; 7 with 12; and 5 with 13.*

*In the cases of shared accommodation, the following figures apply to
houses with two families.   **Two bedroom** houses with two families, 47
had 8 persons belonging to 2 families. 30 had 9; 18 had 10; 10 had 11; 8
had 12; 5 had 13; 2 had 14 and 2 had 16.*

*Of the **three bedroom** houses that had two families sharing   there were
64 that had 8 persons in each; 47 had 9; 19 had 10; 13 had 11; 5 had 12; 7
had 13; 2 had 14 and 2 had 15.*

*There were also a number of houses in the town that had three families in
them.*

Comparing the figures with the census of 1919, Councillor
Lewis said that there were more than twice the number of houses
containing two families now, in 1929, than there had been 10 years
before.   In fact, although David Lewis did not draw this
comparison, back in the early years of the chemical industry when
there was a rapidly rising population, the overcrowding was not
much worse. For example in 1861 when the population of the
town was 6,893, there were 1,150 inhabited houses, giving an
average of 5.99 people to each house.   In 1921, the average was
5.22.

In 1929, Widnes and its housing problems were mentioned in
The House of Commons when the member for the Widnes
Division, Mr. Alex Cameron, made his maiden speech.   He took

part in a debate about *The Housing Bill* (which included slum clearance, fair rents, and rent allowances). He made an earnest appeal in support of The Bill. During this debate another member of the Chamber had remarked:

"That, even if better houses were provided for these people, the vast majority had no desire to leave the slums, and would soon reduce better houses to the state of those they had left". In response to this, Alex Cameron said that: *"to the contrary, ninety-five percent of the poor people who were today living in slum areas were not there by choice, but because they were the victims of circumstances. All of them would move to brighter and better surroundings if they could only do so. They simply could not pay what was called an economic rent, and that was why the Government was compelled to do something to assist them".* Mr. Cameron went on to tell The House that *"it had been reported to him only two days ago that there were hundreds of houses in Widnes with only two bedrooms where there were from 8 to 24 persons living in each house, and its Medical Officer of Health had pointed out to him that, today, there were twice the number of houses carrying two or three families as in 1919, and that housing was twice as bad as it was then, not withstanding the efforts of past Governments. If he had his way he would treat the slum property owner in just the same way as he would treat the vendor of bad food, who had to stand the risk of imprisonment for his offence. As to compensation, he would not give a moment's consideration to persons who owned property which was injurious to health"*[34].

The problems encountered by Widnes Corporation with regard to housing, were being mirrored all over the country. Ordinary building had ceased completely during the war years and for some time afterwards. Before the war, Widnes had been provided with an annual addition of 100 new houses, that meant that with no building for seven years they were now 700 houses short, and this

[34] *Widnes Weekly News* – 1934
Hansard - 1934

shortage was difficult to overcome. In order to go some way to alleviate this deficiency, the Housing Committee recommended the building of additional houses on the Kingsway Estate. These additional houses were to be constructed on land bounded on the north by Wavertree Avenue, on the south by Milton Road, on the east by Kingsway and on the west by land occupied by *The Widnes Cricket Club* and *The Widnes Football Club* respectively.

The new housing scheme programme was not without controversy, as the designated areas meant that the sites of the football and cricket grounds would be absorbed into the plan. There was widespread anger in the town that these sites were under threat and *The Widnes Weekly News* became a forum for numerous angry complaints from sports lovers. *"Housing or Recreation?"* was the theme, and the different groups "for or against" held frequent meetings. In the end, the matter was put into perspective, the plans tweaked, and an acceptable compromise reached. This meant that the planned addition to the Kingsway Housing Estate could go ahead and provide much needed homes.

Despite the progress that was being made in town planning and building during the 1920s, the town's image was still a rather dismal one to the outsider. An architect from Bolton who visited the town in 1927 said of it:

"One could go on indefinitely on the laxity of things generally in Widnes. The appalling sight of the waste land in the centre of the town which should be hidden by a fence at least (not similar to the atrocity bordering Kingsway of course). The buses rackety and dismally illuminated, the fares charged for the stages being double what is required if the buses are run properly, the streets, dirty and equipped with a few decrepit lamp posts, which at night emit a feeble glimmer only equalled by the same glimmer oozing from the gas brackets in the houses. The narrow, straggling main street, dusty and cluttered with orange papers, straw etc. and lined with shops the sameness of which frontages would do justice only to the back streets in a progressive town. No, Widnes seems to be a

decided back number, when viewed from outside, calling for a clean sweep of its old and feeble ideas, and a clean sweep generally of the shop fronts, the Town Hall Square, and the bus interiors".

It seems that others were of a different opinion. After a lapse of seventeen years, the members of *The North Western Sanitary Inspectors' Association* made a return visit to Widnes in the spring of 1928. The visitors, who were entertained by the Mayor and senior members of Widnes Corporation, were representing different parts of Lancashire and Cheshire. Alderman David Lewis, who was present on the occasion of their first visit in 1911, said they would see many changes in the town and asked them to note the splendid type of houses that had been erected and the pleasing layout of the schemes. The Chairman of the Sanitary Inspectors' Association said:

"He was agreeably surprised to find that Widnes was not as bad as it was painted – that no one had a need to enter the town armed with a gas mask and afraid of walking through an atmosphere charged with poisonous chemical gases. He thought, on the whole, it was a rather pleasant town."

Whilst this decade saw the rise of new housing developments in the town, it also saw the loss of some old landmarks. During the widening and straightening of Lower House Lane early in the decade, much attention and consideration was given to preserving the old walls, gate, and horse block of *Widnes House*. However, by 1926, the lovely old house was in a state of dilapidation and the structure was unstable. Despite appeals to *The Society of Arts* in London, sufficient funds were not forthcoming to preserve or renovate this valuable piece of history. In February 1928, demolition work commenced and within a few weeks the house, which was thought to date back to 1670, was gone. The name *Widnes House* was a modern appellation as the old house was originally called *Upper House*. Another house, known as *Lower House* stood a short distance away, both were sited in the "modern" Lower House Lane area.

As the 1920s drew to an end, it seemed that the inhabitants of Widnes were experiencing a marked improvement in living standards. New houses had been provided for those who had lived in some slum clearance areas, new roads were installed, a maternity hospital, child welfare clinics, and other welcome services had begun to appear in the town. Another new and welcome facility was the provision of public conveniences to enable people to "spend a penny" if they needed to. In October 1928, Peter Walker & Sons made a gift of land, at the rear of The Bradley Hotel and fronting Cross Street, for the site of a "Public Convenience".

Education

"The purpose of education, apart from the obvious, is also to teach children the conventions and courtesies of society and to enable them to cultivate a positive attitude to life".

(Councillor David Lewis)

Since *The Fisher Act Education Act* of 1918 there had been numerous improvements in local education provision. This Act had abolished all fees in elementary schools, called for the school leaving age to be raised from 12 to 14, and for the establishment of "continuation" schools. Although some of these provisions were not immediately implemented because of economy cuts in Government spending, they were nevertheless gradually phased in. The school leaving age was raised in 1921, and Local Education Authorities recognised the right of all young workers to have access to release education.

In 1920 the following figures were given for Widnes Schools.

School	No. On Roll	Av. Attendance
St. Bede's	*747*	*663*
Farnworth C. of E.	*445*	*383*
St. Marie's	*988*	*876*
Widnes C. of E.	*425*	*367*
St. Patrick's	*583*	*521*
Simms Cross	*1585*	*1442*
Warrington Road	*879*	*802*
West Bank	*882*	*812*
Central	*156*	*147*

As in previous decades, there were regular occurrences of parents or guardians being summoned to appear before the Education Committee for contraventions of the Education Act. In one period there were 96 people summoned. Many of these were just given a verbal warning, however there were also a number of prosecutions for those who had regularly absented their children from school, and some children were sent to Industrial Schools and Reformatories, for continued truancy or absenteeism.

At that beginning of 1920 the Widnes Local Authority's contributions to Reformatory and Industrial Schools was 12 shillings per week. In October that year only one child was committed to an Industrial School, which was The St. Thomas Industrial School, at Ashton-on-Ribble. However, during the remaining years of the decade a fair number of Widnes children were sent to these establishments. In 1928, the Home Office closed down a number of Industrial Schools in the north-west including The Hightown School in Manchester and Holy Trinity School in Liverpool, both of which were schools used by our Local Authority. The local children resident in those schools at that time were either transferred to The Barnes Homes, Heaton Mersey, or sent home to Widnes on licence.

The investigation of absences or truancy was the domain of the School Board Officer. In much the same way as many jobs today offer the use of a company car, in those days transport was provided by the Council. Mr. Charles Bingham, of Victoria Road, was given the contract to supply a "Raleigh Bicycle" at a cost of £8 for the use of Mr. J. Asprey, the School Board Officer. An aptly named Mr. T.E. Boardman supplied the uniforms. He charged the Council £26.12s.6d, for 3 suits, 3 pairs of trousers, and 3 mackintoshes.

Of course, not all absences from school were down to truancy or lax parenting. Some of the reasons were a sad reflection of the times. The Log Book for St. Marie's Boys' School for the 1920s tells us that in one instance attendance was low due to *"cases of ringworm and conjunctivitis"*. Another entry said that attendance was very poor because *"the weather is snowy and many children have little or no footwear"*. On another occasion, poor attendance was owing to children being sent *"cinder picking"* during a coal strike.[35] These reasons again highlight the awful poverty of the times and make sad reading. In 1921 the Local Education Authority made arrangements for needy children to be supplied with breakfast on their arrival at school. These children were mainly pupils at St. Marie's and St. Patrick's schools, which were located in areas where unemployment was high.

In 1922 the Government stated that a quarter of all classes had more than 60 pupils. Many of the schools were old, and here in Widnes there were problems with overcrowding. The raising of the school leaving age meant there were inadequate provisions at that time for secondary education. Recognising these failings, *The Hadow Report* in 1926 condemned the small percentage of children aged 11 to 16 who were receiving secondary education. The report planned a total reorganisation of the system. It was proposed that a break should be made at 11+ and that the adolescent should then be educated in a separate Secondary School with an appropriate curriculum. The Board of Education encouraged this reorganisation, which meant that education for 11+ would fall into three types: existing Grammar Schools, new "modern" Secondary Schools, and Junior Technical Schools[36]. The selection process for secondary education was also set out in this report. Selection would be by means of an 11+ examination, which incorporated an intelligence test. Children would then be streamed into an appropriate school. However, these reforms required the building of new schools. In Widnes, work on these new schools did not accelerate until the following decade when building costs were lower.

---

[35] *SL565/4917* – County Archives, Cheshire Record Office
[36] *Educational Reform 1900-1950* – M.J. Hoskins (Oxford, Thesis 1976)

Although a planned building programme for "Secondary Schools" was in the pipeline, some older schools were already being replaced or improved because of their age or condition. In 1925, the old St. Bede's School was demolished and replaced by a new building which was built in the same sandstone as the original school. The Technical College in Victoria Square was renamed The Widnes Municipal Technical College.

For many of the local schoolboys the woodwork lessons were an enjoyable break from the strict discipline of the three "R's". What was particularly enjoyable for the pupils of West Bank School, as well as for St. Patrick's and St. Marie's Boys' Schools, was the fact that they were required to leave their own school environment and walk to Simms Cross. The Simms Cross Handicraft Centre was opened on 1st September 1924, with Mr. Jones, of the Farnworth Handicraft Centre, as its Head teacher. Both of these centres offered basic tutorials in the craft of woodworking for the schoolboys of Widnes.

By this time, advances in health and welfare provisions also extended to schoolchildren and arrangements were made for additional health services, which would be initiated in the schools. At school, children received medical and cleanliness examinations by nurses who made an average of 34 visits per year to each local school. Among the persistent problems encountered were: head lice (which was higher in girls than boys); ringworm; scabies; bronchitis; rickets; chorea; tuberculosis of the glands, spine and joints; and cases of suspected pulmonary tuberculosis. Impetigo was a major problem, as were ear infections and eye conditions such as conjunctivitis.

In 1926 the administration of the Schools Medical Service was divided into four districts. Each of the districts was provided with a clinic where the treatment of minor ailments, the inspection of special cases, and the examination of infants were carried out. Routine inspections were carried out which included the correction of eye defects. Mr. H. V. Foster was appointed to examine and treat defects of the throat, nose and ear, and Mr. E. Fox carried out the "X-ray treatment of ringworm". In 1924 Mr. H B. Davies was appointed as a part-time dental surgeon with Nurse Turton as his dental assistant. Also appointed were Mr. T. P. McMurray for orthopaedic treatment and Miss. E. L. Bartlett as an after-care nurse.

In 1926 the Medical Officer's Report for Schools said that:

The only schools of modern construction are St. Marie's Boys' and Ditton Council Schools. It is not to be expected that the older schools conform to the standard of modern requirements of school hygiene, but with perhaps one exception, no radical structural alteration can be considered imperative. Substantial improvements have been effected at St. Bede's Boys' School, and minor alterations in various directions have been carried out from time to time at the Council Schools. The cloakroom accommodation in some schools is inadequate both in amount and in quality and satisfactory arrangements for the drying of wet clothes do not exist.

The striking improvement in the class lines of the children since the beginning of medical inspection continues to be maintained. Rarely do we now come across a child in a very verminous condition. The improved cleanliness of children is also shown in the marked reduction in the number of scabies. In 1921, there were 194 cases and last year there were 14.

The incidence of pulmonary tuberculosis amongst children is not high. It is estimated that there are 30 children of school age who have definite signs of pulmonary tuberculosis. The total number of children suffering from tuberculosis of joints or bones is 16 and those with tuberculosis of the skin 8.

The most prevalent external eye disease was, as usual, conjunctivitis, and the majority of those found among the special cases examined, since such cases do not attend school owing to the condition being contagious. One of the beneficial results of the child welfare work has been the early detection and treatment of squint. In the majority of cases of squint if the condition is allowed to go untreated until the child is over six years of age, the squinting eye becomes blind from non-use.

Defective hearing in a marked degree imposes a serious handicap on children during school life. All children found to have defective hearing are referred to the ear specialist for examination.

In the same report, the Medical Officer addressed the subject of providing an "Open Air School" for Widnes:

No provision has yet been made for the establishment of an open-air school. The arrangements that have been made, for attending to the health of school children in the Borough, cannot be regarded as complete until and open-air school is provided. There are at least 100 children who are physically unfit to attend the elementary school for sufficient period to enable them to benefit educationally. They are examined by the School Medical Officer at regular intervals, receive some treatment and improve in health, but they quickly relapse if allowed to attend school. Such children are not only physically handicapped in later life, but their range of occupation is further limited by their lack of knowledge. The ideal site for an open-air school is undoubtedly Pex Hill, but its distance from the most populous parts of the Borough is a disadvantage from the administrative standpoint. An alternative site would be Victoria Park, and it would be possible to so design the building that it could be utilised for other public needs when not required for school purposes.

At that point in time, the Education Committee resolved to form a sub-committee to consider the provision of an Open-Air School. Following on from this, a temporary school for "delicate children" was opened in 1928. There was only accommodation for 22 children. A permanent building, accommodating 120 children, was erected later at the rear of the old Farnworth Grammar School. The staff of this new school consisted of the headmistress, Miss M.

A. Griffiths, and three assistant teachers, Miss Aspinwall, Miss Hardman and Miss Southwood. The building contractor for the school was Mr. J. E. Farrell of Widnes. An additional note of interest was that the bricks for this building were obtained from Messrs. Wood & Co. who operated from the well- known "Old Teapot Works" in St. Helens. Around the same time as the provision of an Open-Air School was being discussed, the Local Education Authority also made arrangements for the care of what were classed as "mentally defective children". In 1929 a temporary school was opened for these children at the Baptist Chapel Schoolroom in Deacon Road.

In the month following the General Strike, in 1926, members of the Widnes Education Committee discussed the necessity of feeding needy school children in the Borough. Councillor Squires told the members that a letter had been received from Mr. W. Roscoe stating that at a joint meeting of the Labour Party, the Trades and Labour Council, the local branch of the I.L.P.[37], and the Widnes Women's Co-operative Guild, the question of feeding the school children was considered.

"It had been brought to their notice that a lot of distress prevailed in the town and it was becoming more acute. A month ago, the total number on the unemployment register was 1,450 and the present total was 2,572, an increase of 1,122 with a tendency to increase still further. In the Widnes district, there were 200 miners who, with their wives and families, would total something like 800 to 1000. All these people were getting was Poor Law relief. He had been requested to bring the matter before the Education Authority with a view to The Act being put into operation".

Councillor Squires said that he had been in close touch with the attendance officers for the past few weeks. Up to the present, the committee had had no real evidence that would lead them to

---

[37] *Independent Labour Party*

believe that at that moment there was any absolute necessity for setting *The Act* in motion. However, they had decided to call Head Teachers together and enquire into the situation. None of them wanted a child to go hungry, but they recognised that the position was different today than the time when there was no real relief and the children depended on voluntary effort. If the Local Authorities set *The Act* in motion The Guardians would, of course, stop the relief that was at present being given for the children. Councillor Hanley said 80 to 100 children were being supplied daily with dinner and tea. He appreciated the great difficulty that the teachers had in getting information. There was still a great amount of pride left in some people[38].

The subject of corporal punishment in schools has always been a contentious one. In the early days there did not appear to be any hard and fast rules as to how this should be administered, or by whom. By the early years of the twentieth century, things had begun to change. However, some teachers seem to have been over harsh with their administration of corporal punishment. In 1922, the father of a pupil at St. Patrick's School came into the school and struck a teacher because he had severely chastised his son the day before[39]. In March 1927, the father of a pupil at Warrington Road School complained of irregular infliction of corporal punishment on his daughter. Two months later, at a meeting of the Education Committee it was agreed that the following rules should be imposed.

Corporal punishment of all kinds should be discouraged, and that discipline and good conduct in the schools should be secured by other means. All irregular forms of punishment, such as boxing the ear, striking on any part of the head, or shaking the body, are strictly prohibited.

---

[38] *Widnes Education Sub Committee Minutes* – June 1926

[39] *SL429/2/4* – County Archives, Cheshire Record Office

In order to provide for exceptional cases, corporal punishment may be administered in the schools under the following conditions:

Head Teachers shall be directly responsible for the infliction of corporal punishment but they are allowed in certain cases to delegate to a Certified Class Teacher the power to administer punishment. All delegation or withdrawal of same must be given in writing and a record of this must be entered in the School Log Book.

If punishment of a more serious nature than the infliction of two strokes is necessary, the Head Teacher must administer it.

There was serious overcrowding at St. Marie's School, Newtown, in 1927. The increasing number of pupils had caused the local parish priest, Father Corcoran, to write to The Education Committee to suggest that the new Parochial Hall, in Lugsdale Road, be used to provide temporary accommodation for two classes of senior girls. Although at that time, this was said to be a "temporary measure", the Parochial Hall continued to be used as classrooms for decades.

In 1927 Lancashire County Council announced the Junior Scholarship awards and the following pupils were named as recipients.

Stanley Griffiths	*Simms Cross County School*
Annie Gallagher	*St. Bede's R.C. School*
Benjamin Scott	*Farnworth C. E. School*
Florence Edwardson	*Warrington Road School*
Frederick Coleman	*Warrington Road School*
Sadie E. Wendt	*Farnworth C. E. School*
Kenneth Woodroofe*	*Halebank C. E. School*
James Dutton*	*Farnworth C. E. School*

---

* * All children were 11 years of age with the exception of * who were 10 years old.

Harry Broome	*Simms Cross County School*
Leslie Quinn	*Simms Cross County School*
Alfred G. Atkin	*Simms Cross County School*
John Morgan	*Warrington Road School*
Edna Burgess	*West Bank County School*
Arthur Harper	*Simms Cross County School*
Gordon L. Unsworth*	*Farnworth C. E. School*
Marion Taylor	*Simms Cross County School*
Dudley Fildes	*Farnworth C. E. School*
Roger Hodson	*Simms Cross County School*
Gertrude Wright	*Widnes C. E. School*
Leonard Bower	*Simms Cross County School*
Herbert Lightfoot	*Warrington Road School*
Ada Barton	*Simms Cross County School*
John Middlehurst	*Simms Cross County School*
Kenneth Ormroyde	*Simms Cross County School*
George K. Barber	*Farnworth C. E. School*
Frederick Welding	*Simms Cross County School*
Arthur Hampson	*Simms Cross County School*
Clara E. Meredith	*Simms Cross County School*

A number of new assistant teachers were appointed in 1928. The following teachers were named as probationers that year.

Mr. Samuel Powell	*Central School*
Miss Hilda B. Crake	*St. Bede's School*
Miss Mabel Rushton	*Simms Cross School*
Miss Edith Galvin	*St. Marie's School*
Miss Catherine Dolan	*St. Marie's School.*
Miss M.J. Hart	*St. Bede's School*

In September 1928 the Education Committee considered a request from Mr. J.A. Hutchin, of the *"Lancashire and Cheshire Band of Hope and Temperance Union"*. Mr. Hutchin was seeking permission to pay his annual visit to the local Council Schools to give lessons on temperance. His request was granted. In education those days, a great deal of emphasis was placed on moral values and codes of behaviour. Indeed, standards that had been set by the earlier educationalists were still in place during the 1920s. *The Elementary School Code of 1904*, which was designed to implant in the children *"habits of industry, self control, and courageous perseverance in the face of difficulties"*, was still very much adhered to.

An "Essay writing competition" for children over the age of 11 years was held in April 1929. The competition was open to children from the counties of Lancashire, Cheshire, and Derbyshire and there were over 10,000 entrants. The winner of the competition was 11½ year old Tommy Giblin, a pupil at St. Marie's School, Widnes. His essay was about "Ovaltine". Little Tommy Giblin was presented with 10 volumes of *The Children's Encyclopaedia*, value 6 guineas.

Everyday Life

In 1920 it had been less than 80 years since John Hutchinson had brought the first significant chemical manufacture to Widnes. At that time, in 1847, the population of the town was little more than 2000 and our inhabitants had earned their living in a variety of ways including agricultural work, maritime occupations, weaving, clock making, tool making, and other varied small cottage industries. The inception of the chemical industry had brought with it other service industries and a dramatic increase in population. In July 1921, the Widnes population statistics tell us that the estimated number of inhabitants was 37,000. The birth rate was 26.7 per 1000 and the death rate 14.7 per 1000. Later that year the population figure was 38,861. This increased population growth was linked to the extension of the Borough boundaries. *"The Widnes Extension Bill"* went before Parliament on 13th July 1920. The result of this was an extension of the boundaries to the parishes of Ditton, Halebank, and part of Cuerdley bringing these areas into the Borough of Widnes. It was also agreed at the inauguration of this *"Bill"* that a review would be made at a later date with a view to extend the boundaries further to include several other rural districts.

Those of you who read *"Into the Crucible"* will be familiar with the details of the origins of our local society. The rapid industrialisation that came about during the 19th century was responsible for large waves of immigration into the town. People came from all corners of this island and also from Ireland and other European countries. The Irish were by far the largest ethnic group in the town and consequently Irish affairs and events were of great interest to a large percentage of the Widnes population.

During the 1920s there were a number of important political and military events taking place in Ireland, which culminated in a civil war. The signing of *The British-Irish Treaty* was viewed as a compromise, and was far from satisfactory for any side. All those concerned accepted The Treaty with the greatest reluctance. The main issues were that the Northern Ireland Protestants were committed to remaining in the Union, whereas the Sinn Fein Irish leaders were committed to independence. However, this is an over simplification of a situation to which there is no simple interpretation. I think it is fair to say that the *"Government of Ireland Act"* went a long way in preparing for partition. The Conservative Government of that time had a strong aversion to Irish Home Rule, let alone independence. As Lloyd George was dependant on the Conservative Party for support in his coalition Government, it is not surprising that the terms of The Treaty meant that the six counties of Ulster were kept in the Union. Modern historians have asked if perhaps there was an alternative solution, or maybe another politician or statesman, rather than Lloyd George, may have come up with a better result. In Widnes, the Irish population were closely following these worrying developments.

In March 1920 there was a huge Irish demonstration in Widnes. A meeting was held at The Alexandra Theatre under the auspices of the newly formed Widnes Branch of *Irish Self-Determination League of Great Britain*. The theatre was full to capacity and an Irish Pipe Band supported the proceedings. One of the guest speakers was The Rev. Eugene Nevin, from St. Helens, who said:

"I believe there are 10,000 Irish people in Widnes so we expect something great and glorious we expect a smashing blow for the freedom of Ireland. Keep your eye on Widnes, and if the Irish people of Widnes disappoint the hopes of Ireland my eyes very much deceive me this afternoon"

Following the signing of *The Government of Ireland Act* in December 1920 there were numerous meetings held by the various Irish groups in the town. *The Widnes Weekly News*, through its "letters columns" became a platform for ventilating views. In February 1921 there were angry letters from "Widnes Irish" demanding self-determination for Ireland. Some letters drew comparisons with the French Revolution and championed the cause of Irish nationalism. Other sections of the Widnes population reacted to this by penning angry replies. Amazingly, some of the pro-"Irish Independence" letters arrived at *The Widnes Weekly News* from as far away as Montana in the U.S.A. The anonymous author of these letters used a pseudonym. [40]

Sadly, in May that year a young man from Alpha Street, who was serving in the British Army, was killed in action during the troubles in Ireland. The young 18 year old bandsman and his brother were stationed at The Richmond Barracks in Dublin. He had joined *The South Lancashire Regiment* in 1919 and 18 months later transferred to *The King's Own Royal Regiment*. As a boy, he attended St. Bede's School and prior to joining up he worked at the Pilkington Sullivan Works. On the day of his death, the two brothers and several other soldiers had been instructed to go to the barracks to collect the mail. When only 200 yards from the building, a party of *"Sinn Feiners"* opened fire on them and the young Widnes man was fatally wounded. On the day of his funeral, the route to the cemetery was lined with townspeople. Comrades from *The Kings Own Royal Regiment* accompanied the cortege. Preceding the hearse were members of *The 335th Battalion R.F.A.* (Widnes) and the band of *The 2nd Cheshire Regiment*. The Rev. Dean Clarke conducted the funeral service in the cemetery chapel, and at the conclusion of the committal service, there was a rifle salute followed by the "Last Post".

---

[40] *The writer of these letters has now been identified, by this author, as Widnesian, Jack Carney. Jack Carney was working as a journalist at that time in Butte, Montana.*

Less than a month later, *The Widnes Weekly News* reported on a number of arrests in Garston and Woolton in connection with a series of incidents that had occurred the previous week. There had been several disturbances at various locations throughout Merseyside. It would seem that these were planned to happen simultaneously to create the maximum impact. All these incidents were attributed to the activities of local *"Sinn Feiners"*. Prior to the official press report, rumours had spread like wildfire throughout Liverpool and its hinterlands, including Widnes. These rumours ranged from open riot to organised murder on a large scale. Fortunately these stories were untrue, although guns were actually used and some shooting did occur but without injury to either police or civilians. There was a shooting incident at Wavertree, and also one at Mossley Hill, where telegraph wires had been cut near to the railway embankment, causing disruption to telephone and signalling apparatus. Telegraph wires were also cut at Fazakerley. Similar acts were taking place at the same time at Hunts Cross, Garston and Allerton. In Wavertree, a police constable foiled an attack on petrol tankers at the premises of the North Western Railway in Rathbone Road. Guns were used at this incident and the raiders fired a number of shots. The police constable returned fire but the men escaped capture. At Wheathill Woods, in Woolton, shots were also fired.

Whilst there were small groups of people willing to take aggressive action, most Irish were hopeful of bringing about a peaceful settlement to the "Irish Question" by political dialogue. In Widnes, with its large Irish population, the subject was hotly debated and numerous meetings were held at The Borough Hall and The Alexandra Theatre. John Scurr, an Alderman, from the London Borough of Poplar, came to address a large audience of local Irishmen at The Borough Hall in December 1921. Mr. Pat Hanley chaired the meeting.

In 1927 another Irish organisation was formed in the town. *The Widnes Irish Fellowship Club* held its inaugural meeting at the

Central Hotel in March that year when over sixty members sat down to dinner to celebrate its formation. The Rev. Dean Kenny was the President of the club. Among its members were the Mayor, Councillor Millar, and Councillors P. Hanley, R. Graham, and J. Connaughton. In proposing a toast the Mayor said when referring to the Irish of Widnes:

"During the 34 years of incorporation many Irishmen in Widnes had played their part and there had been five mayors of that nationality who had given 12 years of service. He was pleased to be among them and associate himself with their new organisation".

The traditions and culture of the Irish population was kept alive by local Catholic parish clubs, who counted the Irish as the major group in their congregations. During the 1920s, and for a number of following decades, the Irish parishioners of St. Marie's in Lugsdale and St. Patrick's in West Bank, were able to enjoy Irish ceilidhs in their Parish Halls. For those who were not Irish born, and maybe did not know the steps of the traditional set dances, special "beginners classes" were held on a frequent basis in St Marie's Hall.

Like the Irish, the Welsh residents of the town continued to promote and exhibit a pride in their national heritage. The Welsh chapels had large congregations and at this time many of the services were still conducted in the Welsh language. Welsh musical traditions found expression in the Eisteddfod, an annual event originally started in 1895 by some of the early Welsh residents of the town. This musical festival, which included choral concerts and competitions, marked its quarter century in 1920 and was at that time still well attended and enjoyed by all sections of the community. In fact, in the 1920s, non-Welsh people were actively encouraged to participate in order to keep the Eisteddfod alive. In 1923 the organisers voiced concern about the shortage of competitors in the "male voice" section. It was said that the lack of patronage was due to the small amount of prize money being offered and also the fact that *"The Highfield Choir"*, from Runcorn, were considered to be "unbeatable". The following year, the President of the Eisteddfod Committee, Mrs. J.C. Crawford, on opening the event said:

"She was a Welsh woman and although she had lived in Widnes 74 years she could speak the Welsh language today as well as ever she could. Her father and mother were the two people who had started the Welsh cause in Widnes and she had always done what she could for the various Welsh Churches in the town". In conclusion, Mrs. Crawford gave a brief address in Welsh to the children.

The Widnes Welsh also had a local branch of the association known as *The Society of David*. Each year, on St. David's Day, they met at Moor Lane Welsh Congregational Chapel to celebrate this event. One event in the 1920s was described thus:

The meeting was opened by the singing of the Welsh National anthem "Hen Wlad fy Nhadau" the solo being beautifully rendered by Miss Towena Thomas. The children's choir, in picturesque Welsh costume, led the chorus singing. The national flower, the daffodil, was very much in evidence and a strong sentiment of love for Wales and the Welsh language pervaded the gathering. Mr. H. W. Hughes, the chairman, urged the Welsh people in the town to keep the language alive by speaking Welsh in their homes.

In 1920s Widnes, there were still a considerable number of Lithuanian and Polish immigrants who had not yet mastered the English language. Whilst their children had integrated and were bi-lingual, speaking English at school and Lithuanian or Polish at home, for many of the older age group the language was still a huge problem. The Liverpool Catholic Archdiocese made provisions for a bi-lingual priest to attend St. Patrick's Church each month in order to hear their confessions. This monthly hearing of "Poles'Confessions" continued until well after the second war, until such time as this facility was no longer required, as the older generation died out[41].

In Widnes at this time, there was still a network of social clubs and societies with different pedigrees and contacts that had 19th century origins. Charitable organisations drawn from a desire to help or reform, as well as numerous philanthropic associations founded in churches and chapels, were abundant in the town. The young people of these churches were also encouraged to join junior sections or societies. The Anglican *Boys Brigade* was hugely popular and offered opportunities for boys to develop a sense of adventure as well as encouraging a strong Christian discipline. *The Widnes Catholic Young Men's Society* also provided a fraternal atmosphere with a strong Christian flavour. In February 1920, this society was honoured by a visit from the writer and poet, Mr. Hilaire Belloc, who came to speak to them.   The following year, 1921, *The Knights of St. Columba* was established in the town. In February 1929 *"The Knights"* opened their own Hall in Frederick Street. The building was estimated to have cost in the region of £4000. During this same year, other churches and organisations were also providing new halls for their members. The parishioners of St. Mary's Church in West Bank built a hall in Davies Street, and *The Albert Road Wesleyans* opened their new Memorial Hall.   By the 1920s *The Widnes Freemason Lodges* had also outgrown their premises, because of increased membership, and found it necessary to relocate to a larger venue at St. Paul's Chambers in Victoria Road.

Musical societies were also much in evidence and many of these had their origins among the Welsh community of the town. Miss Towena Thomas, who had been associated with the Eisteddfod, was continually engaged in promoting musical events and staged many concerts with her choir, *"The Widnes Musical Society"*. Early in the 1920s another group of people formed *"The Widnes Amateur*

---

[41] *St. Marie`s R.C. Church – (Parish Archives).*

Players" under the musical leadership of Mr. Herbert H. Wilkinson and the theatrical directorship of Mr. Gar Kiddie of The Alexandra Theatre. This group staged musicals, light opera, and various popular and classical music events.

Apart from the social activities of church, political, and musical organisations, another type of club was developing in the form of "Works Recreational Clubs". Gossage's provided a recreational ground for their employees which included a cricket pitch, tennis courts, bowling greens and two football pitches. In 1925, the United Alkali Company opened their swish new premises, which catered for all types of sporting tastes including tennis, hockey, cricket, bowls and football. Following the absorption of the U.A.C. into I.C.I. the club was renamed The I.C.I. Recreation Club.

Less than a year after *The Widnes Extension Bill* had been passed by Parliament, another, though smaller, type of extension took place in town when "St. Luke's Graveyard" at Farnworth was extended. In April 1921 the Bishop of Liverpool performed the consecration ceremony. On that occasion he said, when explaining the meaning of the service of consecration, that:

"Consecration did not infuse virtue into anything. It simply set it aside for the service of the Lord; it set it apart from all the profane and common uses. When hundreds of years ago that beautiful church was consecrated, no virtue was breathed into its stones; the building was simply set apart from all secular purposes and devoted to the service of God. That day they had set apart a particular piece of land where the bodies of their loved ones might be laid to await resurrection of the dead. Henceforth no one would be allowed to build on that land; cattle could not graze on it; or games be played on it. It was holy ground. Ever since he had known their churchyard it had been beautifully kept and he felt quite sure that those who had done so much for that church would not allow it to become otherwise".

When reading about Widnes in the 1920s, one is acutely aware of the terrible poverty experienced by a greater part of the population. Indeed, poverty was usual and pauperism was not unusual. The inquisitorial procedures of The Poor Law and the very minimum relief offered, plus the general air of grudging charity that appears to have permeated its activities, must have made it the last resort for all but the desperate. The effects of high unemployment, the aftermath of the war that had left many families fatherless, and the general impression of gloom and depression paint a dismal picture of the town. However, perhaps we forget when we view this through modern eyes, that this was the norm at that time. A correspondent, writing in the *Widnes Weekly News* in the summer of 1921 gives us another glimpse, with an altogether much brighter impression, as he describes *"Widnes Sea Shore"*:

On a bright sunny day, Widnes by the river looks like some fashionable watering place only much more interesting. There is the blue sky, the rippling silver sea, the silver and gold sands, the clean white promenade, and above the refreshing gardens. Adding to these joys are the glimpses of the neighbouring town of Runcorn, the parish church looking as silent as if it were just in a picture book, the row of red houses in Bridge Street, the sunny towers and chimneys, the suspension bridge, and the outlines of many boats.

Now and then, a train passes over the old bridge, and one looks up at the famous construction and notices its towers, its battlements, and its shields. As always, the stately Transporter Bridge is busy, now at Runcorn, now at Widnes, "never hastening, never resting". At ebb tide the children gather underneath the car begging for coppers, and the impatient motorists awaiting transport amuse themselves watching the urchins scramble in the mud. Then off to the water, for another swim or once more to sail their boats, or to catch shrimps and crabs, now in harmony, now quarrelling furiously.

Then there is for them the joy of building sand castles in the sand or a long walk along the warm dry stretches of land. Seeing it at low tide one can hardly realise that large ships can sail down there. From the gardens above, the happy children are watched by elders, who in this quiet spot, seek rest from the worries of business. Here, occasionally, the children sit on the grass and eat lunch talking "nineteen to the dozen" "Aw! Our Robert's ad more'n me!"

It will always be interesting to watch the busy signs of life all around, and hear the newsboys cries mingle with the sound of the children's happy shouts, and the conversations of the elders. Time passes very swiftly and pleasantly by the riverside.

To compound this impression, another pleasing report appeared in the same month when *"The Widnes Yacht Club"* held their annual Regatta. A record of the event stated that:

A spanking westerly breeze and sparkling sunshine combined to make almost ideal conditions for both sailors and spectators. The decorated "steamer" was a bright spot in a very lively nautical scene, while the promenade and the approach to the Transporter were lined with interested spectators. Of the two principal races, one was confined to members of the Widnes Yacht Club and the other open to Widnes, Warrington and Runcorn. The course was from New Ferry to a mark boat off Cuerdley Marsh and back to the winning post – the aforementioned "steamer" moored near the Accident Hospital. Sports for the youngsters followed the sailing events once the tide had retired far enough to permit. A sand-building competition produced some very pretty designs, to select the best of which must have been something of a puzzle to the judge.

The children of various Sunday Schools in the town also enjoyed innocent and unsophisticated summer pleasures. During the summer of 1921 The Milton Congregational Sunday School travelled to Lea Green, Rainhill, by charabanc. They enjoyed a pleasant afternoon of games and races followed by a substantial picnic provided by the Misses Hodgkinson. The children of

Trinity Chapel, in Waterloo Road, were conveyed by corporation bus to Hough Green for their annual treat. The afternoon was spent in a field near Ash Lane, loaned by a Mr. Wright, where they had the usual games and races and in addition to an excellent tea, they were given bags of sweets.   Children from The Lacey Street Sunday School also benefited from the loan of Mr. Wright's field and their annual treat followed on the same lines.   A similar excursion was experienced by the children from St. Paul's Church, this time the field was provided by Mr.Humphries.

During the same era, another type of "Sunday School" was regularly taking place in the area of Spike Island.   This school however was not a religious but a gambling one.   Each Sunday large groups of men (and also some women) would assemble to bet on games of "pitch and toss".   The police often raided these illegal gambling schools and there were regular prosecutions, although often these would only be for trespassing on railway property.   Each summons usually involved a significant number of people. On one single occasion, in 1921, no fewer than 36 people were prosecuted, including four women.

In September 1921 a young child was allegedly "cured" at Holywell in North Wales. The beneficiary of this cure was a 6 year old child from Widnes.   The little girl had been born with a clubfoot.   Despite numerous operations at Myrtle Street Hospital in Liverpool, all attempts to put her right foot into a normal position had failed. The child, whose tragic background almost resembled a Dickens novel, lived with her father and stepmother in Albert Road.   Her mother burned to death in an accident when the little girl was just six months old. Her father had lost his sight in the war, and was working as a matchmaker from his home in Albert Road. The father, having heard of the healing waters of "St. Winifred's Well", decided to send the child on a charabanc trip to Holywell in the care of a lady from Midwood Street.   According to reports, the child was placed into the waters at the Well, and when

she emerged the foot had moved into a normal position and
remained so from that time onwards.

This story highlights a sad fact of life as it was then. The
numerous birth and other defects due to, amongst other things,
lack of proper nutrition or adequate antenatal care. The number of
children in the town who were suffering from physical disabilities
or deformities was recognised by a fund opened by the Mayor,
Dan Garghan, some years later. *"The Crippled Children Fund"* was
intended to raise money *"for provision of operative treatment for the
crippled and deformed children of the borough"*. Money was raised
through concerts, carnivals, whist drives and collections
throughout the town. At the end of the first year, a report of
expenditure was produced. The secretary, when reporting to the
committee said:

*"The natural questions now arise. What are the practical results? What
can be shown for the money given? At the last meeting of the committee,
Dr. Jones, the Medical Officer of Health, submitted a summary of the
cases treated, from which the following will serve to answer the questions
raised: 2 cases of congenital dislocation of hips (result, hips placed in
position); 6 cases of paralysis of legs with deformity (deformity corrected
and children able to walk); 5 cases of club foot or severe deformity of feet
(deformity corrected); 7 cases of knock knee or bow legs (legs
straightened); 3 cases of wry neck (corrected). But why go on? The
result to the child, no less than to the community, is beyond words.*

*During the year, 350 cases have been through the hands of Dr.
McMurray, the Orthopaedic Specialist. At the present time 7 children
are in the Children's Hospital at Heswall, 3 with congenital dislocation of
hips, 1 very deformed legs, 1 severe rickets, 1 paralysis of shoulder with
deformity and 1 paralysis of legs with deformity. The cost whilst in
hospital is 33 shillings per week per child. In addition, 120 children are
attending once, twice, thrice or even every day in the week for massage
treatment by Miss Bartlett at the centre at Mill Brow".*

The establishment of this clinic at Mill Brow was facilitated by a loan of £900 to Widnes Corporation from the Ministry of Health in November 1920. The money was used to enable the Council to purchase the building known as "Cliffe House" in Mill Brow, which was to be used as a permanent Child Welfare Clinic.

For many, poverty put constraints upon social life. Nonetheless, sport, for the workingman, was an important part of the local scene. Spectator sports particularly, served as light relief from the mundane drudge of factory life, for those lucky enough to be in employment! *Widnes Rugby Club* offered thrilling performances at their weekly matches. Notable players who made their debut during this decade included the famous *Nat Silcock and Jack Higgins, Fred Kelsall, Albert Ratcliff and Jack Dennett.* For the cricketing enthusiasts *Widnes Cricket Club* resumed play after the war in 1919, although the full playing strength was not resumed until 1920. In 1921 both of its teams were entered in *The Southwest Lancashire League.* S.H. Wynne took over captaincy of the second eleven in 1925 and this team went on to win the second division in seasons 1926, 1927 and 1928. Among the notable local cricketers during this decade, the names of *H. Ireland, S.H. Wynne and L. Callon* are always likely to be mentioned[42].

Like football and cricket, boxing also provided an outlet for those wishing to participate on a practical level as well as for the spectator. Even though boxing had been around for generations, two things happened to this sport in the 1920s. Firstly, it became more scientific, and secondly it became a "popular entertainment", particularly in America where boxing matches offered huge monetary prizes. Jack Dempsey and Gene Tunney were the legendary World Heavyweights of that era. Here in Widnes, Tom Mallinson, of Deacon Road, was well known in local and national boxing circles during this decade. His ability in the ring led to

---

[42] Information on *Widnes Cricket Club* was kindly verified by Club President, Mr. Gordon Gilmour.

him being invited to America where a number of opponents were lined up for him. In 1922 Widnes sporting aficionados received news of Mallinson's spectacular win in America. On the 18th August, he met Billy Carney in a 10 round contest in New Bedford. The fight went the distance with Mallinson winning on points. An American newspaper, in New Bedford, gave the following description of the fight:

Billy Carney, of this city, who usually leaves the ring after a fight with a new scalp added to his collection, got as merry a jousting as ever went with a roller coaster ride when he tried conclusions with Tom Mallinson, of England, at the Elm Rink last evening.

The Englishman demonstrated that he is quicker than the New Bedford welter, and he gets his punches over faster. Carney flashed in the ninth round and made a bid for an encore in the tenth, but Mallinson was always ready to slug it out with him, and had such an overwhelming lead at the finish that it was impossible for the Englishman to lose except by a lucky knockout"[43].

A different kind of fight was in the news from time to time. "Dog-fights" were, thankfully, outlawed. However, this did not deter those who wished to gamble on the outcome of this cruel clash, where an animal could be killed or maimed for the entertainment of the gathered "sportsmen"! In 1924 a number of local men were heavily fined for organising illegal dog fighting in the town.

Whilst the male population of Widnes at this time were able to watch and participate in a number of leisure activities, womens' leisure was subject to a series of financial, domestic, and moral constraints. They were mainly excluded from some of the larger arenas of mass entertainment, such as spectator sports. They

---

[43] *In the 1930`s, in his retirement, Tom Mallinson acted as promoter for two other local boxers, brothers Ned and Mick Lucas.*

Laying the Foundation Stone for the Cenotaph – 28th August 1920

Procession to Victoria Park for the unveiling of the Cenotaph – 28th September 1921

A class of boys from St. Marie's School – June 1927

depended instead upon the networks provided by family or neighbourhood for most of their social life.

On 10th December 1922 Widnes Catholics were mourning the loss of Dean Clark, the patriarch of Catholicism in Widnes. Dean Clarke had come to Widnes in 1873 to serve as a priest at St. Marie's and remained in that parish until his move to St. Bede's in 1906, where he served until his death. He was involved, as a member, in numerous public services including The Education Committee and The Prescot Board of Guardians. He, and the good Doctor O'Keeffe, had done inestimable work on behalf of the poor communities in the south end of the town. These two men also shared the regretful distinction of having been summoned to attend the horrific scene after the murder of Patrick Treacy in 1879. Both were called as witnesses at the trial of his murderers, who were subsequently hanged for this monstrous crime[44].

The following summer the parishioners of St. Marie's, in Lugsdale Road, were looking forward to their first social event in the new Parish Hall. The first dance in the new hall took place in July 1923. Dancing was from 8.00 pm. till 11.00 pm. and the admission price was 1s.6d. The following week the dance started at 7.30 p.m. and the cost of admission had been reduced to 9d for Gents and 6d for Ladies. The new hall was a great asset to the parish. Apart from the weekly dances on Saturday nights, there was a weekly concert on Sunday evenings. The concerts played to full houses and the entertainment was usually provided by a number of local parties. The regular entertainers were: *The Lugsdale Party; The Black and Whites; The Lugsdale Jazz Band; and Mr. Alf Radley's Party.* The front seats were 6d and seats in the rest of the hall were to be had for only 3d. There were also regular boxing contests held in the hall as well as a weekly whist drive and Irish ceildhes.

---

[44] *"Into the Crucible"* – Jean M. Morris (Countyvise 2005)

Local churches were the heart of social activity in the communities. Outings and trips were organised in the summer months by churches of all denominations. In August 1923, St. Marie's had their annual parochial picnic and went to Rhyl by charabanc at a cost of 7s.6d per head. Because of the limited transport available, it was necessary for the "charas" to make a double journey[45].

In the first month of 1923 Widnes Borough Council made arrangements for the removal of "Simms Cross Lamp". The "lamp" was in fact an old Victorian air vent, one of a number that were once scattered around the town. The locations where some of these were originally sited were: Victoria Square; Frederick Street/Widnes Road; Lugsdale by the Bridge; Mill Brow; Warrington Road near the Castle; Birchfield Road/Derby Road; Birchfield Road/Highfield Road; two in Moss Bank, one near The Golden Bowl and the other near Bowmans Works.

Widnes received a royal visit in July 1925 when King George V and Queen Mary made a fleeting visit to the town. The Mayor, Dan Garghan, welcomed the royal party in Victoria Square where an enthusiastic crowd had gathered. Among those given a special place at the event were a large number of disabled war veterans. St. Paul's Church bells rang out in greeting, and a musical welcome was provided by *The Nazareth House Boys' Band*. The national anthem was sung by the members of *The Widnes Musical and Operatic Society*, although it was reported that St. Paul's bells had drowned out their voices.

Early in this decade, the owners of commercial businesses in the town voiced their concerns about people going out of town to purchase larger items while only using shops in Widnes for smaller items and groceries. These comments provoked a series of angry letters to *The Widnes Weekly News*. One correspondent

---

[45] St.Marie`s Parish Archives.

claimed that the reason she, and other local people, travelled to Liverpool and other neighbouring towns to purchase food, clothing and furniture, was because the local traders were *"a horde of pirates"*. However, some people gave a more acceptable reason...more choice. The members of The Runcorn & Widnes Co-operative Society were advised, *"Not to take the bus or train and carry trade away to distant towns"*. Shortly after this, The Co-op introduced "hire purchase" into their furnishing department, possibly as a means of keeping trade in the town. The Co-operative Society also added to their string of premises. As well as extending their central drapery department in Victoria Square, they opened another new shop, in Gladstone Street, in 1927.

Notwithstanding the fact that some may have preferred to shop out of the Borough, Widnes Market attracted custom not only from the inhabitants of Widnes but also from neighbouring towns. The Market Hall, near to the Town Hall, was erected in 1875. In addition to this, there was a large open market. In the early years, it had run at a loss but from the arrival of the bus service, in 1909, it never looked back. In 1925 the open market was covered over, creating the large market building that was to serve the town well for generations. The new covered market was considered to be a boon to both buyers and sellers, particularly in wet weather.

By the 1920s the bus service that began in 1909 had expanded considerably. With the development of more routes, the service was well used. With the increase in service, there was also an increase in accidents. A number of minor accidents involving buses are reported during the 1920s. However, there were a small number of serious accidents as well. One of these occurred in November 1921 when an Irishman, who lodged in Rock Lane, Upton, was struck down by a bus in Birchfield Road and killed. The driver of the bus was traumatised by the incident but the Coroner returned a verdict of misadventure and attached no blame to anyone. Motorcars were also becoming more common and, as with the buses, we see reports of accidents involving cars increasing.

On November 27th 1925 the steam ship *"Sutton"* owned by The Overton Steamship Company, of Liverpool, was sunk in Cardigan Bay. The shock and horror of this tragedy was felt all around this area especially in our sister town, as there were nine Runcornians on board including a 16 year old youth. The *"Sutton"* left Aberystwyth on the night of the 27th in the command of Captain Terretta, and along with his crew of nine, his wife and daughter were also on board. The *"Sutton"* was bound for Antwerp. It had just taken on board a part cargo of zinc and lead concentrate, which had been loaded that evening at Aberystwyth. They set sail after dark and apart from their night lights being seen at Aberporth, a little distance down the coast, the *"Sutton"* and her crew were never seen again. A Board of Trade Inquiry found that the cargo of zinc and lead concentrates would have been kept "alive" by the vibration of the ship and that it would be an unstable cargo to carry in bad weather. At the Inquiry, the designer of the *"Sutton"* said *"that if the "Sutton" had met a rough sea and a beam wind and the cargo shifted suddenly, he thought she would go down quickly, but she would "hang" for a fairly long time, and the crew would not be able to walk on the deck"*. The ship had been in a seaworthy condition when it was inspected in September, so it was decided that the cargo, and its unusually wet composition, was probably the major factor in the loss of the *"Sutton"*.

Because of our geographical location on the banks of the river Mersey, employment in trades associated with the river was part of our heritage. Many local men were employed as mariners, master mariners and bargemen. Flat-bottomed barges, commonly known as "flats", were used for transporting materials for a variety of industries along the river. The United Alkali Company owned their own vessels and employed numerous local men on their barges. The barges owned by William Cooper & Sons were mainly engaged in the sand and gravel trade, and these were generally crewed by Widnes men. The "sandhooking flats" operated by Cooper's were employed in loading sand from off the banks of Eastham and Bromborough, on the Wirral. This sand was destined mainly for the works of Pilkington Brothers, of St.Helens, where it was used in the glass making industry. Sadly, as has often been the case in all communities that have men employed in sea or river occupations; there has frequently been loss of life[46].

Less than two and a half years after the loss of *"The Sutton"*, Widnes and Runcorn were again faced with loss of life in a shipping disaster. In February 1928 a dreadful storm hit the area causing extensive damage, especially in Newtown where roofs were stripped of their slates and whole chimneys were blown down. The covered Market Hall was also damaged and half the roof of St. Ambrose Mission Hall, in Page Lane, was blown away. At sea, and in the Mersey, many ships were battling these elements. That night two vessels carrying local men were to be involved in separate disasters. *"The Grinkle"*, a sandhooking vessel owned by Cooper's, was sunk in the gale off the Oglet and all hands lost. A lifeboat was found a few days later on Frodsham Marsh, but the bodies were not recovered until some weeks later. Six men died in that disaster, three from West Bank, one from Lowerhouse Lane, one from Runcorn, and the Captain, a Runcorn born man who was at that time residing in Aigburth. *"The Grinkle"* was an iron vessel, 136 feet long by 36 feet wide, with a carrying capacity of 400 tons. She was regarded as a strong and seaworthy boat. Cooper's had only owned her for two years prior to the disaster but she was considered to be "the latest thing" as she had special self-loading apparatus fitted.

Another local man, from Grenfell Street, the Captain of *"The Ferndale"*, lost his life when his barge, and other barges, went adrift in the Mersey during the gale. A survivor described how the crew

---

[46] See Notes

had had to lie flat on the deck to avoid being swept into the water. The barge had loaded up with sugar at Liverpool and was bound for Preston Brook. However, the weather had been too bad for them to move and they were laid up at Princes Dock for two days before setting sail. When the accident happened the weather was very rough and it was dark. They were only about seven miles from Runcorn.

There were numerous previous nautical disasters claiming lives of local men, many of the boats belonging to William Cooper & Sons.

February 1916 – *A "flat" "The Weaver" owned by William Cooper & Sons sank off Hale Head. Two Widnes men were drowned[47].*

March 1918 – *The Steamship "Severn" owned by Messrs. Abel of Runcorn, and manned by a crew of three, crashed into the approach of the Transporter Bridge on the Widnes side. All the dead were Runcorn men.*

April 1920 – *The steam flat "The Forth" owned by Lighterage & Co., Liverpool, sank of Hale Head during a gale, and the captain, a Widnes man from Water Street, was drowned.*

February 1923 – *The steam flat "Sandmail" belonging to William Cooper & Sons, sank off Garston and the crew of three, all from West Bank, were drowned.*

October 1927 – *The steam barge "Vulcan" crashed into the dock wall at Garston. There were three men on board, two, from Runcorn, managed to jump to safety. The third man, from Widnes, was drowned.*

The Transporter Bridge was also the scene of a terrible accident in 1927 when a large steam wagon and its trailer plunged from the "Transporter Car" into the Manchester Ship Canal. The driver of

[47] See Notes (re: Downer Fyldes)

the wagon, a young married man, lost his life in this tragedy. The car was full of early morning passengers heading for their workplaces in Widnes. The steamer and wagon had boarded the car at the Runcorn end at 7.30 a.m. and within a few minutes of the bridge car clearing the dock the locomotive began to move backwards. The wagon quickly gathered speed and burst through the gates, plunging into the canal below. Some men standing behind the wagon managed to jump clear but one man was unable to do so. This man, who had been in its path, was knocked into the water but was rescued by another passenger who quickly dived into the waters some 20 feet below. However, the driver of the vehicle was trapped and the vehicle quickly sunk beneath the water. Divers retrieved his body some time afterwards.

Of course, not all of the river disasters were associated with employment. There were also many swimming and other fatalities. In August 1929 three Widnes men were drowned off Rock Ferry when their punt accidentally capsized. The men, members of a party of four, had been on a pleasure trip when the accident happened. One man was rescued but three others lost their lives. One of the drowned men, who lived in Lacey Street, had survived the rigours of war, having served in *The Royal Garrison Artillery* in August 1914. After a few months training, he was sent to France in early 1915 and was one of the first 25 men to form the first French trench mortar battery. He was badly gassed in one of the first gas attacks that occurred on the Western Front, at Hill 60. He was sent home and hospitalised. A few months later, in January 1916, he returned to France and from then on he saw action in several places, the most notable being at Cambrai on 30th November 1917. At this battle, he picked up a rifle alongside the retreating infantry and helped to stem the tide. For this act of bravery, he was awarded *The Military Medal*. It is sad and ironic that this man should go through all that, and then lose his life in the pursuit of pleasure on his local river.

However, some tragedies were not accidental, as in an extremely sad and horrific case that occurred in the 1920s. Three bodies were discovered in a house near the Ball O'Ditton. A husband, his wife, and their 17 year old daughter. The wife had her throat cut, the daughter had been brutally attacked with a hammer, and the husband had taken his own life by attaching a rubber tube to a gas fitting. At the inquest the jury returned a verdict of murder and suicide. The man had been employed as a labourer at Gossages and was described as hard working and temperate. We will never know the reasons for this crime but it was suggested that an accident at work some years before, in which he received an injury to his head, had left him morose and taciturn. It was indeed a shocking and very sad crime.

In 1926 the Corporation agreed that land at Pex Hill, not presently required for "water undertaking" should be utilised for the purpose of a pleasure ground. A few years later, a correspondent wrote: *It is a circumstance worth noting that, during the summer, large parties from the neighbouring towns (Liverpool included) organise picnics to Pex Hill, a natural eminence situated about two miles from the Town Hall. This is the property of the Corporation and the public have free access."* The same source tells us that Widnes could boast over 60 acres of parks, gardens, and open spaces.[48] It also said that residentially, municipally, and industrially, Widnes was no mean place to live.

The wireless set was now becoming a part of everyday life. It was both informative and entertaining. At the time, it was considered to be something of a "communications revolution" because it was a new way of imparting information to a mass audience. The broadcasting of regular news bulletins with impartial summaries no doubt had some effect on the sales of newspapers, and it was from this period that editors began to present their news in a more sensational manner. Newspaper

---

[48] Corporation and Chamber of Commerce Handbook 1929

headlines became bigger and in order to boost circulation, content underwent subtle changes that included more feature writers.

The radio in a strange way was a counterpart of the silent films at that time – whilst the films offered pictures without words, the radio offered words without pictures. From the very beginning, it was necessary to pay a licence fee to the BBC for operating a radio receiver. But, because it was possible to construct a radio quite reasonably from a kit, or to buy a crystal set cheaply, there was no real way of estimating how many unlicensed sets were in use. The crystal sets of the 1920s cost between £1 and £2. The early receivers were run on batteries and accumulators and a headset was needed to listen in. In those early days, tuning in was something of an art. In order to receive the chosen station it was necessary to fine-tune the set. This process was not without problems. An irate wireless enthusiast wrote to *The Widnes Weekly News* in 1926 with the following complaint:

"Will you grant me the space in which to voice my indignant protest against the user of a wireless receiving set somewhere in the neighbourhood of Highfield and Birchfield Roads, who persistently oscillates with reaction his aerial to the infinite annoyance of other users. The nuisance has been particularly noticeable on between 6 and 7 p.m. and on the Daventry wavelength only. The high crescendo and decrescendo of howls from my loudspeaker has been most weird and nerve racking. Surely, it is time all users of sets knew when they were causing this sort of annoyance".

An article in *The Widnes Weekly News* suggests that the population regarded this "new entertainment facility" with some trepidation.

"Statistics have been published which prove how universal the demand for wireless receiving sets has become. In most homes are to be found apparatus of some kind or other, but there are still many people who hesitate in the belief that the working of a set is a complicated job. The

announcements on this page should be convincing evidence that notwithstanding the moderate prices of reliable sets, they are delightfully simple to operate. The recent foggy weather has convinced the majority of people who have had to stay indoors that radio is not merely a luxury but a positive necessity".

In June 1921 the General Purposes Committee of the Town Council resolved to draw the attention of the Postmaster General to the inadequate accommodation and postal facilities generally in the Borough, saying that it was a great inconvenience to the public. Five years later, in 1926, the new Widnes General Post Office opened its doors for business.   One of the first customers described the building thus:

"The front doors give access to a glazed vestibule, beyond which is a counter running the full length of the room.   A wire screen or grille rises from the edge of the public side of the counter, for the discouragement of irregular transmissions of post office valuables and to the discomfiture of the clutching hand.   Every device for facilitating business has been installed, and the maximum of convenience has been achieved by the arrangement of the furniture and the fittings.   A letter may be posted either within or without the building, and the two telephone boxes unobtrusively occupy the left end of the room, the telegram desks being under a window to the right of the door.   Sliding glass panels allow those who carry on the front shop business quick communication with those whose lives are devoted to the performance of the less spectacular but not less important duties behind the scenes".

In the late 1920s Widnes was "dance crazy".   "Rag-time" rhythms had come in before the war, along with other dances like "The Charleston", "The Black Bottom", and "The Tango".   The "Flat Charleston" first made its appearance in the district in 1926 and was popular among the dancers at all dance venues in the town.   In Runcorn, in January 1927, there was great controversy over the fact that the Master of Ceremonies at The Baths Assembly Hall had banned "The Charleston" on the grounds that it was indecent. He also made racially derogatory comments about the origins of the dance and stringently imposed the ban on it, despite the fact that it was continuing to grow in popularity all over the country.   Some of the older people thought these new dances were another symptom of the social and moral decline among the younger population. Despite the moral outrage "The Charleston" provoked, it gained in popularity in the Widnes Dance Halls of that time, which included: The Borough Hall; The Liberal Club; The Carlton in Lugsdale Road; and The Widnes Dance Academy in Albert Road.

There is no doubt that the war had a huge effect on the behaviour of society. The war had broken up families and it had not been an easy task to "keep the home fires burning".   Peoples' lifestyles had changed dramatically during wartime conditions. There was now a flood of moral criticism, ranging from dress to drinking, most of this criticism was aimed at women, who now wore shorter skirts and frequented pubs. Although convictions for drunkenness on the whole had dropped considerably, there was an increase in the number of women being convicted for drunkenness.[49]   The popularity of smoking among women had also increased during the 1920s. The number of women smokers prior to the war had been negligible but now it was increasing steadily and was generally accepted, although smoking in the street was still frowned upon.

In 1927 a potential fire hazard was discovered at Pitt Street where a man was running his own cinema from a wooden shed in his back yard. The police visited the premises and discovered 35 children, ranging in age from 3 to 13 years, seated on wooden benches with a gangway of only 9 inches between them. The shed itself was only 18 foot wide by 12 foot long. Highly flammable materials were stored inside the shed. Along the wall of this room were two lighted candles and an overhead gaslight that got its

---

[49] In 1922 there were only 54 convictions for drunkenness in Widnes.

supply piped from the main house. When the police inspected the shed, there were 13 other children in the back yard waiting for admission. The owner of the "cinema" charged one penny for admission and gave each child a ticket. The man was brought before the court and received a substantial fine. Some people thought that the police had been over strict and that it was harmless entertainment for their children. However, not long before this date there had been a horrible tragedy in Ireland where a large number of people had died in a cinema where there had not been proper fire precautions. The Magistrate cited this case and praised the actions of the police in acting to prevent a similar tragedy. In the case of the shed in Pitt Street, it is too horrible to contemplate what might have happened had a lighted candle fallen into the material stored there.

Although this illegal cinema had been closed down, other "certified establishments" were flourishing and providing entertainment for the masses. In fact, not too far away from the site of this "illicit" cinema, the residents of West Bank were enjoying the facilities offered by their new local cinema, "The Century", which opened its doors in September 1922[50]. In the same week of the Pitt Street prosecution, "The Picturedrome", under the management of Mr. F. Barnes, was showing *"The Outlaw's Daughter"* starring Josie Sedgewick, (The Riding Queen of the West). Further up town, at Mr. Martin's "Bozzadrome", the western fan could see Tom Mix in *"No Man's Gold"*. The films at "The Bozzadrome" also had a "singing cartune" which was an audience participation singalong. The organist would play the tune and a little bouncing ball, or marker, would highlight the lyrics. This cinema continued to show silent films until 1931

In May 1927 the people of West Bank were saddened to hear news of the death of 69 year old Dr. Creighton Hutchinson. Like

---

[50] *"The Century"* cinema closed in 1959, along with *"The Picturedome"* in Victoria Road.

many of the doctors of that era, he was greatly loved and respected by his patients, many of whom had been regular recipients of his benevolence. Over the years, the poor of Widnes were fortunate to have had in their midst men such as the good Dr. John O'Keeffe and Dr. Creighton Hutchinson. These were medical men who put humanitarian considerations above that of monetary gain. Some time later, a committee was formed for the purpose of providing a suitable memorial for Dr. Hutchinson. Later a statute was erected in his memory on West Bank Promenade. Sadly, there are no memorials dedicated to Dr. O'Keeffe.

An outbreak of typhoid fever caused great alarm in Widnes and the surrounding districts in July 1927. Sixteen cases were confirmed at Nazareth House Orphanage in Ditton. The victims, all children, were removed to the Isolation Hospital at Crow Wood. At that time, there were 130 children resident in the home, most of them having come from Liverpool. More than half of the infected children were members of *The Nazareth House Band* and it was thought that they might have contracted the disease during visits to neighbouring towns, as typhoid had been absent from Widnes for a number of years. Nazareth House and its occupants were put into quarantine until the outbreak was eventually brought under control.

The spread of disease through rats and mice infesting food was a constant worry. The Ministry of Agriculture & Fisheries put posters up to warn people of these dangers. Local Authorities were urged to make special efforts to destroy rats and mice in their areas by periodically designating special "Rat Weeks". In Widnes, 31st October to 5th November 1927 was one such occasion.

Pawnbrokers were a familiar and necessary part of the social environment in poor communities. Although they served merely as a temporary relief to a long-term problem, they were nevertheless viewed as a "saviour" to many families. Pawnbrokers were strictly regulated and required a certificate to trade. In July 1927 the following people applied for renewal of their certificates.

Mr. J. Abrahamson	41/49 Waterloo Road
Mrs. L. Carroll	172 Widnes Road
Mr. N. Cornberg	16 Waterloo Road
Mr. W. Harvey	77 Mersey Road

In the early days of industrialisation, Widnes had a serious problem with drunkenness in the town and at that time it was thought to be the main cause of crime in the Borough. In 1928, the local Police Superintendent, Superintendent Wilkinson, presented his annual report to the magistrates, in which he gave figures for prosecutions for drunkenness and licensing offences in the Borough. This is an extract from that report:

"The district contains 87 licensed houses. The present estimated population is 44,212, showing one licensed victualler for every 703 inhabitants; with beer-sellers "on" and "off" added, one for every 543 inhabitants; and with other licences added, a licensed house for the sale of drink of some description for every 506 inhabitants. The houses generally have been found to be well conducted. In 1922, attention was called to the fact that only 17 out of 79 licensed houses had separate lavatory accommodation for females. During 1923, six more licensed houses provided such accommodation, one in 1924, one in 1925, and six in 1927. Forty-four males and four females were convicted of drunkenness, a decrease of 11 males and an increase of 2 females. There are 19 registered clubs in the division, with a total membership of 8,481. Proceedings were taken against Widnes Trades and Labour Club, Lugsdale Road, Widnes, for a breach of the intoxicating laws, and the club was struck off the register for twelve months. The other clubs have been well conducted".

The magistrates at that time were in the process of renewing licences. There were objections to the renewal of the licence for "The Sea View Gardens" in Farnworth, run by Mrs. Eliza Baldwin, because of the age and condition of the premises. The rooms were described as dark and the ceilings very low. It was decided that this house was not required to meet the needs of the neighbourhood. The "Railway Hotel", in Hale Road, kept by Frederick Hicks, was described as a respectable working-class hostelry, but this house was no longer necessary to meet the needs of the neighbourhood. "The Blackburne Arms", near Ditton Junction, licensee Horace Prince Hillyer, was also regarded as unnecessary for the district as 59 of the 70 houses, which were adjacent to the premises, had recently been demolished resulting in a severe decrease in business. "The Brown Cow", on Liverpool Road at Hough Green, did very little business and therefore the magistrates again decided that this pub was redundant. All these houses belonged to Messrs. Greenall Whitley. Licences for all these pubs were refused on the grounds that the premises were redundant.

Among other pubs destined to close their doors for the last time during the 1920's were:

Commercial Hotel	*Marsh Street*
Commercial Hotel	*Ann Street*
Coopers Arms	*Waterloo Road*
Bath Spring Vaults	*Waterloo Road*
Britannia Vaults	*Marsh Street*
Ivy Green Vaults	*Wellington Street*
Kings Arms	*Ann Street West*
Queens Arms	*Warrington Road*
Rams Head	*Suttons Lane*

The traditional method of cooking with the help of heat from the fire was being challenged in the 1920s as the "gas cooker" started to make an appearance in the home. Prior to this time, almost all houses used the "black-leaded grate", with its integrated oven, for most of the family cooking needs. In 1928 Widnes Corporation Gas Department organised a series of free cookery demonstrations at the Conservative Club in Victoria Road. The aptly named lecturer, Miss Margaret Trainer, used a "New World Gas Cooker" for the demonstrations. It was around this time too that we first began to see the gas cooker used for an entirely different purpose – as a means of suicide.

In March 1928 local businessman Mr. A. E. Calvert was celebrating his half century in the drapery business. Mr. Calvert, the son of a Primitive Methodist Minister, began his association with this trade in February 1878 when he started his apprenticeship with Mr. George Hill, in Pendlebury, Manchester. Some years later, in 1885, he came to Widnes and opened a hosiery and fancy drapery business at 34 Victoria Road. At that time, the main shopping area was Ann Street, but Mr. Calvert, aware of the steadily increasing population, recognised the potential development of Victoria Road as an important shopping area. Mr. Calvert's business grew rapidly and in no time at all he had doubled his accommodation in Victoria Road. Shortly afterwards he purchased an additional property in order to cater for increased trade. Some time later Mr. Calvert amalgamated his business with that of Mr. David Lewis, who was a grocer and provisions dealer. The new company traded under the name of "Lewis and Calvert" and they owned joint premises in Church Street in addition to Mr. Calvert's Victoria Road shops. However, in 1919, the two sections of this company decided to separate and Mr. Calvert once again concentrated on the drapery and outfitting side of the business. *"Calvert's of Widnes"* was renowned for its quality merchandise and good service. It was a very sad day for the town when the business finally closed its doors in the 1980s, after over a century of trade in Widnes.

The members of the Wesleyan Chapel in Moss Bank celebrated their "Diamond Jubilee" in March 1928. The small chapel, in Moss Street, first opened its doors for worship as far back as 1868, when the chemical industry in this town was barely 20 years old. The celebration of their 60th anniversary was marked by special services and a number of visiting preachers praised the efforts of the congregation over this long period of time.

   In the early days of the chemical industry, Widnes had accepted immigrants from other countries, namely Ireland, Lithuania and Poland, as well as countless internal migrants.   Thus, the social fabric of our town was woven from an interesting multicultural mix.   With the arrival of *The Empire Settlement Act of 1922*, opportunities were created which encouraged many Widnes people to seek their fortune in other lands, in much the same way earlier immigrants into this town had done.   After the war ended, in 1918, the Canadian Government created a new *Department of Immigration and Colonization* in the hope that they could attract large numbers of British agricultural immigrants.   The British Government, aware that unemployment here was reaching unacceptable levels, encouraged people to leave by offering subsidised travel to many parts of the Empire, including Australia, Canada and South Africa.   In Canada, there was plenty of good, cheap, arable land for sale.   The two national railway companies, Canadian Pacific and Canadian National, primarily owned this land and they advertised extensively in England.   Many men thought that if they worked there for a while they would be able to save enough to buy their own land.   While the Canadian Government supported the railway companies in this initiative, they were also mindful that agricultural immigrants were desperately needed all over Canada.

   Early in 1928 a general notice issued by the Canadian Authorities appeared in English newspapers appealing for 10,000 men to go to Canada to help with the harvest.   The response was so great that the lists were closed within a very short time.   It was said that over 25,000 applied within the first week.   Each area was allocated a certain number of applicants and the Merseyside quota was strictly limited.   There were 121 hopeful candidates from Widnes and from that 121 only 60 were selected for interview by the Canadian authorities in Liverpool. After the final selection process, and medical examinations, just 30 men were accepted.

The scheme offered transport assistance and other benefits, but due to the fact that these men had experienced long periods of unemployment, many did not possess a decent suit of clothes. In fact, many of the men attended their interviews in borrowed clothing. Mr. A. B. Lloyd, the manager of The Widnes Labour Exchange, appealed to a number of local firms for help. There was a swift and generous response in cash and kind and the 30 men were all kitted out with new suits and a cash sum of 10 shillings each, to help them on their way. In the summer of 1928, the men left Widnes Central Station on their journey to Liverpool where they would join a fleet of steamers bound for Halifax, Nova Scotia. The men were given a civic send-off and the Mayor addressed them as "*Gentlemen of Widnes*" he went on to say:

"You are a few out of a big number leaving the Mother Country to go and assist one of her daughters to get in her harvest, some of which comes back to us again in the shape of food to keep the home fires burning. I wish you all god speed, a pleasant journey and good luck in your new venture. Our best thanks to those who have in any way helped to send you out as well equipped as possible"

The men were kitted out so well that each man left with a new suitcase, two new suits of clothes, a blanket, and also writing paper and envelopes. These men came in the main from Newtown, Simms Cross, and West Bank but there were also some from Moon Street, Kent Street, Greenway Road and St. Michael's Road.

Within a few weeks, some of the men were writing home complaining that the whole scheme was in disarray. One man wrote:

"I've been left badly at this place; seven of us got to this place, no one to meet us and no directions. We tried two or three farmers but no luck –

they were French Canadians and did not want Englishmen. The farmers did not know why we were sent, and I don't know either, and it is a rotten shame to leave us stranded. There we are making tents of our blankets with four dollars between us, and if we don't get work God help us. We have only had a cup of tea since yesterday"[51]

However, a short while afterwards, this man wrote again saying that he had found work and that everything was fine[52].

By the end of the year the demand for labour in Canada had increased further and a free training scheme was offered for those willing to go out as farm labourers. A series of addresses and films were presented at various venues throughout the country. In Widnes, the Ministry of Labour and *"The White Star Colonization Department"* gave a joint presentation to a large audience at The Premier Cinema just before Christmas in 1928. A film was shown depicting farm life in Canada. The scheme was for single men aged between 18 and 35. It was intended to alleviate the burden of Government unemployment payments in this country, as well as supplying much needed labour for Canada. A man going out to Canada under this scheme was guaranteed work for a period of four years.

I am sure the irony will not escape you when I draw analogies. How curious, that these chemical workers from Widnes should now be seeking agricultural occupations. The early immigrants into Widnes had been primarily agricultural workers from rural communities, forced to seek employment and subsistence in the "new chemical industries" of Lancashire. These people had formed the basis of our early industrial society. Industry was totally new to them. They came here and learnt how to live amid a pall of smoke and noxious odours, far from the green fields and fresh air of the countryside. Now, here we find their descendants,

---

[51] Widnes Weekly News
[52] Correspondence in possession of Mr. F. Pilkington

in the 1920s, being retrained to work as farm labourers and once again taking the emigration trail!

Some years later, a Widnes man who had gone out to Australia earlier in the decade, arrived back in the town.   This man appeared to be completely disillusioned with the whole emigration programme.   It transpired that after he had spent 5 years in Australia, having gone there under a Salvation Army emigration programme, he returned to Widnes and made an application to go to Canada. When he arrived in Canada, he discovered that there were thousands out of work because the country had just experienced one of the worst harvests in living memory. He said that many of the English men committed petty crimes in the hope that they would be arrested and jailed. They reasoned that it was better to be housed and fed in jail than to be homeless on the streets.   This man, penniless, jumped a freight train over the border into Seattle.   However, he was arrested there by the American authorities, and subsequently transferred to New York from where he was deported back to England.

It was interesting to note the involvement of *The Salvation Army*. In fact, The Salvation Army and other voluntary organisations played an important part in sponsoring and assisting those who wished to emigrate. Their scheme included assisting widows and children of ex-servicemen to migrate to Australia.   The Salvation Army took responsibility for their employment and welfare for a period of three years, or in the case of widows, for four years after their arrival. Most of those who emigrated under this scheme were secured employment as domestic servants or farm workers.   The Salvation Army's migration activities, like all their other humanitarian works, were non-sectarian.

The Salvation Army, a product of the "darkest England" of the 1880s, was well established in Widnes and had a large congregation in the town. The Widnes Corps was first set up on 7th July 1881. In earlier days they used a number of temporary venues such as the Volunteer Hall, the Lacey Street Schools, the Snig Pie Dance Room, a shop in Alforde Street, and Mallin's Hall in Hibbert Street[53]. In 1907 they made their base at the Salvation Army Hall in Widnes Road. The building cost £900. The money was raised with a generous donation of £500 from Mr. Sutton Timmis, and the remainder by other donations from Messrs. Thomas Bolton & Sons, Messrs. Thomas Vickers & Sons, and Messrs. J. H. Dennis & Sons. Earlier in the decade, in 1922 and 1923, the town played host to members of the Booth Family, descendants of General Booth the founder of *The Salvation Army*. On both these occasions they were the guests of Councillor David Lewis, a member of the local *Free Church Council*. Both these visits ended with a mass rally and enthusiastic meetings in The Picturedrome, where the Salvation Army bands from Bootle and Widnes played hymns and musical selections to an appreciative audience.

Towards the end of the decade, a Local Government Act brought about the transfer of the functions of The Poor Law Authorities from the Board of Guardians to committees of the County Councils. Widnes Corporation nominated Aldermen Berry and Garghan, and Councillors Connaughton, Kennion, Ludden and Marsh for appointment by Lancashire County Council as members of the committee for the Prescot area. The inclusion of Daniel Garghan is particularly significant, when we remember that he was the man who led the march of over 1000 hungry unemployed men to the Whiston Institute in September 1921. On that occasion he made an impassioned appeal to The Guardians on behalf of the unemployed and their families. His actions, over decades, bore testament to his compassion and proved that he was, without doubt, an appropriate candidate for this committee. The same Local Government Act that had transferred this administration also permitted Local Authorities to take over Poor Law infirmaries and institutions (workhouses) and convert them to municipal hospitals. Thus, the Whiston Institute became Whiston

---

[53] Salvation Army Archives

Hospital. Incidentally, the term *"workhouse"*, in name, was not abolished until 1948.

Politically, like the rest of the country in the 1920s, Widnes was far from stable. At the beginning of the decade there were three General Elections in less than two years. Arthur Henderson, our first Labour MP, held his seat for only three years before the election of November 1922, when Dr. G. C. Clayton beat him by a majority of 1782. Just over a year later, in December 1923, Dr Clayton was again returned but with a reduced majority as this election was split by a three party vote. In January 1924 Ramsey McDonald formed his Labour Government. 15 of the 20 members of his cabinet had no previous ministerial experience and all, with the exception of Wheatley, who was responsible for some of our greatest housing reforms, were moderates. Arthur Henderson, who had previously represented Widnes, was part of that cabinet. However, the Labour Government of 1924 did not reign long, and in October of that year there was another General Election. In Widnes, Dr. Clayton was again returned as our MP with a greatly increased majority.

As the decade came to a close there was to be another election in 1929. This particular election was a fiercely fought one and brought some of the principal British politicians of that time to Widnes to speak on behalf of their candidates. Mr. Ramsey McDonald spoke in support of the Labour candidate, Mr. Cameron, at a public rally in Victoria Square to a crowd estimated to be in excess of 3000 people. Mr. Stanley Baldwin, the Prime Minister, also arrived in town to speak on behalf of his candidate Dr. Clayton. The Prime Minister was shouted down and continuously heckled by a large crowd who had gathered near the market to hear him speak. The outcome of that election was that the Labour candidate, Mr. A. J. Cameron, was returned with a slim majority of only 749, thus Widnes ended a very troubled decade, once again represented by a Labour MP.

It is impossible to end this section without referring once again to the social and economic conditions of those times. The incidence of acute poverty had hardly diminished since the end of the previous century, although the Government had made some attempt to provide relief and improvement with various social reforms. In the south end of the town, the smoke polluted air and crowded streets remained. In these areas, people shared a common culture of bare subsistence and survival. Housing conditions and overcrowding were a major factor in the spread of disease. Tuberculosis was one of the scourges of those times and, not surprisingly, instances of death from this disease were higher in the Victoria and Waterloo wards than in any other areas of the town.

The Medical Officer of Health for Widnes, in a summary of vital statistical data, gave the following information regarding instances of Tuberculosis in the Borough during the 1920's.

The Mortality Rate from Pulmonary Tuberculosis 1920-29
(Figures per 1000 of population)

Ward	1920-24	1925-29
Farnworth	0.7	0.4
Halton	0.7	0.7
Simms Cross	1.0	1.1
Victoria	1.7	1.1
Waterloo	1.2	1.4
West Bank	0.7	0.8
Ditton	0.8	0.5

Although the treatment of tuberculosis was in the hands of the County Authority, a locally appointed officer was based at

Brendan House, in Widnes Road[54].   All suspicious cases were referred to this officer.

---

[54] *Brendan House* was originally built for Dr. John O`Keeffe. The building served as both his home and surgery. This might answer questions for those who may have pondered over its architectural stone relief, which included entwined shamrocks.

The 1930s

Numerous writers and historians have described this decade as
"The Hungry Thirties". The Wall Street Crash in America in 1929
signalled the start of the worst period of depression both in
America and in global markets. Here in England, this country was
also suffering from the effects of this worldwide depression as
unemployment peaked just below 3,000,000 in 1932. In January
1930, a market analyst, reviewing the chemical manufacturing
business in 1929, could offer no hope for an improvement in 1930[55].
The worst period of depression was 1931-1934. It was not until
1935 that unemployment figures began to decline, although the
worst of the depression was not really over until the period
immediately prior to the Second World War.

The basic cause of this depression was a decline in staple
industries such as textiles, steel and iron. A downturn in these
industries also meant there was less demand for coal. Although
we tend to think that the slump was countrywide, this was not the
case. In fact, it was concentrated into limited geographical areas
such as South Wales, Lancashire, Yorkshire, Cumbria, the North-
East and Clydeside. The social effects on these districts were dire.
These places became known as *"Depressed Areas"*, although in 1934
the Government renamed them "Special Areas", no doubt thinking
this new description would be less demeaning to the people living
in them. However, the changing of words meant little to those
struggling to survive without work. For those living away from
these areas things were much different. In places like the West
Midlands people were enjoying a mild prosperity due to the

---

[55] *The Chemical Trades Journal* (January 1930).

development of new industries. These included the motor industry, as well as electrical and aircraft industries – all these catering for the home market rather than export.

The 1930s unemployment problems caused great hardship. The Government introduced new methods of payments to those no longer entitled to unemployment benefit. These transitional payments were subjected to the dreaded "means test" which was first introduced in this decade. These changes to the benefit system were brought about after the Government received details of *The May Committee* in July 1931. This report estimated that the budget deficit could reach £120 million. The proposed economies resulted in a cut in unemployment benefit. There was a huge split in the Labour Party that resulted in the Prime Minister, Ramsey MacDonald, resigning on 24th August. The following day he formed a National Government with other parties in order to balance the budget. The Labour Party subsequently expelled MacDonald and his two of his colleagues, Philip Snowden and J.H. Thomas. Our erstwhile MP, Arthur Henderson, was made leader of the Labour Party.

Numerous historians have stated that the primary reasons for poverty during the 1930s were attributable to three things. Inadequate unemployment benefits, old age, (pensions did not meet minimum needs) and to earnings being below the minimum subsistence level. But maybe it is worth remembering when considering the cuts in benefits, that though the war had dimmed to a waning memory, the country was still weary under its debt. The British budget of 1930-31 amounted to £822,000,000 and of this sum no less than £523,000,000 was allocated to war debts, war pensions and preparations for further war!

By 1939 there were signs that the country was slowly recovering from "the depression". There was an upturn in the building trade and a growth of new industries. Although there was a significant fall in unemployment nationally, the figures were still high in many areas, including Widnes. Consumer spending was limited because of low wages, and a lack of public spending meant that demand was restricted. Towards the end of this decade it was apparent that full recovery was still a long way off, although rearmament and, regretfully, war helped.

Industry and Employment

The 1930s was the period of *"Hunger Marches"*, when large masses of unemployed took to the streets and appealed to the Government for help. The first national Hunger March had actually taken place in the autumn of 1927 but the 1930s was marked by numerous protests of this type, the most famous being "The Jarrow March" of 1936, in which 200 men from the north-east town of Jarrow marched 300 miles to London. The Jarrow marchers wanted Parliament, and the people in the south, to understand that they were decent law abiding and responsible citizens who were living in the poverty created by 70% unemployment in their area. One of the marchers described his home town as *"a filthy, dirty, falling down, consumptive area."* Their MP, Ellen Wilkinson, elaborated by saying *"that if people have to live and bear and bring up their children in bad houses on too little food, their resistance to disease is lowered and they die before they should"*[56]. When these men arrived back home, they found that their dole money had been stopped because they had not been available for work – even though there was no work to be had!

In Widnes in the 1930s the sight of men standing at factory gates hoping to get a day's casual labour was a common scene. In many ways, it was not unlike a "slave market". In the same manner as the slave owner had chosen his labour, the foreman would come out and select the man who looked the fittest and most able. The others would return home dejected and demoralised.

---

[56] *Jarrow March* --Tom Pickard: (Allison & Busby 1982)

Government *"Unemployed Grants"* were paid to Local Authorities, for help in funding work on which the unemployed could be given temporary work. Here in Widnes, in March 1930, approval was given for work to be carried out under the terms of "relief for the unemployed" on land abutting Lowerhouse Lane and Dundalk Road. Mr. J.C. Gerard Leigh had given this land to the Corporation for the purpose of a public recreation ground. At that time, it was being used as allotment gardens but the proposed relief work would involve the clearing, levelling, and laying out of the land as a recreational ground[57].

The Government issued strict directives regarding the work done under the terms of the "relief fund". Local Authorities were sent a circular saying:

"That all materials should, as far as practicable, be of United Kingdom origin and all manufactured articles should be of United Kingdom manufacture, and that the Minister looked with confidence for the wholehearted support and co-operation of local authorities in the policy hitherto pursued by the Ministry in the matter. It was hoped that these conditions would not be confined by local authorities to work specially expedited for the relief of unemployment but would be observed as widely as possible in connection with all expenditure".

Unemployment often meant that households were reduced to near destitution. The Poor Law, or unemployment relief, was not sufficient to maintain those who had no other source of income. Even workers, who were in the lower ranks of the unskilled, had a standard of living not much above the poverty line[58]. It was obvious that official social policy did not adequately meet the needs of our society. It was then left to our local communities to respond in a practical way.

---

[57] Minutes of Widnes Council (1930)
[58] *Trends in British Society since 1900* – A.H. Halsey (Macmillan 1972)

The Widnes Relief Committee was responsible for issuing clothing to workers who had been given "relief" work. However, in January 1930 the Committee passed a resolution calling for the discontinuance of this clothing issue because they considered that they were not used for the purposes intended by The Guardians. It appears that "detectives" had been employed to monitor the men. The detectives discovered that some men had pawned their shoes. All in all 20 pairs of shoes had been pawned. These detectives also provided evidence of clothing being sold to friends. Representatives of the unemployed men expressed concern that everyone would suffer because of the acts of just a few.

Recognising the need for some form of insurance system, Widnes inaugurated a Contributory Hospital Scheme in 1930. The rates agreed at that time were that an adult male should contribute 2d. a week, and women and juveniles would pay 1d. a week. The scheme had been in operation for only two years when it was realised that the income from the contributions was inadequate and subscriptions were increased to 3d. for men, and 2d. for unemployed men over the age of 21. Males under 21 would pay 1d; 2d. for women with dependants, while women without dependants would pay 1d. Employees of I.C.I. and Orr's Zinc White Ltd., opted out and administered their own insurance schemes. Membership of the Widnes scheme offered the following benefits:[59]

1. *In-patient and out-patient treatment at a hospital.*
2. *Travelling expenses for the patient.*
3. *2 weeks in a Convalescent Home if recommended.*
4. *Maintenance at Whiston Institute for 13 weeks.*
5. *Payment of charges made by Local Authority.*
6. *Operative treatment for throat and nose defects for children under 14.*

---

[59] Currency conversation - £1 was equal to 20 shillings in pre-decimal terms. 12 pennies was equal to 1 shilling. (s)shilling. (d)penny.

7.   *Payment for spectacles for schoolchildren.*
8.   *Grant of £10 for necessary operations or £2 for a child's operation.*

By 1935 there were 6222 employed contributors to the fund and 2887 voluntary members[60].

At the end of April 1930 the Government released the "*Local Unemployment Index*"[61]. The report showed that Lancashire held the record of having the highest unemployed figure of any county in England. There were just four areas with a larger percentage of unemployed than Widnes. The worst centre in the country was Mossley, Manchester, where more than half the insured were on the unemployment register. Wigan came just above Widnes and Widnes only slightly above Liverpool whose lower figure was accounted for, to some extent, by the large amount of casual labour.

At the end of the year, the unemployed register in Widnes reached 3827. In 1925, prior to the General Strike, the number on the register was 1516. By December 1931 the jobless figure for Widnes was still well over 3000 and rising. A public meeting was held at "The Picturedrome Cinema", in Victoria Road. The result of that meeting was the forming of *The National Unemployed Workers' Movement*. Councillor Millar was the President of this new movement, with Mr. P. Myler as Vice President and Mr. F. McDonnell holding the position of Secretary. Over a period of time, the members of *The Widnes Unemployed Workers' Association* were able to gain representation on the Public Assistance Committee and the Labour Exchange Advisory Committee. This Association was also instrumental in bringing about a number of significant local benefits for the unemployed. They raised

---

[60] *Minutes of Widnes Town Council* – Medical Officer's Report 1935/36
[61] "*Government Employment Statistics.*" - Insured persons registered as unemployed on 14th April 1930 (PRO. Kew)

numerous questions about various issues such as employment schemes, the position of ex-servicemen, the feeding of needy schoolchildren, the desirability of reduced admission fees for the unemployed wishing to attend football games etc. A social club was also set up and a hut was built with the assistance of donations and subscriptions from local industries and individuals. The unemployed men themselves constructed the building and it contained billiard tables as well as a canteen, which served light refreshment.

Unemployment Benefit was paid for 26 weeks after which time all payments automatically ceased. On 12th November 1931 a *Transitional Payment Order* was introduced. This meant that all persons who were not entitled to unemployment benefit (which had been reduced a short time before)[62] had to apply for a transitional payment. When a man's benefit was exhausted the Labour Exchange would refer him to the Local Public Assistance Committee, who would establish the claim and circumstances of the claimant. The Public Assistance Committee's decision was absolute and final; there was no provision for "appeal". Once granted, this payment, which became known as the "dole", was subjected to the much-resented *Household Means Test*, which was introduced in 1931. Under the regulations of the "test" the wages of all the family members, and any household or personal assets, were taken into account. Even the accumulated dividend *("Divi")* paid to members of "The Co-op" was included as income, and this money had to be used up before any payment was granted. In addition to this, the disability pensions men had been granted because of injuries received during the war were also taken into consideration and classed as an "income".

---

[62] *Unemployment benefit for a man, wife and 2 children was 27/3d in 1931. This had been reduced from 30/0d in 1930.* (Royal Commission on Unemployment Insurance, Final Report) Cmd.4185
Note: actual benefit paid was less than one third of the average wage.

There was a widespread concern about the workings of the "means test". Deputations of MPs from northern constituencies had repeatedly approached the Ministers of Health and Labour to complain about aspects of this system. One of the main concerns was that different interpretations of the "test" were being applied in different areas. That there were different principles and methods applied to the payment of "relief" is demonstrated by the fact that at an earlier meeting of The Prescot Board of Guardians, a report submitted by an inspector for the Ministry of Health, stated that:

"With reference to visiting by the Relieving Officer, at present only in Widnes and Ditton districts are each case visited before relief is given. In the Prescot district very little visiting is being done. In the four St. Helens districts, the position is not at all satisfactory as regards the amount of visiting".

In January 1932 about 2000 Widnes "test" cases had been dealt with and about one third of these had been struck off the list for various reasons. Among the cases for continuance of transitional payment was the application of a single man who had £1000 invested. He was congratulated by the Chairman of the Board for his thrift and was subsequently struck off. The rule was that people who had savings or assets of £100 or more were automatically disqualified.

In that same month, the local Public Assistance Committee received a communication from the Lancashire Authority at Preston, regarding the application of the "test" to disabled ex-servicemen. The Prescot Committee said they would inform Preston that they would not take into consideration a man's disability pension, but they would judge each case on merit. It is worth remembering here, that records show that there had been in the region of 1400 Widnes men incapacitated by the war. It is not known if many of these were involved in the "test". The harshness of the "means test" was also hotly debated in the Widnes Council

Chamber. In April 1932 Councillor Millar asserted that the test was cruel in its administration. A motion was submitted that stated:

"That this Council is of the opinion that the operation of the means test in this district is arbitrary and that its administration is detrimental to the health of the families who are the recipients of the reduced scale, and also to the business people of the community, whose loss has been very substantial; that the Council endorse the opinion as expressed by the Prime Minister that the hardships should be removed at the very earliest date; and that a copy of this resolution be forwarded to the Prime Minister, the Minister of Health, and the Member of Parliament for this division".

Councillor Millar told the members of Widnes Council that he, and the unemployed of the town, believed that the "means test" had gone beyond what was intended. It was harsh and cruel. He was concerned that homes were being wrecked and broken up because thousands of young men and women were being forced to leave decent homes and go into lodgings and model lodging-houses. It seemed that this was the only method of securing the miserable maintenance during periods of unemployment. Many children in the town were going to school hungry and ill clad. Councillor Miller also believed that unemployment should be faced as a continuing fact of life, owing to the new scientific methods constantly being introduced in industry. However, he was of the opinion that *"the captains of industry were making fabulously huge profits and should be prepared to keep people in a decent standard of life".*

Within a few weeks of this resolution, a case was brought before the Widnes Magistrates Bench, in which the local "Relief Officer" was charged with embezzlement. The previous administrative Board of Guardians had appointed this man to the position of Relieving Officer for the Widnes Relief District in 1924. After the re-organisation under the Act of 1929, he had maintained this important position and held it until his fraud was uncovered. One of his duties was to act as collector on orders made by The Board. These orders made relatives liable for the maintenance of patients in the Whiston Institution and the Rainhill Mental Hospital[63]. In some of the cases cited, he appears to have pocketed this money himself. A widow, who had been paying maintenance for her husband, a war veteran, who resided as a patient in Rainhill Mental Hospital for three years prior to his death, told how the officer had gradually increased her payment liability. In fact, her payments had never been officially increased —the additional money was never paid in. The case against this man was proved and he was given a 6 month prison sentence.

There is no doubt that the high level of unemployment in the town in the 1930s was the cause of great economic loss and social and individual waste. Unemployment threw households into poverty. One can only imagine the psychological effects of continued unemployment on these men – anger; shame; loss of social confidence; depression and finally apathetic resignation. We should also consider that the number on the Widnes Unemployed Register did not represent the full picture of "effect". Because of reduced spending power in these communities, many small businesses were also struggling for survival. Only the pawnbroker thrived in the 1930s.

There were a number of schemes designed to keep the unemployed occupied in some task. One of these was the "Allotment Scheme". This was for able-bodied men who were in receipt of "relief". It was not intended to replace ordinary employment, but was a type of "job creation scheme" of the day. The Widnes District Relief Committee rented land in Halton View,

---

[63] *It is worth noting that many men who had returned from the War with "shell shock" had been patients in these hospitals.*

near to the bridge,[64] for the purpose of creating work for the unemployed who were receiving relief payment. It was said that the aim of the scheme was to *"provide work of health-giving properties in order to maintain men in a physical condition, which would benefit them to take their places in the ordinary labour market when the opportunity arises"*. The fresh vegetables grown on these allotments were sent to The Whiston Institution and Infirmary.[65]

Widnes, with its acute unemployment problem, was prominently featured in a report carried out by Manchester University for the Board of Trade in 1932[66]. The southwest corner of the survey region, which included the towns of Widnes, Runcorn, St. Helens, Earlstown and Warrington, showed that unemployment in the chemical industry had not fallen below 9% since 1923. Conditions were not uniform throughout the area, for while employment seemed to be declining in the chemical industry in Widnes, it was expanding in Runcorn. The employment capacity of the building and engineering trades, which were closely associated with chemicals, was also declining. It was said that at that time Widnes had a surplus of over 3,000 men of which less than 1,000 could be absorbed into the existing industries. The report said:

"In these circumstances, it is desirable that the surplus should be drained either by the creation of new forms of employment within the Widnes area or by the voluntary movement of male labour into other areas".

In the summer of 1932 Lever Brothers Ltd., who had earlier taken over the Gossages Soap Works, announced their intention to reorganise their home and export market. This meant that products produced at Widnes would be manufactured elsewhere.

---

[64] At a later date, Widnes Corporation rented land in Derby Road, Farnworth, for the "Allotment Scheme".
[65] Whiston Workhouse
[66] *Employment Survey for Board of Trade* (Manchester University 1932)

For some time prior to this, there had been a gradual reduction in the number of employees at the Widnes works. The older ones were pensioned off and some of the younger ones had been transferred to works at Warrington or Port Sunlight. This marked the beginning of the end for the old soap-works that had been for so long a feature of the Widnes industrial landscape. By the end of the year it had closed its doors for the last time.

Some seven years later, in June 1939, the massive chimney, an industrial landmark and a reminder of the days when Gossages soap had been exported to all corners of the globe, was finally razed to the ground. Many of the old Gossage pensioners, perhaps with a tinge of nostalgia, assembled in the neighbourhood of Waterloo Road and Mersey Road to catch a last glimpse of the structure as it fell to the ground.

No sooner had the death knell rung for Gossages Soap Works than another enterprise stepped into the breach. Grannox Ltd., based in West Bank, announced their intention to embark upon a business venture that would once again bring soap manufacture to the town. It was said that in the course of their present business they carried out a large amount of refining work in ingredients that were essential to the soap-making industry. They had already approached local traders and asked for their opinion and support. The new venture, known as "The Widnes Soap Company Ltd.", was set up in an old "Pith and Size Works" in Factory Lane, off Derby Road. The total area of the works covered around two and a half acres.

The site chosen for the new "soap factory" already had an interesting industrial history. On an ordnance survey map of 1846-47, we can see that a sailcloth factory, owned by Bushby and Allen, was operating there. Directories tell us that after the demise of this industry, sometime around 1876, it became the "Farnworth Pith and Size Works"[67].   The Directors of the newly established soap company announced their intention to produce a good brand of soap for domestic trade, as well as for technical use in laundries and factories[68].   Subsequently, a new brand of household soap, which they marketed under the name of *"Double-Seven Soap"*, was produced.   There were also plans to progress into the manufacture of soap powder and soap flakes in order to reach a wider field of user.   The first "boiling" at this works took place in June 1933.   An advertising poster for the Widnes Soap Company described their *"Double Seven Household Soap"* as a superfine soap – 4d for a 1lb (pound) carton.   *"Double Seven Carbolic Soap"* was a halfpenny dearer.

A few years later, another local company, Bowmans Ltd., were producing shampoo at their Widnes works.   Their new product was described as a "non-alkaline tonic and soapless shampoo".   They claimed that this shampoo, marketed under the brand name *"Delilah"*, was destined to become world famous.   A local competition was launched with a prize of £10 for the person who could come up with the best slogan.   The winner was a lady from Kingsway who said: *"Delilah Brings Beauty to the Head"*.

On the 14th October 1932 a nationwide Hunger March with marchers from all over England, including Widnes, set off for London to present a petition to Parliament for the abolition of *The Means Test and Anomalies Act*[69] and cuts in social welfare and unemployment benefit.   Most of the country was behind them. Soup kitchens were set up for the marchers in the numerous towns and villages they passed through and they were accommodated overnight in local schools en route.

---

[67] Widnes Official Handbook - 1948

[68] Some of the Directors were ex- Gossage employees.

[69] It is worth noting that the "means test" was not completely abandoned in its original form until 1941.

A few weeks after this Hunger March, the town received a visit from The Prince of Wales, (later King Edward VIII and afterwards the Duke of Windsor). He had visited various depressed areas around the country to view the effects of unemployment on their communities. It appears that the tours of these areas were little more than public relations exercises as almost no useful help resulted from these visits. His visit to Widnes was something of a gala occasion and thousands of people waited in the pouring rain to provide a loyal and enthusiastic welcome. The Mayor and civic dignitaries received him in Victoria Square where the local scouts and guides were also assembled. *The Nazareth House Band* provided music and there was community singing. After the official welcome and reception, there was an opportunity for him to visit the Technical College, which had lately opened up an occupational centre where the unemployed could learn a new skill. He also spoke to members of the "Unemployed Club" before leaving for a visit to Warrington.

The *"Means Test"* was again debated in Parliament in November 1932. It was agreed that proposals to remedy the anomalies in the administration of this benefit should be adopted. Definite rules would be laid down that only one half of the income from a disability pension would be taken into account when assessing the needs of a claimant. The same rule would apply to workmen's compensations. Capital up to £25 would be disregarded, and above that amount but below £300, would be treated as the weekly equivalent of a shilling for every complete £25.

In 1934 *The Unemployment Act* set up a National Unemployment Assistance Board. This board was intended to regulate and standardise "Dole Payments". One elderly Widnes resident, who remembered that period, described the procedure to me:

"You would have to go to the "Board Office" in Lugsdale Road, to apply for assistance. Before the money was given to the family, a "means test"

man called at the house to see what money the family had and what possessions were in the house. The family were told to use their savings, if they had any, (which they never did), or they would have to sell some household goods, their assets, before any money would be given.   There was a great deal of shame attached to visiting the Board Office.   People felt degraded by the whole process, it was like begging!"

The industrial face of Widnes was to change drastically during the 1930s.   Whilst some of the old established factories closed down, this period also saw the arrival of new industries in the town.   In 1933 the old Muspratt Woodend Works became the site of the new Albright & Wilson Factory.   Albright & Wilson had previously manufactured white phosphorus at their Oldbury Works, but ceased production of this material there in 1919. From that time on, The Electric Reduction Company of Canada supplied all Britain's needs.   However, in 1931, it was realised that the demands for phosphorus would increase beyond that factory's production capacity.   Albright's then decided to resume manufacture in England on a new site which would require a cheap source of power and easy transport facilities to a major sea port.   The old Muspratt Works met all the essential requirements. Garston Docks was nearby, and there were preferential railway freight rates to the Muspratt site, which had previously been written into the Garston–St.Helens Railway Acts.   This meant that Ann Street was an ideal choice[70].

Other changes and additions taking place in this decade included the reorganisation of I.C.I's administrative operations. In 1934 a new office block was built in Waterloo Road to serve as the main administrative centre for The Gaskell Marsh Works.   Two years later, in 1936, the West Bank fertilizer works owned by Thomas Vickers & Sons was taken over by Fisons Ltd.   That same

---

[70] Phosphorus production ceased at the Ann Street Works in February 1959.

year, Messrs. Thomas Ward Ltd., a well-known industrial company of Sheffield, acquired Widnes Foundry.

Following the First War, Widnes Foundry had gone through a difficult period, as that time was neither auspicious nor encouraging to the heavier engineering industries. Following the purchase by Thomas Ward Ltd. the company was reconstituted as a separate autonomous undertaking known as The Widnes Foundry & Engineering Co. Ltd. With the onset of World War II, The Foundry was kept busy with Government commissions of the highest priority. These assignments were as diverse as they were important. In the construction area of the business, varied equipment was manufactured such as: parts for Bailey Bridges, munitions, steel huts, and other war equipment.

Mention should also be made of youth unemployment in the 1930s. At an annual meeting of the Widnes Advisory Committee for Juvenile Employment in 1935, it was pointed out that there was a constant surplus of boys and girls available for employment. It was said that this surplus was likely to increase as a consequence of the high birth rate of the previous 14 or 15 years. Because chemical manufacture was the main industry in the town, and due to the heavy nature of that work, it was not possible to absorb many juveniles. It was estimated that there was a constant surplus of approximately 300 boys and 200 girls available for employment. From information detailed in education records, it was ascertained that 360 boys and 353 girls left school during the previous year. 75% of these subsequently registered as unemployed. Details of the number of juveniles in employment showed that there were about 100 boys between the ages of 14-17 employed in the chemical industry, and about 40 girls in the same age group were employed in tin-canister making and the packing of light chemicals. The Shirt Factory was also employing young girls and although I do not have statistics on the number taken on each year, I know that there were 123 girls employed there in 1933. The asbestos-cement business (The Everite) also employed in the region of 200 juveniles, mainly boys.

In earlier times, young girls leaving school often went into "domestic service", but once industry had opened its doors to female labour there appeared to be a gradual revolt against this type of work. Apart from the obvious strain of being isolated from family and friends, live-in domestic servants were required to work long hours and had just one day off each week. Some live-in servants were provided with a uniform, which they had to pay for themselves, by having a shilling a week deducted from their wages. Many girls found they were tied to their employment simply because they had to stay until their uniform had been paid for! Factory work offered greater freedom, better pay, and leisure time in the evenings and at weekends. In 1938, a newspaper article said that many young girls would sooner be unemployed than go "into service".

I have not dealt in detail with the question of industrial deaths in this section. This is not because there were none, but simply because they occurred with the same appalling regularity as they had done in the past decade. There were numerous fatalities and cases of accidents and industrial diseases. A large number of the accidents were preventable and were often down solely to bad working practice and lack of any proper health and safety rules, or training. Sometimes equipment had not been properly maintained or fitted, these conditions resulting in the deaths of workmen on numerous occasions. As in the previous and earlier decades, there were some horrific accidents, such as the one in which a worker at Albright & Wilson was enveloped in phosphorous mud, which caused his clothing to set alight. At the inquest, the brother of the deceased man said that: *"some suggestions had been made about protective clothing and safety measures but they did not apply to this plant"*.

Some factories had a pretty high level of accidents and indeed some companies had ominous nicknames, as in the case of Messrs. Todd Bros. Ltd., in Ditton Road, who made steel drums. This factory was known as *"The Leg and Arm Shop"* because of the high number of people sustaining accidents to or loss of these limbs. During the course of production, the metal was formed into shape by the use of levers and guillotines. There were frequent accidents due to unguarded machines. In the early days, the only medical facilities consisted of a first aid box containing bandages and iodine. Serious cases were despatched to the Accident Hospital. Later on, as in most factories, a full-time nurse was employed.

Cases of industrial diseases feature largely in this decade, particularly silicosis. Earlier, the Government had set up a Medical Board and people with industrial diseases were often referred to this Board and another, *The Silicosis Board*, when seeking compensation for disease. However, often it was too late. It was only after the disease had done its worst that the post-mortem examination revealed the evidence of an industrial acquired disease. Today, we all know the dangers of working with asbestos. The workers at The Everite Works were constantly, but unsuspectingly, exposed to this danger. In factories like Dennis's Cornubia Copper Works men worked surrounded by dust and zinc oxide fumes. Most of the workers developed chest problems. It would be possible to list factory after factory in this period and in almost every one would be found some serious hazard detrimental to health.

One industrial accident I will mention, because of its magnitude, was the Gresford mining disaster of 1934. Although not occurring locally, the people of Widnes were moved to expressing their horror and sympathy in a variety of ways. There were memorial services held in local churches and a special fund was set up to help the widows and orphans of the 261 men who lost their lives. The trades unions of Widnes and district organised a memorial service at the Victoria Road Methodist

Church and a large procession, led by *The Clock Face Colliery Band*, walked the short distance from the Town Hall. As this catastrophe happened in North Wales, the Welsh residents of Widnes were particularly distressed and a Welsh Concert was held to supplement the fund. Speaking at the Victoria Road service, Mr. G. Cameron, the prospective parliamentary candidate, said:

"The average wage for a miner was £2 to £2.14s. a week. Was that enough for such magnificently courageous men? He would remind them that the compensation fund for accidents amounted to 1½d per ton on all the coal raised while royalties were 9d a ton. If compensation was levied at 9d. a ton there would be no need to make charitable appeals when disaster overtook the industry".

The unemployment situation was to remain a constant feature of the early years of this decade in much the same way as it had in the 1920s. However, by 1936 the numbers were steadily decreasing as the Government re-armament programme eased the situation. A local employment survey in 1936 revealed that there were 4326 men; 223 boys and 277 women employed in the chemical trades in Widnes. There were 738 men; 248 boys and 237 women employed in the asbestos trade in Widnes. Widnes Borough Corporation employed 425 men, and 34 women, in a variety of occupations. The jobless figure in this year was reduced to 1600.

At this time, some local companies were actually expanding. Such was the progress at "The Everite" during 1937 that they were able to absorb the majority of excess juvenile male labour in the town as well as some female juvenile labour. Orr's Zinc White Ltd., as a result of a merger with The Imperial Smelting Corporation in 1931, had also been extending their business. By 1935 their work's site had greatly increased as additional land, to the west side of Bower's Brook, and also further west over Lugsdale Road, was acquired. The merger with The Imperial Smelting Corporation had enabled Orr's Zinc White to weather the storm of depression during the early decade. Company records show that their output during 1930-1939 had more than doubled. This meant that almost 40,000 tonnes of Lithopone was produced annually. Not only did they manage to sustain their full workforce during the "trade depression" they were also able to take on additional workers.

Of course, despite the expansion of The Everite and The Vine Chemical Works, the unemployment situation never really went away, and there were still long queues at the Labour Exchange. In March 1939, our local MP, Richard Pilkington, voiced his concern during a House of Commons debate on unemployment. With distinct reflections of a speech made by an earlier Widnes representative, Mr. Moss Edwards, in 1882, when the subject of "alien labour" was discussed, Mr. Pilkington now alleged that "Irish labour" was being preferred to local men[71]. He said:

"As to the question of Irish labour, it was in no spirit of an attack on the Irish that it had been raised, as had been suggested in some quarters. There was no question of racial persecution. It was only a question of whether or not our own people should come first. Surely a Dominion's first responsibility was to its own citizens, and ours should be to our own people. The taxpayer had a right to know the number of people they were supporting who were not citizens of this country".

It appears that most of the jobs being undertaken by "Irish labour" were transient, such as work in maintenance construction and improvement of roads and bridges. In general, this work was done by outside contractors who brought these workers with them. Mr. Pilkington asked the Minister for Labour, Mr. Brown, for the numbers of men employed in this work. However, Mr. Brown could not supply them, as this type of work was not separately distinguished in employment statistics.

---

[71] Hansard – *Unemployment Debate, March 1939*

Obviously, the march of time had seen the industrial face of Widnes change drastically. Although conditions were still far from satisfactory, some people who remembered the chemical industry of earlier days were able to reflect, with some appreciation, upon the improvements.   In 1937, at a meeting of chemical workers on Merseyside, the conditions of industrial Widnes over a century were reviewed.   To some of the younger men present, a recounting of conditions in Widnes factories a half-century earlier were thought to be almost "unbelievable".   Mr. Holbrook Gaskell told the audience that in Widnes *"the industrial revolution blotted out well nigh every blade of grass.   For half a century it was accepted as indisputable that no green thing could grow in proximity to a chemical works – and there were sixteen dotted over Widnes"*.   He recalled buildings of pitch pine posts with Belfast roofs sheeted with inch boards.   The only artificial light had been given from gas jets or *"from hand held duck lamps which generally smelled, always smoked, and generally burned the legs of one's trousers when carried about"*.   He also mentioned how the welfare and social conditions of the chemical worker had improved.   The chemical workers of yesteryears had never dreamed of medical services, holiday pay, retirement pensions, or indeed of recreational facilities for their leisure time. Yes, for those in employment in 1937, factory work had greatly improved, although from a health and safety viewpoint there was still a mountain to climb.

Another modern development, which Mr. Holbrook Gaskell omitted to mention, was the setting up of joint industrial assemblies of workers and management.   By the early 1930s, I.C.I., and other large companies, were beginning to shed their favoured style of autocratic management by establishing industrial democracy in the form of works councils.   These councils consisted of democratically elected representatives of the workforce and designated members of the management.   It is interesting to see that a number of women gained places on the first Greenbank Works Council.

Building for the Future

The Housing of the Working Class Act (1890-1919) had made provisions for the building of public housing schemes, and expectations of standards in housing and health care had risen considerably since the publication of the *Tudors Walter Report* in 1918. There were over 4 million houses built in England between 1919 and 1939. One and a half million of these were municipally provided council houses. The 1930s' had brought a housing boom throughout the country, and here in Widnes we saw the large-scale development of the private housing sector in the town. Statistics show that during this period there was a sharp rise in the proportion of owner occupied houses.

In the early days of industrialisation in Widnes, the houses had grown up alongside the factories. One of the reasons for this was that public transport was at that time virtually non-existent and therefore it was necessary to house the workers conveniently close to their place of work. With the development of the bus service in the town, it was no longer necessary to reside close to the factories. By 1930 Widnes had 23 buses in operation and ran special services for workmen.   Of course, town planning now recognised the need to keep residential and factory areas separate, therefore housing was placed at greater distances from the established industrial areas of the town.

The various Housing Acts that had been brought in during the 1920s gave subsidies to Local Authorities and private builders. *Wheatley's Housing Act* increased subsidies to Local Authorities for building houses at controlled rents. A further Act in 1930 gave them additional powers to demolish slum properties and the

Government provided further subsidies for this purpose. This was a major social reform and encouraged a number of large building projects here in Widnes. In 1933 the Government said its aim was to sweep away all slum properties within five years. Health Officials also supported the idea that slum clearance would help to eradicate tubercular cross infection, however this did not seem to be the case[72]. The Government supposed that the financial provisions it was offering would make slum clearance a very attractive proposition to Local Authorities. In theory, the subsidies meant that slum dwellers could be re-housed at rents no higher than those they were presently paying for sub-standard housing.

During a meeting of the Housing Committee of Widnes Council in the summer of 1933, one Councillor remarked that:

"He could not say that they had got slums in Widnes, although they had a large number of houses of very poor quality. Slum was a peculiar word. He had known rich people living in slum conditions in big houses, so that it did not always follow that people living in a poor quarter were living in slums. He had been through Lugsdale and had been struck with the fine condition of the children, and he had thought what would be their condition physically if they were living in better surroundings. Everybody realised that there was a problem to be dealt with, and he thought all the Churches should be helping the Town Council in the matter. The Churches had failed badly in their energies and publicity on the question of slums".

However, despite this gentleman disputing the fact that there were slums in the town, there were others who strongly disagreed. In 1933 the question of slum clearance in Widnes became elevated to one of national importance as the Minister of Health, Sir E. Hilton Young, cited this town as one of eleven authorities throughout England that had inadequate slum clearance strategies. The Minister, speaking on a BBC radio programme, said he would

---

[72] *The Coming of the Welfare State* – M. Bruce (Batsford 1968)

be setting up a Government Inquiry into the Widnes slum clearance scheme. Following this broadcast, and subsequent national newspaper coverage, the Widnes Town Council received an official communication from The Ministry informing them of the Inquiry. Members of the Council were outraged that the Minister had seen fit to air this matter publicly, and nationally, before they had been informed[73].

As the Council set about confronting the problem of inadequate and unhealthy housing in the Borough, negotiations were started for the acquisition of land abutting upon Moor Lane and Lowerhouse Lane. One councillor congratulated the Housing Committee on tackling the slum clearance question before the Ministry took official action. He said that they now faced another problem, in the allocation of houses. He suggested that:

"The Housing Committee should familiarise themselves with the people and the conditions under which they lived before deciding on the type of house in which to re-house them. Some people living in the worst property in town would do credit to the best property they had to let, in regard to cleanliness of person, of house and of furniture. They had houses in which he would not hesitate to stay; yet the next door would offer quite a different problem".

The Ministry of Health Inquiry into the Widnes slum clearance scheme began early in 1934. Among those giving evidence were the Town Clerk, Mr. E.W. McNorton, and the Medical Officer of Health, Dr. Albert Jones. By June, the Inquiry was complete and Widnes Town Council outlined a revised scheme, which involved the clearance of buildings in the Waterloo area. The "Clearance Order" related to buildings in Barn Street, Water Street, Sankey Street, High Street and Albion Street. In all, this Order referred to 91 dwelling houses, 1 common lodging house, 8 dwellings with shops combined, 1 garage and 3 yards. There would be 535

---

[73] *Widnes Council Minutes* - 1933

inhabitants displaced by the demolition of these slums. The area
was low lying being only 23 feet above ordnance datum. It was
bounded on three sides by industrial works and on either side by a
thoroughfare to the river and there were no through roads. The
properties were over 70 years old and had been built quickly and
cheaply to house the rapidly growing population of industrial
workers who had arrived in the area during the 1860s. A
description of the state of the area and the houses was given at the
Inquiry:

*The arrangement of the streets (which of course embraced the passages)
and the widths had the result that there was a minimum of sunlight and
air space, and it was also significant that in no single case were the
bylaws for the Borough complied with. As to the exterior condition, the
properties were 70 or 75 years old, the bricks used were handmade and
porous, the walls were solid with no cavity or damp-proof course, and the
pointing, generally speaking, was exceedingly defective. The roofs,
gutters and downspouts were defective and the yards wholly
unsatisfactory. The sub soil was clay and one of the most important
features was the serious condition of dampness from rising damp and
percolating damp. All those elements went to make a lamentable
condition of things in that particular area. The sanitary condition was
deplorable, the walls and ceilings generally had the plaster torn down;
some 60 percent of the floors were defective and some 50 percent windows
were worn out and the staircases were in a bad condition. Only in nine
cases were handrails provided and only in six cases was there natural
light to the staircases.*

*The death rate for the area was 23 as compared with 12.7 in the whole of
the Borough; the infantile mortality rate was 182 against 82; the death
rate from diarrhoea was 65.6 against 10.7; the death rate from pulmonary
tuberculosis was 2.46 against .97 and from respiratory diseases 5.7
against 2.1*[74]

---

[74] *Widnes Council Minutes* – June 1934

As the local debates progressed, and the new clearance plans were outlined, the Town Council met with strong opposition from the owners/landlords of these properties. Dr. Jones, the Medical Officer for the Borough, when giving detailed evidence to the Inquiry, said:

"that no repairs of any magnitude had been carried out for many years prior to this. Once the Council had stated that the properties were "unfit for human habitation" and would be the subject of "demolition orders" some of the owners had started to do repairs, however none of these repairs could be regarded as permanently remedying the condition of the houses. As School Medical Officer, he was responsible for the health of all the school children and he had conducted a weekly clinic in the Waterloo area for 12 years, and he felt that the lowered vitality, the incidences of rheumatism and other debilitating conditions were in a large measure due to the poor housing conditions. He also said that compared with the whole of the Waterloo Ward the scheduled area had a higher death rate and infant mortality rate than other parts of the district. Going further down towards the Transporter, in West Bank Ward, which was entirely and definitely working class without open spaces, the death rate was 12.5 and infant mortality 82 both being much lower than the scheduled area".

At the beginning of June that same year, Widnes was again publicly, and nationally, criticised. The Labour MP for Plaidstow, Mr. Will Thorne, raised questions in the House of Commons regarding the infant mortality rate in Widnes. He asked if the Minister of Health would make known the infant mortality rate from the various wards in the Borough of Widnes, and what action he was taking in view of the gravity of the figures in some of the wards. He also asked if the Minister would make public the report of the Inquiry held by his inspectors, in connection with the demolition of property in the Waterloo area of Widnes. The Minister advised him that the documents relating to this were confidential. For his final question, Mr. Thorne asked: *"Does not the Minister think that some of these Widnes landlords should be pinched for taking rents for these houses?"*

To the tenants of some of these houses the identity of the true owner of their property was not always apparent. The so-called landlords in many cases were in reality only "Lessees" and in fact other people or organisations owned the properties. An example of this could be found in Wellington Street where the registered owners of a number of properties were The Minister and Church Wardens of St. Mary's Church[75].

Apart from the appalling structural conditions of the houses, infestations of vermin were common in most slum areas, not only in Widnes but also in all parts of the country. Bedbugs were such a problem that the Ministry of Health found it necessary to send a circular to all councils on the subject of bedbugs and how to deal with them. The Minister pointed out, especially when dealing with the clearance of slums, *"that it was essential that bedbugs should not be transferred to new houses when the tenants have been residing in infested premises"*. Councils were asked to take immediate action for securing disinfestations wherever the nuisance was found to occur. Widnes Corporation workmen carried out a fumigation process in infested houses with an electric spray containing a substance known as 4-cide. The furniture of tenants who were being moved from condemned houses was also treated.

Some of the first people displaced by the Waterloo slum clearance order were subsequently re-housed on the new Moor Lane housing scheme. The first residents moved in on 13th December 1934. Although pleased with their new improved living conditions, many were keen to maintain their previous communal life. Sociologists tell us that all areas have their own social identity where there are evident continuities in ways of thinking, feeling and behaving. So, it is quite understandable that people would wish to retain the comfort derived from that social "belonging". The new residents of the Moor Lane Scheme did not waste any time in putting that intent into action. They formed a new club,

---

[75] Building and Slum Clearance schedule: *Widnes Council 1934*

called *The Waterloo Social Club*, as a means of maintaining the community spirit of the old area. It is interesting to read contemporary observations of this new relocated community. A local reporter visited the Moor Lane estate to talk to the first group of new residents and recorded this passage:

"Not a blade of grass would have grown in the Waterloo area had there been any gardens or open spaces and it is a revelation whence comes the latent desire for the "lovesome thing". Digging, trenching, liming, and clearing the ground of scutch grass and brick bats are the prelude to what promises a bright appearance in summer. Actually, some tenants have already planted shrubs, and cuttings, and roots of perennials. "I suppose you must find it a great change from the old place?" was one question put to a woman who was busy in her front garden. "I should think we do, and you would agree if you had had to live in houses that let the rain through the roof." Then she went on to lament the loss of children from pneumonia, adding "You don't like to lose your babies and feel all the time that they could be saved". "And to think we have a bathroom, and we don't use it like it says in Gracie Fields' song – to put the coal in. Now the lads enjoy a good bath". At another house, I was informed that while at the old place it was the greatest trouble to get the children in to have a wash in the tin bath, at the new house, the trouble was to keep them out of the bath. One man exclaimed "it is only costing me a few coppers extra a week for rent and it is worth it all to have hot water and open air".

Around this time, the Corporation sent out a circular to over 1200 new tenants regarding their gardens. The local Horticultural Society had made overtures to the Council and negotiations were in progress with a view to helping with the cultivation of their new gardens. As only 5 replies were received from the tenants, the scheme was abandoned. Whilst these new Corporation tenants were enjoying their newly acquired green spaces, another group of new house owners had acquired a plot of land opposite their recently built homes in Beaconsfield Crescent. The builder, Mr. Joseph Penney, wrote to Widnes Corporation in July 1935 informing them that the owners wished to present this land to the Corporation free of charge, on the condition that the Council would set out and maintain this open space. The offer was accepted[76].

Prior to the occupation of the new Moor Lane houses, the Council fixed the rental amount at 7s.6d per week for a three-bedroom house with modern amenities, built at 14 or 15 to the acre. The controlled rents on the old slum properties had been only 3d. or 4d. a week less than the proposed rents on the new properties. At this point, there appears to have been a great variation in rent prices on the different estates. How these rents were calculated depended on the rules of *The Housing Act of 1924*. This presented great difficulties for the council as large numbers of existing tenants started to ask to be transferred to cheaper houses. The matter was resolved, in part, when the Ministry of Health agreed to let the Council calculate the rentals over the whole number of houses erected by the Corporation under the provisions of The Act.

Another Ministry of Health Inquiry was held at Widnes Town Hall in August 1935 to investigate further schemes proposed by Widnes Council. Seven areas in Farnworth were under consideration, and the Ministry Inspector carried out a personal inspection of the properties designated for "slum clearance". Some houses in Farnworth Street, Derby Road, and Birchfield Road were earmarked for demolition despite fierce protests from the owners of these properties. Some of these houses were said to be between 120 and 200 years old. One local commentator said that he feared that *"the area would lose its quaintness and picturesqueness when the little low cottages, some with gardens back and front, have been demolished"*. The tenants from this "clearance area" were subsequently re-housed on the Lancaster Road/Derby Road estate, which was in the process of being constructed at that time.

---

[76] Widnes Borough Council Minutes – July 1935

In 1936 further plans were unveiled for another new Corporation housing development. This plan was to develop three sites which had been acquired by the Corporation at an initial outlay of just over £5,000. The land was bounded by Widnes Road, Brynn Street, Oxford Street, Suttons Lane, Waring Street and south of Lacey Street. It was proposed to build 120 houses on the Widnes Road side and a further 36 houses on the Lacey Street site. The new streets would include Cambridge Street, Keble Street, Trinity Place, and Pembroke Street.

As this new development was nearing completion, Councillor Pat Hanley questioned the choice of names for these new streets. Because Oxford Street already existed, the Highways Committee thought that the new streets should also be called after colleges. Councillor Hanley said he would prefer streets to be named after well-known Widnesians. He said that they should remember one distinguished man who had lived in the neighbourhood, and had for many years represented the people of that ward. He called for an amendment to the name of one street and the Highways Committee gracefully accepted this. It was agreed the name of Pembroke Street would be changed into the now familiar "Quinn Street" in memory of the late Alderman Samuel Quinn.

During the process of knocking down condemned houses in the town, an alarming incident happened while workmen were demolishing houses in Pleasant Street. Three young boys, who had been playing in one of the empty houses, were buried under rubble when the house collapsed. The ceilings of the downstairs rooms had been removed, together with their wooden joists and woodwork. This left the walls unsupported and in danger of "swinging". A workman had earlier warned the boys of the danger and chased them away. However, boys will be boys, and they ignored his warning and sneaked back to the house. The roof and wall of the building subsequently collapsed burying these children. The workmen on the site, under the direction of their colleague, a Mr. Gandy of Midwood Street, responded rapidly and the boys were quickly dug out from beneath the rubble. They were unconscious, and were transferred swiftly to the Accident Hospital. Miraculously, apart from concussion, shock, and a few bruises, none of them suffered any serious injury. This was due in total to the prompt action of Mr. Gandy and his fellow workmen.

We can see that despite the earlier criticism of its slum clearance programme, Widnes Borough Council had a commendable building record. In the eleven years from 1922 to 1933 they built 1274 houses on the Fairfield and Kingsway sites. Another 500 houses built by private enterprise had supplemented these. The Council also built 84 houses as part of a re-housing scheme at Halebank. All of the new Corporation housing schemes had constituted a real effort to deal with slum clearance. The total number of houses built in the Borough between the periods 1919 to 1939 were 4692, of these 2092 were built by Widnes Corporation and the rest by private enterprise.

Such was the rapid rate of building in the private sector during the 1930s that the Borough Engineer, James Holt, informed the Council that because of the quantity of new building work in the Borough at that time, he did not have an adequate number of staff to ensure efficient inspection and compliance with bye-laws. He suggested that his department's work had been very difficult. He also said that the general standard of building in the Borough is *"acceptable, though not wholly satisfactory"*. Mr. Holt, along with Dr. Jones, the Medical Officer of Health, had additional concerns with regard to the large number of houses built by private enterprise, as very few of these were for the rental market. Dr. Jones was particularly critical of the fact that those that *were* available for rent were beyond the reach of the ordinary workingman. In his annual report in 1934 he said:

"The need for additional houses is still great, but the rentals charged for many of the houses built by private enterprise are in excess of the amount the average workman can afford. Therefore, for an industrial community,

such as exists in Widnes, the demand for a cheap house cannot be supplied by private enterprise"[77].

Although a great number of people had been successfully rescued from bad housing, a most distressing case was brought to the attention of the public when the results of an inquest on a lady who died at Whiston Institute were made known in the spring of 1935. Widnes Corporation was severely criticised for not providing her with proper accommodation, and for allowing her to live in the most abysmal conditions. It appears that this lady, a widow aged 71, had previously lived with her husband in a caravan in a field off Moor Lane. After her husband died, she lived alone in the caravan for a few years until she was given the use of a hut behind the mortuary at the Corporation Depot in Lowerhouse Lane. The hut did not have any sanitation provisions or heating. She lived here in the most squalid conditions for over a year until she had an accident and was taken to Whiston Institute where she died a short while later. The Coroner, addressing the representative of the Council, said: *"if you or anyone else in connection with Widnes Corporation can justify her existence in that hut for one year, considering her age and infirmities, I shall be extremely surprised".*

This case highlighted the fact that there were many individuals living in improvised accommodation. The dire housing shortage, and lack of money, had forced some into living in conditions that made even the slum houses seem desirable. There were numerous people living in caravans and huts and other types of temporary shelter throughout the town. In the Moor Lane vicinity there were five disused and dilapidated railway carriages being lived in. In the Crow Wood area, two old omnibus bodies, connected by a wooden structure, were home to a man and his wife and four children. This family had been evicted from their previous home, as the landlord wanted the house for another family.

---

[77] *Annual Report of the Medical Officer of Health - 1933*

During this decade building costs were cheaper than they had been, and Government grants were also an incentive to private builders as well as the Local Authority. The following selection of building schemes demonstrates how the urban face of the town changed drastically during the 1930s, as new streets of housing rapidly appeared on what were previously green field sites.

Barrows Green Lane	*1938*
Dykin Road Estate	*1936-38*
Ireland Street	*1933-35*
Joseph Street	*1938*
Warrington Road	*1936*
Gregson Road	*1936*
Castle Street	*1936-38*
Knowles Street	*1934-38*
Lytham Road	*1936*
Fairhaven Road	*1936*
St. Annes Road	*1936*
Millfield Road	*1934*
Claremont Drive Estate	*1936-38*
Deirdre/Shelagh Avenues	*1933-39*
Green Lane Estate	*1936*
Mayfair Grove area	*1933-34*
Ditchfield Road	*1936-37*
Hale Road	*1936-37*
Berry Road	*1935*
Grange Drive	*1936*
Heath Road area	*1937*
Hayes Road	*1937*
Highfield Crescent	*1931*
Beaconsfield Road area	*1934-38*
Keble & Cambridge Streets Council Estate	*1935*
Lacey Street Council Estate	*1935*
Quinn Street Council Estate	*1935*
Suttons Lane Council Estate	*1935*
Shakespeare Road Estate	*1938-39*

Kingway private housing   *1936*
Windsor Road   *1937*

In addition to these there were also a large number of individual private houses built in Cronton Lane, Coroner's Lane, Norland's Lane, Birchfield Road and other areas of the town.

In 1938 there were 78 licensed premises in the town.[78] Planning permission had also been sought for a number of new public houses that year. These included the following:

> *The Angel and Elephant, Appleton*
> *The Prince of Wales, Kent Street*
> *The Albion, Liverpool Road*
> *The Cricketer's Arms, Lowerhouse Lane*
> *The Church View, Lunt's Heath Road*
> *The Derby Arms, Widnes Road*[79]

The building of The Albion Hotel caused much discussion in the town. There had been a lot of opposition to the plans from residents and also from the *Widnes Council of Christian Witness*. The licence, in the name of Alfred Radley, was removed from the original "Albion Hotel" in Waterloo Road and transferred to the new premises. By this time, the Waterloo area had seen a considerable decline in population due to slum clearance schemes. A *Royal Commission on Licensing* had previously indicated that when populations moved, that licensing facilities also, within reasonable limits, should follow that movement. The application for the transfer of this licence said that this new type of public house would be a place *"where men could go with their wives and families and take refreshment in decency and comfort"*. The Albion Hotel eventually opened for business in October 1940.

[78] *A History of Widnes* – George E. Diggle (Widnes Corporation 1961)
[79] This was the reconstruction of older premises

Whilst some new public houses were being built, the 1930s also saw a number of the old pubs close their doors for the last time. Amongst the pubs taking their "last orders" that decade were:

The Engineers Arms, Victoria Street
The Moss Bank Hotel, Moss Bank
The Rose & Crown, Moss Bank
The Brown Cow Inn, Liverpool Road
The Blackburne Arms, Warrington Road
The George Hotel, Waterloo Road
The Wellington Hotel, Wellington Street
The Central Hotel, Derby Road

In 1933 an article in *The Widnes Weekly News* outlined the "lure of house ownership" and claimed that Widnes was an excellent place to buy a home because:

Widnes as a residential town wants some beating. It is built on sold bedrock, so there is no fear of subsidence; it is well drained, so there is no fear of floods; its roads compare favourably with many others; its gas has been the subject of many headlines; it is "linked to the world" by its many industrial, political and educational associations; and linked to the rest of the country by its bridges and excellent facilities for travel by road, bus or rail.

A number of builders advertised properties for sale on forthcoming developments:

H. Beech of Milton Road
Houses and bungalows in Hall Avenue, Hough Green, also properties in Highfield Road, at a cost of £400 each.

T.Gleave of Eccleston Park, St. Helens
New houses, in the course of erection at Derby Road, Barrows Green. Only £335.

Amos Limited of Liverpool
Modern homes at Liverpool Road, Ball O'Ditton.   - £375 (a £25 deposit would secure).

F. Tuson, Birchfield Road, Widnes.
Houses now being erected at Upton Lane, Widnes.

G.A. Weate, Barrows Green Lane, Widnes
Houses now in progress at Tennyson Road and Crow Wood

J.A. Gallagher, Moorfield Road, Widnes
Splendid semi-detached houses in Moorfield Road.

The enterprising Gas Department of Widnes Corporation was always keen to attract new customers for their appliances.   The showrooms, in Widnes Road, displayed examples of new "gas fires" as well as cookers and water heaters.   Many of the local builders co-operated by allowing their show houses to be used as "All Gas Exhibition Homes".   In May 1934 Mr. J.A. Gallagher had just completed his new houses in Moorfield Road.   These houses were priced at £395. One of them, 146 Moorfield Road, was to be an exhibition house.   It was described thus:

"The house itself is a splendid example of the builder's craft and examination will show how excellently the workmanship is executed in every detail.   It contains three bedrooms, bathroom, dining room, sitting room, scullery, hall and wash-house.   The rooms on the ground floor are wood blocked and the bathroom tiled.   The visitor will be able to see in full operation everything of the latest labour and drudgery saving gas equipment, cooking, heating, lighting, washing and cleaning.   All the gas and water appliances seen can be obtained from the Corporation Gas Department at the showrooms in Widnes Road."

The housing boom of the 1930s was due, in part, to a fall in building costs. A statistical survey outlined by M. Bowley in his book *"Housing and the State"*[80], shows a marked fall in both material prices and wages after 1927. Between February and June 1932 there was also a sharp reduction in the Bank Rate and low interest rates increased the attraction of buying rather than renting houses, as rents continued to increase. After 1936 costs began to rise again but this appears to have had little effect on the rate of building in the private sector.

Of course, not everyone was in a position to purchase their own home. However, now that the State had intervened for the first time on a large scale in the provision of houses for the people, the result was a new social form - Local Authority housing estates. The new Corporation estates were populated by people who had been re-housed during the process of demolishing the slum housing in the older districts of the town. In 1935 some houses in Newtown, including parts of Elizabeth Street, Ann Street West, and Suttons Lane, along with houses in Railway Street and additional houses in the Waterloo area, were earmarked for clearance. Many old houses in Ditton and Halebank were also demolished at this time. The residents of these slum clearances were re-housed on the new Halebank Council Estate.

The new houses provided gardens, indoor sanitation, fixed baths, piped water and the provision of power by electricity and gas. Many of the new Widnes Corporation tenants, although delighted with their new modern homes, mourned the breaking up of old communities. Neighbourhood relationships were heightened and deep rooted in districts where families had lived in the same terraced streets for a few generations. Although some were re-housed in new areas with their relatives and old neighbours, they felt that the new estates lacked the character, culture, and welfare network of the old neighbourhoods. Some residents believed that the new districts had no harmonising or empathetic elements. In fact, many people thought them lifeless,

---

[80] M. Bowley *"Housing and the State 1919-1944"* (Allen & Unwin 1945)

silent and dull. This was a natural human reaction to changes in what they considered had been a stable social arrangement. Their new houses did not feel like real "homes" as it took time to learn to live with new surroundings. Some people were able to adapt more easily and were keen to develop new interests such as gardening. However, with time, new communities were built up and a new social structure was established. I suppose it is still too early to do any "historical" research on the emergence of different patterns of social life on these "new" estates. The closer social history gets to our own times, the more difficult it is to be sure we have identified what is important about a period. I suppose this is largely a matter of vantage point as some features of a pattern may not yet be clearly visible.

A lady who was 9 years old when her family were re-housed on the new "Fairfield Estate" told me:

"We had only ever had an outside lavatory, now we had a bathroom and the luxury of hot water, which was supplied by a back-boiler from the coal fire. We also had a garden to play in. My Dad had had an allotment before, but he gave this up when we moved to our new house. I remember my mother saying that the rents were very dear, as there were no subsidies or housing allowances in those days, but my Dad would save by not having to pay for the allotment anymore.

We missed our "old" Street, and things like sitting on the doorstep talking to neighbours. Where we had lived before people were very sociable. All the mothers took chairs outside in the summer and sat chatting to each other while they watched the kids play. The new estates finished all that. People became more reticent - the community spirit had gone. We also missed the corner shop where you could buy almost anything. My mother complained that she had to go all the way to Albert Road if she needed something! The lack of a nearby chip shop was also something we missed. In our old neighbourhood, mothers used to go to the chip-shop for the Friday night tea. They took their own plates and a tea-towel to cover the meals and keep them warm till they got home."[81]

Another person described her old neighbourhood, which was a known "slum clearance area", in these words:

"We lived among people whose incomes were low, and the housing conditions were appalling. But it was an area of domestic peace and neighbourly trust of a standard unknown today. People never thought of locking their doors if they went out. Families raised children, men worked, women ran households. We were poor, but then so was everyone else, so we didn't dwell on it. It might sound strange, but when we moved we were sad to leave it all behind".

The allocation of houses was not without problems. There were numerous complaints of "unfair treatment". *The Widnes Weekly News* was often the vehicle for airing complaints. I include below extracts from some of many similar letters published in July 1933.

"A certain young couple, living in a modern house which they own, apply for and are given a house on the new Lockett Road Scheme, putting their own house not "for let" but for sale, at the price of between £400-£600. If their own house is worth £400 why should they want a council house?"

"Young couple lately married (six months) living with relatives apply and get a house on Lockett Road, relatives who are in a large house, parlour, kitchen, scullery, outhouse and three bedrooms, also receive a house. Now sir, compare the following: Father, mother and two children occupy two rooms, up three flights of stairs, apply – nothing doing. Family of five children and parents living behind a shop, rent 10 shillings, apply for house – nothing doing!"
(Signed: "A Disgruntled Hero")

---

[81] Information given by Mrs. P. Hughes

The chemical industry had been responsible for the creation of the industrial town of the 19th century with its extensive urban problems. Small, badly built houses with inadequate sanitary provisions created health and overcrowding issues. However, the years between the wars saw much effort given to solving these problems. The housing history of Widnes during the inter-war years shows both successes and failures. As we have seen, in the 1930s there was a rapid output of new and "good quality" housing which greatly improved social conditions. But, regardless of the Council's very best endeavours, the housing shortage was still acute and many sub-standard "slums" remained.

Despite the continued shortage of housing stock, in 1936 when the Council proposed the purchase of 35 acres, comprising Lowerhouse Farm buildings and land, for re-housing purposes, there were strenuous objections to the scheme. The Council planned to build 500 new houses to re-house people displaced by clearance. At that time there were 773 families living in overcrowded conditions in the four wards that comprised West Bank, Waterloo, Victoria and Simms Cross. All these houses had been built during the nineteenth century to accommodate the industrial workforce of the town. In those pre-planning days no consideration was given to width of streets, density of houses, drainage, sewage or the removal of refuse. The houses were small and by the 1930s many of these dwellings were considered unfit for human habitation. In a debate on "Housing" in The House of Commons in February 1938[82], our local MP, Richard Pilkington, told the members that there were 75 families in this Borough with more than 10 children, and one family had as many as 25 children. The problem was too large families living in too small buildings. He urged the Minister of Health to offer grants to enable the Council to build larger houses.

---

[82] *Hansard (Housing (Financial Provisions) Bill* – February 1938.

Until the first *Town Planning Act of 1909* there was no plan of development to guide Local Authorities. Each scheme for building was presented in isolation for approval or disapproval according to whether or not the plan complied with the bye-laws. In Widnes, there were many examples of haphazard arrangements where one developer had laid out one side or part of a street and another developer had laid out the other. One example is Cooper Street and Regent Road. The *Town Planning Act of 1932* encouraged Widnes to define the direction in which future development should take place. The draft scheme presented by the Council in 1938 was prepared in the interests of the community as a whole, industrial and commercial, as well as residential/landowners and tenants. The plan was intended to promote the future welfare of the inhabitants of the town. The draft plan was presented for public scrutiny in August 1938, but the scheme could not actually come into effect until it had passed through both Houses of Parliament and been made an Act of Parliament.

By the end of the decade such planning issues and housing problems were far from settled, not only locally but also nationally. Generally speaking, during the 1930s most authorities endeavoured to attack the problems of slum clearance and overcrowding in equal measures, but in spite of this, with the onset of war, these problems had to be thrust into the background where they remained for the following six years.

Schools and Child Welfare

One of the most positive things to have come out of *The Hadow Report of 1926* was the increasing belief that secondary education for all pupils, in separate buildings and establishments, was essential. The report also said that the term "elementary" should be replaced with "primary" and education following on from 11 years of age should be called "secondary". The magic age "11 years" seems to have been chosen for a number of reasons. Firstly, most of the existing elementary schools had been built when the leaving age was 11 and their buildings were only adequate to provide classrooms for children up to that age. Secondly, it seems that 3 years was the minimum which could reasonably be offered as secondary education with the school leaving age at 14. Thus, the report had called for a total reorganisation of secondary education and new schools were required to meet these needs. Once again, economy cuts in Government spending meant that these proposals had limited effect in some places. However, some Local Authorities showed initiative in providing more secondary education. Widnes was one of these.

As well as dealing with the necessary requirements outlined in Government legislation, the Local Education Authority was also charged with the responsibility of providing education and welfare for some less fortunate children. In the first year of this decade, on the 9th September, a School Medical Service Report was issued on the subject of "Mentally Defective Children" in the Borough. The School Medical Officer reported 6 cases of "mentally defective" children, of these, 1 case required institutional treatment in accordance with section 31(c) of *The Mental Deficiency Act, 1913*. Another sad and disturbing fact to emerge from the report was that, at that time, children suffering from epilepsy were sent "away" to special "Homes". *"The Home for Epileptics"* at Maghull, near Liverpool, was the dwelling place for a number of Widnes children at an annual cost to Widnes Corporation of £68.18s. for each child. The parents of these children were not required to make any contribution to these costs

In the 1930s Widnes saw a great deal of educational building progress. The Local Education Authority had set out a programme of building in 1929 which would include Fairfield Infant School, the Fairfield Senior Schools, an additional school in Kingsway and an extra hall for the Central School. The Central School was opened in 1930 and the new Wade Deacon Grammar School[83] followed shortly afterwards. An "Open Air School", to afford facilities for "delicate" children, had also been provided. The effect of "education" on the rates had always been a serious concern for the Widnes Town Council, and Government demands for economy meant that development had been restricted to a certain extent. Nonetheless, it appears that Widnes was well to the fore in its educational provisions at that time. By the end of 1939 Widnes had no less than 9 elementary schools with about 8000 on roll. In addition, there was a Grammar School and two Secondary Schools.

Important proposals regarding the development of education in the Borough were submitted to the Widnes Education Committee in January 1930. A revised programme of educational improvement had been drawn up and was forwarded to the Board of Education for approval. It was hoped that this programme would enable the Council to obtain a special educational grant. In ordinary circumstances, the grant paid by The Board of Education to Local Authorities was three fifths of expenditure on teachers' salaries, one half for special services, and one fifth on approved expenditure for the provision of buildings and furniture. With

---

[83] In 1931 *"The Widnes Secondary School"* was transferred to new buildings in Birchfield Road and renamed *"The Wade Deacon Grammar School"*

regard to the revised Widnes programme, it was hoped that the Borough would qualify for a special grant, which had been put into place for a period of three years from 1st September 1929. This grant offered half the expenditure, instead of one fifth, for re-organisation and development purposes. However, The Board insisted on certain requirements, which included the instruction of all 11 plus children in special schools, specially equipped for advanced instruction. The new programme took into account a number of significant changes which were due to be implemented. Firstly, there was the important matter of the raising of the school leaving age to 15 years on 1st April 1931. A reduction in class sizes was also to be brought into effect. Class sizes should not exceed 50 for children under 11 years and 40 for children over 11.

Needless to say, these changes to the education system placed an increased financial burden on the ratepayers. Despite the prospect of a generous grant, some councillors were not in favour of the revised educational programme because of the cost. The total estimated expenditure would amount to £70,000. It appears that the main criticism of the scheme came from people without children. There were numerous heated debates among the members of the Education Committee. One member said that:

"A considerable outlay was involved, but it would not all represent extra expenditure, and there would be savings in other directions. It was anticipated that the withdrawal of a generation of 14 plus children from the labour market would lead to a saving in the amount paid in unemployment benefit, or alternatively, in Poor Law relief". However, Alderman G. I. Neil, who opposed the scheme, said he had *"heard nothing said about the labouring classes. Suppose they gave all the children the education suggested, were they going to educate them all to be parsons or doctors? Where were they going to get their labourers?"* [84]

---

[84] *Widnes Borough Council - Education Committee* (January 1930)

Apart from the few members of the Education Committee who were against the increasing of the school leaving age, family priorities sometimes shaped parents attitudes to education. Some were unhappy to learn that their children would be staying on at school for a further year. Although most parents obviously wanted their children to be educated to a good standard, economic pressures meant that some boys and girls needed to work as soon as possible to help supplement the family income. Most of the boys became labourers, and the girls went into factories or shops, or left home to go "in to service". Whatever their job, their contribution was a valuable addition to the domestic financial structure.

In April 1933 at the annual meeting of the Widnes Council of Social Service, the matter of providing milk in schools was raised. During that year, the Executive Committee had been concerned about infants in the elementary schools suffering from malnutrition. A milk fund was started and they received a grant from the local branch of the N.U.T. The money was handed back to the teachers to be spent on milk for those who needed it. This had an unexpected development, it made the Education Committee realise that there was a need for something of this kind, and as a result, the Education Committee took over the responsibility of providing milk for needy children.

In November of the following year, it was reported in the proceedings of the Education Committee, that of the school population of 7,500, milk was supplied to 3,592 children, 1,450 receiving free milk and 2,142 receiving a third of a pint for a halfpenny. During school holidays, provision had been made for the supply to continue on the condition that the children went to their own school and drank the milk on the premises.

By 1937 the daily supply of milk to schools was well established. However, in July of that year the local dairymen were up in arms over the Education Committee's decision to discontinue the supply of non-pasteurised milk to schoolchildren in the Borough. It appears that the milk dealers in the town thought that this pronouncement was casting aspersions on the local milk supply generally. The Council said they had consulted experts who outlined the distinct nutritional benefits derived from pasteurised milk as opposed to non-pasteurised. The committee stated that their chief concern was the health of the children, and that for safety's sake they must have pasteurised milk for the local schoolchildren. The difficulties arose with the local milk dealers, because many of them did not have, at that time, proper pasteurising facilities at their farms.

At the end of 1934 the Medical Officer of Health made his annual report to members of the Council. Reports based on the physical condition of children when they first entered school, and the regular inspection of all schoolchildren during the school year, were published. It appears that generally the physical condition of new entrants had improved during a ten-year period. The reasons for this were put down to the establishment of Child Welfare Centres in the town. Cases of rickets were decreasing, however, despite the arrangements made for the supply of fresh milk to schools, there was an increase in cases of malnutrition. The increase in these cases was to be found mainly amongst the Junior and Senior Departments in schools. It appears that the supply of milk was having the desired effect among the younger children.

The School Medical reports for this year show that cases of crippling congenital defects were also reducing. The chief cause of severe defects was put down to Infantile Paralysis. Children found to be affected by this were now being brought to the Orthopaedic Clinic in the early stage and this prevented deformity in most cases. One alarming fact outlined in the reports was the increasing number of children suffering from heart disease in 1934. It was said that:

"The total number of children of school age suffering from heart disease is so severe as to necessitate the provision of educational facilities other than those of a public elementary school". The main causes were rheumatism and chorea. The Medical Officer said:

"That if we are to prevent the development of valvular disease of the heart among children, we must secure the early detection of rheumatism and treat it energetically. Every effort continues to be made to secure attendance of children for examination who are reported to have been absent from school owing to rheumatic pains and of children exhibiting pallor following an indefinite illness".

In the School Report submitted by the Medical Officer of Health in 1935, the subject of nutrition was carefully studied. Earlier in the year, it was decided that the nutrition of schoolchildren should be examined and classified. This study was to be based purely on clinical grounds and not merely on the height or weight of a child. The survey showed that 15% of children were nutritionally subnormal on entering school, as compared with 10% in other age groups. The percentage of entrants who were extremely malnourished was 2.7%. At the end of the report, The Medical Officer made these comments:

"The securing of improved housing conditions will minimise malnutrition and increase resistance of children to disease, provided a great proportion of the family income is not required for rent. The general health of children who have been removed from unfit houses has definitely improved, but it should be remembered that rentals of new houses are low and an adequate portion of the family income is now available for food. The daily supply of fresh milk in schools also continues to improve value".

In July 1937 the children of Warrington Road School were treated to a special viewing of the *Rugby League Challenge Cup*. The local boys who were part of that winning team toured their old schools to give the pupils an opportunity of seeing "The Cup" close up. Among the Warrington Road Old Boys who returned to the school on that day were: *Alec Higgins, Harry Millington, Hugh McDowell, Bob Roberts and Alf Gallimore.*

Later that year a group of "Old Boys" from another school were enjoying a unique re-union, with the purpose of forming an association. These past scholars of West Bank National School vowed to keep alive the traditions of the oldest elementary school in the Waterloo and West Bank area of Widnes. The first National School was built at Widnes Dock in 1839, but this was closed down and replaced by a new building in Waterloo Road in 1858. The new school was called St. Mary's National School and was affiliated to St. Mary's Church. Some of the reminiscences that evening were entertaining and interesting. One man recalled his schooldays in 1867, and gave us an idea of the type of punishment given out to pupils those days. He said:

"During my time, there were some very rough lads. One, I can especially remember, and Mr. Crawford continually caned him, morning and afternoon. He was better known as Downer Fyldes. One day he had been thrashed in the morning and thrashed again in the afternoon. He had split three canes and Mr. Crawford put him across a stool, and then sat down winded. Fyldes got up and said "Have you finished now, well, good afternoon" and he walked down the school. We had our caps and coats in the cloakroom and we found that he had taken every one off the hooks and scattered them over the place. Downer Fyldes[85] didn't come back for a long time"

---

[85] See notes

Everyday Life

The *"Blue Book for the County of Lancashire"* detailed the census returns for the county in 1931. This book tells us that there were 272,009 more women than men in the county. In 9 of the 17 County Boroughs, the population had declined since the previous census in 1921. There were 62 constituencies returning 66 members to Parliament, and the average population and electorate per member returned were 76,245 and 50,260 respectively[86].

The population statistics for the Widnes Borough and Wards in 1931 are below:

District	Total	Male	Persons Female	per Acre
Widnes	*40619*	*20799*	*19820*	*7.1*
Ditton	*4592*	*2385*	*2207*	*2.0*
Farnworth	*8427*	*4154*	*4273*	*6.1*
Halton	*5822*	*3017*	*2805*	*6.0*
Simms Cross	*7553*	*3825*	*3728*	*26.3*
Victoria	*6067*	*3206*	*2861*	*21.4*
Waterloo	*4627*	*2462*	*2165*	*12.9*
West Bank	*3531*	*1750*	*1781*	*15.8*

Because of the increased ownership of motorcars, together with an increase in accidents and collisions, on 12th February 1930, the Town Council discussed the subject of controlling traffic by light signals. The Ministry of Transport had recently issued a circular to

---

[86] *Blue Book for Lancashire* (published 1932) – Lancashire RO

Local Authorities with respect to the rate of financial assistance available to them for the installation and maintenance of traffic lights. At this time, the motorcar was becoming a very familiar sight in the streets of Widnes, although at a cost of around £300 it was still not easily within the reach of the ordinary workingman. However, the ownership of motorcycles had increased and many had sidecars with which to transport another passenger, or two children, in addition to the pillion rider.

In the General Election of 1931 the Labour candidate, Mr. Cameron, was beaten by the Conservative, Mr. Roland Robinson, with a huge majority of 9814 votes. Despite his resounding victory, Mr. Robinson was only to serve one term as our political representative before being replaced by another Conservative candidate, Mr. Richard Pilkington, in 1935.

In July 1931 the town was in mourning as it received the news of the death of Alderman David Lewis. Over the years, David Lewis had served this town well and his popularity crossed all political and religious divides. Although he was born in Runcorn, he had lived in Widnes all his adult life. He left school at eleven years of age and helped to support his widowed mother and five siblings. At the age of thirteen, he was in the employ of Messrs. William Gossage & Sons, and from that time on his life became inextricably involved with Widnes. Over the years, he had been responsible for the development of a great many of the landmarks that are familiar to us today. His drive had pushed these projects forward and his greatest aim was to see Widnes progress. He was, without doubt, a man of great vision who was ahead of his time in many ways. In the Council Chamber, his fellow councillors gave many moving accolades and paid special tribute to his work as the chairman of the Health Committee of the Town Council. Councillor Dan Garghan said:

"David Lewis was an upright and honourable man who had a strict integrity. He showed ungrudging devotion to his public work and an

ardent sympathy for all undertakings that had as their object the alleviation of suffering or disease. I have lost a good friend, but David Lewis's friendship to me was nothing compared to his friendship for the sick and suffering. It had been his principal objective in life to bring the health administration of the Borough to the state of perfection it had reached, and it was a tribute to his service that the health administration of Widnes was second to none in the Kingdom. The sick and poor of Widnes had indeed lost a good friend in David Lewis".

Fortunately, the town was still blessed by others willing to offer compassion and relief to the poor and needy. In many towns, *The Salvation Army* had opened what were known as "Goodwill Centres". At these centres, thousands of pairs of boots and shoes were collected, repaired by unemployed men, and distributed free. Cast off clothing was also collected and special facilities were started for the unemployed where refreshments were provided. This *"Goodwill League Scheme"* was in operation in Widnes throughout the 1930s. The doors of The Widnes Salvation Army Hall were always open to needy persons. They also provided a "cheap food kitchen" where it was possible to get a dinner for only one penny – or in some cases, free meal tickets were given to deserving cases.

Other organisations were also taking an interest in different problems in the areas. At the annual meeting of the Widnes branch of *"The National Society for the Prevention of Cruelty to Children"* (N.S.P.C.C.), in 1932, the Secretary reported on the number of cases dealt with in the town during the year.

224 cases affecting the welfare of 301 children were dealt with. The Inspector had made 775 supervision visits, and 204 children were known to be insured. The classification of the cases was: Neglect 80; ill treatment 8; other wrongs 3, and advice sought 28. Of the number of children affected 144 were boys and 137 girls, of whom 44 were babies under two years of age.

The Government was also considering the welfare of children and juveniles when they introduced a new *Children and Young Persons Act* in 1933.   Under the terms of this Act, arrangements were to be made to form special magistrates' panels to deal with juvenile offenders.   In November that year, the first "Juvenile Court" was held in Widnes.   The Act desired, and the Home Secretary emphasised the point, that the court should be held away from "police atmosphere" and in a separate building where possible.   In Widnes, arrangements were made to hold this court in the Municipal Technical College, as this seemed the most convenient place.   Mr. A.H. Calvert, the chairman of the magistrates, said that:

"The work of the court would be preventative rather than punitive, and, where helpful, justices might call for reports to be furnished as to the home life and school work.   Thus, the juvenile court justices would act in co-operation with the local education committee and the probation officer. In fact, it would be the offender and not the offence the justices would most need to consider with care".

The age of the young persons to be dealt with was raised from 16 to 17 years.   There were other changes to follow in the law courts. In 1934, Widnes was constituted as an *Independent Petty Sessional Division* and in addition to Widnes it would also include the townships of Bold, Hale and Halewood.   In the past, as part of the Prescot division, all important court business was heard at Prescot.   Prior to this, Widnes had been the only large town in the area not to have its own sessions.

It was disturbing to read that throughout the period this book deals with, a substantial number of small boys were given "The Birch" for petty crimes. On one occasion, in 1942, a young child of 10 years was given 6 strokes of the birch and sent to a Remand Home.   He had stolen 1s.1d from a gas meter in Ann Street. Fortunately, the majority of young people in Widnes did not need to avail themselves of the services of a "Juvenile Court".   Apart from parish activities, almost all the local church groups had "a scout troop" and boys were encouraged to join.   In April 1932 "*The Widnes Boys Scout Association*" held a party to mark its 21st birthday!

In spite of the overall feeling of gloom that marked the 1930s out as the decade of "depression" there seems to have been wide and varied entertainment available. By the 1930s the more expensive valve radios had been developed. These were run off the mains and had speakers, which meant that the whole family could listen in. The new radios cost around £5, which was quite a large sum of money in those days.   Other forms of communication were also making an appearance in the town. During this decade a telephone exchange was opened in Brynn Street. To supplement this expanding service, in 1934 the District Manager of the Post Office Telephones Service applied to Widnes Council for permission to erect a number of telephone kiosks in the town. These were to be placed in Waterloo Road, Liverpool Road, Highfield Road, and outside Halton View Post Office.

Despite the unemployment problems in town, it appears that most people had the ability to rise above their circumstances and enjoy themselves in a variety of ways. For those lucky enough to be in employment, a reduction in the average working week increased the demand for leisure activities. The fact that during this decade some workers became entitled, through collective agreements, to take a week's holiday[87] also meant that leisure pastimes became more common.

The unemployed of course had free time forced upon them and they utilised their time in a number of ways. However, they were often excluded from taking part in many of the normal leisure activities due to lack of money. In 1931 one group of unemployed

---

[87] *The Holiday with Pay Act of 1938* - gave workers an entitlement to a paid holiday.

formed a band. The musicians played mouth organs, clappers, tambourines, drums and cymbals, or indeed anything that would provide an acceptable musical sound. The band, which at various times could number anything up to 100 members and also included about a dozen children, practised in Newtown in the premises of the old Lancashire Metal Works, off Lugsdale Road. They called themselves *The Widnes Star Novelty Band* and their popularity quickly spread beyond the town.

Early in 1932 the BBC made a sound film of *The Widnes Star Novelty Band* performing in the yard at the rear of the Technical School in Victoria Square. The original site of this film was to have been at their rehearsal base in Lugsdale, but howling wind and rain had made this impossible so later it was decided to transfer to the Technical College where they performed in the presence of the local MP, Mr. Roland Robinson, and his wife. Later, on 14th May 1932, they were invited to the BBC Studios at Manchester to do a live radio broadcast. The members of *The Widnes Star Novelty Band* each contributed 2d per week to help pay for their outfits. A draper in Newtown allowed them to "spread the cost" of the material and a local lady volunteered to make the suits. Other local people, in Newtown, Lugsdale, Marrabone and Moss Bank, made voluntary contributions to their fund. The band's leaders, Mr. Foster and Mr. Whitfield, had devised an ingenious method of amplifying the sound from the mouth organs by attaching a metal trumpet to each instrument. None of the musicians were able to read music and they played solely "by ear". In May 1932 Mr. Martin's "Bozzadrome", in Albert Road, was full to capacity when the film of our local band was first shown.

In 1934 it was estimated that in excess of 45% of the population went to the cinema at least once a week. The cinema had by this time progressed to "talkies" and during the 1930s it was one of the most popular forms of commercial leisure among both young and old, and seemed to bring all elements of society together. The films provided enjoyment and relaxation, as well as a few hours of escapism from their normal lives, in warm and comfortable surroundings. Most cinemas had two showings of the main feature and it was not unusual to see long queues of people outside Widnes cinemas, waiting to be admitted to the "second house". Indeed, queuing was to be a feature of this decade as it was often said that long queues formed alternately outside the Labour Exchange and the cinemas. Local man, Nor Kiddie, the son of Gar Kiddie, who had a lengthy association with The Alex Theatre, appeared in one of the early "talkies", a film long since consigned to forgotten things called *"Bad Companions"*. It was shown to packed audiences at The Century Cinema, in West Bank, in October 1932.

Also in 1932 "The Alex Theatre" changed ownership and after extensive renovations was transformed into what its new owners described as "a super-cinema". The Alex Theatre had for something like half a century entertained the people of Widnes and many famous artistes had trodden its boards, including the likes of Stan Laurel and Charlie Chaplin. The "Alex" was built it in 1887 to replace an old wooden building in Wellington Street that had previously served as the local theatre[88]. An enterprising group of people comprising Dr. Tom Gerrard[89], Mr. James Kiddie and Mr. W. Bray were responsible for building the theatre, and were the original owners. In the latter years, Jim Kiddie and his brother Gar Kiddie were the owner/managers. This old building had echoed to the cheers and interruptions at big political gatherings, local amateur performers had scored triumph after triumph and many fund-raising events for local charities had been staged there. In 1916 as cinematography increased in popularity, it was converted to a cinema. However, in the 1920s it reverted to live performance again as well as showing films. It would be accurate to say that the people of Widnes had a special affection for The Alex. The new

---

[88] See Notes- *(Preston's Theatre)*
[89] Licensee of *The Alexander Pub* in Victoria Road, from whom it got its name *"The Doctor's"*

owners, brothers Harry and Joseph Buxton, had interests in a number of entertainment venues in the north of England through their association with The Regal group.   They also had another claim to fame in that they were known to have made substantial sums of money gambling at the tables in the Monte Carlo casino. On taking over The Alex, they assured the public of Widnes that they would continue to promote local talent and, that as well as providing a new deluxe cinema; live theatre would also still be staged from time to time[90].

Apart from "The Alex", other changes were taking place further up the town in Albert Road. "The Albert Hall" later renamed "The Bozzadrome" was demolished in 1935 and replaced shortly afterwards by "The Regal Cinema".   The Albert Hall had originally been a roller-skating rink.   Roller-skating was a very popular pastime in Widnes at the turn of the century.   In fact, in 1909 there were three roller-skating rinks in the town.   The Borough Hall in Irving Street, The Empire Hall in Frederick Street, and The Albert Hall, which was owned by Mr. Charles Edwin Martin, who was known to all by the nickname "Bozza".   When the roller-skating craze died out, "Bozza" Martin covered his rink over and converted it into a cinema.   The Hall closed for renovations in 1915 and when it was reopened it was officially named "The Bozzadrome".

By the end of the decade, further developments were taking place and Widnes had two new cinemas, The Plaza and The Empire.   Both of these were opened in 1937 and were the ultimate in art deco luxury and décor.   The official opening of The Plaza was a glittering occasion attended by the Mayor and Mayoress, Councillor and Mrs. Pat Hanley, and other invited guests.   This new building, owned by Cheshire County Cinemas, was definitely in a class of its own.   It was the only cinema in the town offering

---

[90] The new *"Alex"* reopened in October 1935. Gar Kiddie was appointed new Managing Director with his son, Nor Kiddie, as his assistant

air conditioning and a "Western Electric Mirrorphonic Sound System". The architects of this magnificent building were Messrs. William and Segar Owen and the builder was Walter Peak of Warrington. The first public screening was on 25th October 1937 and the film shown on that evening was *"Feather Your Nest"* starring George Formby. Harold Cookson, known to generations of children as "Uncle Harold", was the first manager of The Plaza, and remained in that role for countless years.

When speaking about entertainments, I should not forget to mention the Sunday evening band performances in Victoria Park. The great brass bands had been a wonderful feature of local entertainment. In Widnes, in the early days, there were works bands, district bands and church bands, all providing entertainment and pleasure for both listener and performer. Among the very early bands were *The Widnes Subscription Band; The Star Temperance Band; St. Mary's (Marie's) Brass Band; Oakland Street Wesleyan Band* and of course *Gossages Brass Band*.

In the early days, *Gossages Band* was one of the finest brass bands in the country. Their coach and conductor was William Rimmer, who also composed and arranged music especially for the band. However, because of a considerable amount of discord within the group, a breakaway band was formed. The new band was to be known as *The Widnes Subscription Band*. This band needed to be self-supporting and so subscriptions of one penny a week were levied, in addition to this the members also had to provide their own uniforms. Among the names associated with both of these bands were: *W. Harper, T. Roberts, W. Roberts and T. Hynes.*

The *St. Mary's (Marie's) Brass Band* first played at The Volunteer Hall in 1879 on the occasion of the visit of Cardinal Manning. The band at that time was under the leadership of Mr. John Coleman, a professional musician who later spent 27 years as a member of The Alex Theatre orchestra. The uniform of the *St. Marie's Band* consisted of green suits with slouch caps, and this distinctive attire earned them the nickname *"The Robin Hoods of Lancashire"*. Like *Gossages Band*, this band travelled all over the country. In 1907, the band travelled to Ireland to take part in the Irish Brass Band Championship in Waterford. They raised funds for the purchase of their instruments by playing on street corners, at garden fetes, and for Catholic processions. Among the early members of this band were:

W. Burke; J. Redmond; J Collins; E. Fitzgerald; H. Harrison; T. Connolly; J. McCafferty; M. Corrin; J. Mosdale; J. Gallagher; J. Sunderland; J. Coleman; H. Fitzgerald; P.Mitchell; P.Osborne; J.Oldfield; T. Brady; J. Pinnington, T. Sunderland and G.Maguire.

Unfortunately, over the years, it was difficult to maintain these wonderful local brass bands and they have now passed into fading memory. Among the other regular performers in Victoria Park were *The Highfield Choir* from Runcorn, *The Widnes Musical and Operatic Society Choir, Gossages Brass Band*[91] and other well known Brass and Silver Bands from around the country. In the early days there had been a great deal of controversy about Sunday entertainment and many of the religious groups were opposed to live music in the park on the Sabbath Day, unless it was in the form of hymn singing. However, local councillor, John Millar, who was also a Wesleyan preacher, raised no objections. He felt that these performances were uplifting and indeed many of the bands and choirs played and sang hymns.

Councillor John Millar was also among the large congregation who were assembled at St. Ambrose Church in February 1932 when the Bishop of Liverpool, Dr. A. David, dedicated memorial gifts to the parish. Among the gifts was a black and white marble pavement made by local stonemason, Thomas G. Robinson, at his Monumental Works in Derby Road. When the church was

---

[91] After many glorious years *Gossages Band* became obsolete in 1922

originally built, the space beneath the floor had been filled in with chemical waste[92]. Over the years, this material had had an adverse chemical reaction with the floor material, causing it to become loose and unstable. Later the chemical waste was removed and replaced with something more suitable, before the new marble pavement was installed.

At the end of that same year, just before Christmas, the parishioners of St. Patrick's, in West Bank, were celebrating the successful completion of a great effort, in the provision of a Parish Hall. Tradesmen and labourers belonging to the parish had given the whole of the labour, both skilled and unskilled, as a voluntary offering. A large number of men in that district were unemployed so they were happy to utilise their time in this worthwhile project. The hall took over two years to build because of lack of finances. It was built as and when there was money available to buy the materials. The hall was to be a base for the *"St. Patrick's Confraternity Club"* as well as for meetings and social gatherings. Later, this hall became well known not only among the parishioners of St. Patrick's, but also throughout the neighbourhood, as a splendid place for dancing.

A few years later, in May 1937, another hall was erected in a similar manner, when the old residents of the Waterloo area were relocated to the new Moor Lane Estate. Anxious to maintain their communal way of life, the residents built a clubhouse on land given at a nominal rent by the Trustees of the Hutchinson Estate. The Town Council gave them an old hut, which had formerly housed the Widnes branch of The British Legion. The hut was in a bad state and the men of the district, providing voluntary labour, set about renovating it during their spare time. On completion, the new *"Waterloo Social Club"* provided facilities for billiards and

---

[92] Chemical waste was used as filler in many other local buildings at that time.

other recreations as well as a large public room for socials and dances.

The ex-residents of the Waterloo area still talked with a great deal of nostalgia about their old neighbourhood. One resident, who was interviewed in the 1980s[93], spoke fondly of growing up in this district in the 1930s. She said that the local "chippy", owned by Minnie Cosgrave(*sic*), did a good trade, with a portion of chips costing just 3½d. The local pawnshop also provided an essential social service. The money from items pledged was used to tide the family over from one payday to the next. On Mondays, the women would queue up outside *Cornberg's Pawnshop* with their parcels of shoes, clothing, and other items. On Fridays, they would arrive to redeem these items if they could afford it.

On Friday evening, the Doctor's clerk would do his "rounds" collecting sixpence from each house, for medical expenses. It was a reflection of the community that this sixpence could be left on the step, no one would dream of stealing it, even in times of such appalling hardship! It is apparent that despite the obvious poverty in this area, community and family ties were seen as central to the moral and individual welfare of the society as a whole.

Another person doing a brisk trade was Mr. Wilkinson, the clog maker in Hutchinson Street. Most workmen wore clogs to protect their feet from the tremendous heat in the workplace. One oft repeated story is *"of a workman falling asleep in a bogie in a local chemical yard. The bogie was later filled with acid and all that remained of the workman was his clog irons"*. Indeed, clogs were the most usual form of footwear for men and children and there were many clog makers in the town. The clogs lasted for ages but the irons usually needed to be replaced every few months. For the less

---

[93] From an interview carried out by the staff of *The Chemical Museum* during the 1980s. Copies made by this author, with the permission of Paul Meara of *The Catalyst Museum.*

fortunate, free clogs were distributed to schoolchildren by the School Board or even sometimes by the local police.

Dancing had been popular since the 1920s and there were numerous dance halls around the town, all providing live music in the form of small trios or a more substantial "dance band". Ballroom dancing was considered to be an essential social skill and there were numerous dance schools and tutors in the town providing basic tuition.   Most of the dance halls held regular dance competitions and prizes were given for the best waltz, quickstep, or slow foxtrot. People usually practised in their front parlours. Apart from being an enjoyable social pursuit, dancing was extremely competitive. Often a couple would team up as dance partners, not through any romantic attachment, but simply because they could dance well together and win prizes. Some couples became well known as good dancers and were considered a big threat to others in dance competitions.

The local dance tutors were also very competitive and a "win" by one of their dancers would reflect favourably on them.   One night, in the spring of 1933, three Widnes dance masters and their wives, or lady companions, were returning separately to Widnes from Runcorn where they had just attended a dance at the Co-operative Café.   Their respective pupils had been entered in a competition that night and there appears to have been some dissatisfaction with the adjudication.   As it was late, and the last Transporter "car" had gone, they were all obliged to walk over the Old Bridge. On reaching the Widnes side of the bridge, a number of people were waiting and a disagreement occurred between the various factions, resulting in an unseemly brawl between the three dance masters and their followers.   The outcome was that two of the dance masters were summoned to appear in court charged with assaulting the third one.   It seems that dancing was a serious (and possibly dangerous) business.

Despite the gloom and doom of unemployment and world depression, the citizens of Widnes were also able to find relief and entertainment in local spectator sports. Football was a major part of everyday life in the town and most workingmen supported the local team. The 1930s was an important decade in the history of *Widnes Rugby League Football Club* as the local team made no less than three appearances at Wembley during that era. During the inter-war years, the town team also had the distinction of having five of her players chosen to tour Australia. They were: *A. (Chick) Johnson, T. McCue, J. O'Garra, W. Reid and N. Silcock.*

Throughout the history of Rugby League in this town, each period provides us with household names and legends of the game. Alas, space does not allow me to mention all the numerous "greats" of this decade, or their many great achievements and contributions to the game of rugby. However, some of those great names would include: *Jimmy Hoey, Nat Silcock, Tommy Shannon, Tom McCue, Alec Higgins, and Harry Millington.*

Home to our town Rugby League team was *"Naughton Park"*. Sadly, this has undergone numerous name changes since the day in 1932 when it was decided to name the ground in memory of Thomas Naughton, the Secretary of the club, who was tragically killed in a road accident that year. One of Thomas Naughton's greatest achievements was initiating the ground purchase fund, which enabled Widnes R.L.F.C. to purchase the ground from Widnes Corporation on 21st April 1932 for the sum of £3,250, thus giving the club a secure home for generations of players and fans.

In the 1932-33 season Jimmy Hoey became the first player in Rugby League history to play and score in every match for his club in one season. The last match of that season was at Barrow and everyone was hoping that Hoey would manage to score. When the news arrived that Widnes had been beaten by 19-9 everyone assumed that Jimmy Hoey had failed to make the record. There was great jubilation when it was eventually known that, in fact, Hoey had scored all three tries in that game[94].

In 1934 the final at Wembley took on a special significance as Widnes fielded a complete team of "local born" players, a feat unlikely now to ever be repeated by any club. The members of the team on that day were: *W.Bradley, H. Owen, P.Topping, P.Jacks, A.Gallimore, T.Shannon, T.McCue, N.Silcock (captain), J.Jones, A.Higgins, H.McDowell, A.Ratcliffe, and H.Millington.* The opposing team, Hunslet, had to play one man short for an hour of the match because one of their players, *Morrell*, had been injured. Despite this, they won the match 11-5.

The Celtic sections of the Widnes population, the Irish and Welsh, continued to celebrate their national days. St. David's Day was celebrated each year at The Moor Lane Welsh Chapel. This event usually involved a service in the Welsh language followed by musical entertainment. In March 1933 the programme included a number of solos on the Welsh harp, played by Miss Gwen Goodwin. Throughout the 1930s the *Welsh Society of Widnes and Runcorn* held their yearly event to pay homage to their patron saint. These celebrations usually included invited prominent Welsh guests and, naturally, a great musical programme. At this time the proceedings were still held in the Welsh language.

The Irish still proudly displayed the shamrock, and the wearing of the green was customary on St. Patrick's Day. Irish concerts and dances continued to be held at regular intervals at both St. Marie's and St. Patrick's Parochial Halls. The multi-cultural composition of our society was also still evident in many other ways during the 1930s. On the sports field also, it appears that cultural attachments were still enthusiastically displayed. A football match that took place at Naughton Park in May 1933 had

---

[94] Information on Widnes Football Club kindly supplied by Tom Fleet *(from his unpublished History of Widnes Rugby League Football Club)*

an interesting composition. A local Lithuanian team played the rest of the League. *The Star Prize Band* presented the musical entertainment and Mr. G. Ireland was the referee. The result of the match was that the Widnes Lithuanians won 23 points to 13. The teams on that evening were:

Lithuanians: *V. Karalius; W.Lowell; J. Lowell; W. Jareh; A. Karalius; J. Pichilingi; W. Mulouski; J. Calocouski; A. Kyouski; J. Lucavitch; B. Karalius; W. Lucavitch; J. Stankevitch*[95]

Rest of the League: *Wright, Edge, Phillips, Roach, Plumley, Gorst, Power, Crompton, Naughton, Condron, Mitchell, Woods and O'Garra.*

Sports lovers admire the qualities of the fighter and the daredevil, exhibitions of strength and muscle, or of speed and daring. Footballers and boxers became heroes because of these skills or for their displays of cunning. In fact, they are not unlike modified counterparts of the heroes of classical legend who were famed for displaying these abilities. Apart from local football, boxing was also hugely popular in Widnes during the 1930s. The Catholic parish clubs often promoted this sport and, in fact, a Catholic priest, Father Francis of Liverpool, founded *The North of England Amateur Boxing Association.* However, there was an interest in boxing in Widnes as far back as 1885, when the first boxing club was opened on the premises of Tom Wright in Wellington Street. The motto of that club, written inside a gloved hand, was *"Nemo me Impune Lacessit"* (No one strikes me with impunity). The motto was stamped on each member's cotton singlet. The well-known pugilists of those days were Wailing[96] and Donnelly who held a famous bare-knuckle fight on Cuerdley Marsh. This was not an evenly matched contest as Donnelly

---

[95] These spellings are taken from the original report. This author recognises that some are incorrect, but in order to maintain the integrity of this work no attempt has been made to change them.
[96] Wailing died in 1938

weighed barely 12 stone and Wailing 14 stone. Later in 1903, Widnes was still producing notable boxers, such as the spirited Tommy Burns. In the 1920s, Tom Mallinson, of Deacon Road, was the local hero of the ring.

I think it is right to say that boxing in Widnes was probably at its peak in the late 1930s. In this decade, there were numerous local clubs producing a cluster of good boxers. Local promoters organised special events in which some world-class boxers came to town to give boxing exhibitions. In June 1935 Freddie Miller, the World Featherweight Champion, appeared before a large crowd in an exhibition match at The Borough Hall.

Here in Widnes, there were two main boxing camps, one run by Tommy Burns and the other by Hughie Doyle. The Burns Club trained in a building at the corner of Lugsdale Road and Major Cross Street, known as *"Cooper's Club"*. Some of the boxers who trained at that club included: *Bert Chambers, Jack Stanner, Wally Gregson, Geoff Caton, the Harding brothers, Charlie Brown and his brother Martin Miller.* The other club, *The Victoria Boxing Club*, run by Hughie Doyle was situated in Market Street in a building owned by a local sporting greengrocer, George Durbin, of Victoria Road. This club was the domain of the brothers, *Ned and Mick Lucas,*[97] *Billy Kenrick, Tommy Byrom, Jimmy McConnell, Teddy Jones, Frank Buckley, Joe Argent, Larry Benson* and many others.

Across the river in Runcorn, there were also a number of boxing clubs. Among the young boxers that Jobie Parkes trained at his *"St. George's Amateur Boxing Club"* were: *Jimmy Stubbs, Ron Britland, Frank (Yankie) Lightfoot and Jimmy Antrobus.* The other Runcorn clubs were *The Princes Boxing Club* and the *Runcorn Amateur Boxing Club*. Of course, there were many more great local boxers on both

---

[97] In the 1940s and 1950s, brothers, Ned and Mick Lucas, ran their own boxing Club *"The Hibernian Club"* which was located in Chapel Street, off Victoria Road.

sides of the river but, sadly, space does not permit their inclusion here. However, one name I would like to mention, along with the other Widnes boxers, is my late friend, the incomparable *Jack (John) Laveric*, a good boxer and a true gentleman. In later years, John was a well-known and much loved figure in the town, along with his equine companion *"Uncle Bones"*[98].

On March 1st 1932 Widnes Corporation, in order to extend their Kingsway housing estate, gave *The Widnes Cricket Club* notice to quit their ground in Lowerhouse Lane. After viewing several possible sites they discovered a field in "Beaconsfield track" which was occasionally used by the Co-op as a sports ground. Subsequently, this site was leased from the Lea family for a period of ten years, and the stalwart members and friends set about the strenuous task of making the ground suitable for laying a pitch. The following year, 1933, the pitch was ready for the season. The first game played on the new Beaconsfield pitch was on 20th May 1933 and featured the second team against Prescot. The Widnes team on that momentous day was: *G. Turton, R. Roberts, J. Fazakerley, J. Hague, T. Critchley, E. Burton, J. Bingham. A. Bailey, W.Richards, L. Hartland and G. Fazakerley.*

Because of their previous experiences, and the fact that there was now also rapid housing development in the Farnworth area, the members felt they would prefer the security of owning their own ground, so a sum of £1,200 was needed in order for them to purchase the ground outright. The Committee managed to secure a bank loan to cover the initial purchase cost. The members then embarked upon an ambitious fundraising project and with the help of appeals to the general public, as well as garden fetes, dances and whist drives, the money was found. By February 1939 the members were able to make a final payment to the bank and *Widnes Cricket Club* finally owned their own ground. During the 1930s people like *Jack Bingham, Bill Richards, George Turton, Albert*

---

[98] See Notes *(John Laveric)*

Fazakerley, Bill Taylor, Harold Baldwin, Jack Griffiths, George Baskerville and Harold Beswick were among the men who made their mark on the Beaconsfield Road pitch. Of course, there were many others worthy of mention but again space does not permit their inclusion[99].

Horse Racing was a sport enjoyed by many – although not in the conventional sense of visiting the racecourse. Betting on horses, other than at the racetrack, was against the law. However, it was relatively easy to place a bet even though it was often done furtively as those taking bets were likely to be prosecuted if caught. Many men acted as "bookies runners", taking bets in the factories or in back entries. Sometimes they would have people acting as look-outs, and I am told that there was an elaborate series of signal codes used by the look-out to warn the runner of the approach of the police. These signals included raising a right hand to touch the face, wiping the face with a handkerchief or raising his cap or hat. The "runner" had a small clock, which would stamp the time on the betting slip, to prove that the bet had been placed prior to the start of the race. Most people used a nom-de-plume so that they would not be incriminated if the "runner" was caught. Some "runners" took bigger risks by receiving the bets in their own homes. There were countless prosecutions and some people appear to have been fined on more than one occasion. Therefore, I must assume that as some of these people were habitual offenders, it was financially worth the risk.

Apart from the "Bookie's runner", another character making a lucrative income from horse racing was the "tipster". This man (or woman), would claim to have inside information which he was prepared to divulge for 3d. Once he had convinced the gullible punter that he had the name of "a dead cert" he would write this

---

[99] Information with kind permission of Gordon Gilmour, President of *Widnes Cricket Club*. Additional information and photographs kindly supplied by Robin Faulkner.

on a slip of paper on payment of 3d. I would think that he must have been able to come up with a winner now and again, or else he would have gone out of business!

Many men kept "homing pigeons" in their backyard. Such was the popularity of this activity that there was a *Pigeon Flying Club* in the town with a substantial membership. During the 1920s and 1930s the breeding and owning of racing dogs was also very popular. A *"Greyhound and Whippet Club"* was formed in 1927 and races were run on Saturday mornings at Moor Lane. *The Widnes Weekly News* had a weekly column entitled *"Tailwaggers"* which gave hints and tips for the care of dogs, with special information on things like "distemper" and how to spot the symptoms. In the 1930s an approach was made to Widnes Council for planning approval to build a Greyhound Racing Stadium on land off Lowerhouse Lane. The application, submitted by Messrs. Brennan and Robinson, was rejected after numerous protest meetings were held in the town.

The "pitch and toss" schools continued to operate in the vicinity of Spike Island. Considerable efforts were made to shield the illicit gatherings but arrests were frequently made. Despite numerous police raids and prosecutions, the gamblers were not deterred. On one occasion, 15 police officers were employed in a carefully planned raid. The police were hiding in a railway wagon. Given the element of surprise, when the raid happened very few of the men were able to get away. The result was that 17 men were transported to Widnes Police Station and charged. The following day, two other men presented themselves at the police station to admit to being involved. In total 19 men were summoned to appear before the court and all received substantial fines. On another occasion, 30 men were caught gambling on ground near Oxford Street, off Lugsdale Road. The police said they were seen to be gambling with coins but the defendants claimed they were just playing marbles. The magistrates did not accept their story and all were fined.

It is obvious that illegal gambling, as a social activity, was widespread among the community. There were numerous events upon which bets were made, such as pitch and toss, horse racing, dog racing, pigeon racing and blood sports. In later years there was a regulatory rather than a prohibitory response to some of these events, particularly bookmaking. Betting Offices were legalised in 1960 and a levy was introduced on all bets placed at these establishments, which meant that the Government received a "cut" from this form of gambling.

In Widnes during the 1930s another type of gambling had also become popular. A new form of *pari-mutuel* (pool) betting, based on the outcome of football matches, had emerged. The *"Football Pools"* opened up the prospect of winning a fortune to millions of people. The Post Office blamed the football pools for delays in delivering post, as the promoters sent out large numbers of circulars each week. In fact, one of the main problems with postal delays arose from the fact that many houses did not have letter-boxes and often the postman was unable to deliver the mail.

In fine weather, the riverside at West Bank still attracted huge crowds of people to its sandy beach. On one Bank Holiday Monday in the late 1930s it was described thus:

"The riverfront at Widnes might have been a rival of Blackpool or Southport, so charming was the holiday atmosphere and so colourful the scene with all the gay apparel and bathing costumes of the many hundreds who disported themselves on the stretch of golden sands when the tide was out. Beach sports, bathing and wading, the enjoyment of ice-cream and cooling drinks transformed the riverside and promenade into a seaside resort, the only element lacking being the music of band or orchestra, or the revelries of Minstrel or Pierrot. Scenes somewhat similar to those on the Widnes side of the river were enacted on the Ship Canal stretch on the Runcorn side, where large crowds enjoyed the sunny conditions".

The arrival of the twice yearly *"Fair"* was always an exciting time and, in those days, seemed to appeal to all ages. The old "Fair Ground" was in Lacey Street, near to the market. Brightly coloured lights, loud music, the smell of candyfloss, toffee apples, and hot dogs filled the air, all adding to this distinct atmosphere. Small children sat in miniature cars on carousels, waving to their patient parents, as they travelled round and round on a whimsical journey. Old fashioned coconut shies, target shooting, and other games of skill were well patronised. Local lads chanced their arm at the boxing booths, teenagers yelled in delight as they bumped around in dodgem cars, and those with no fear of heights queued for a ride on the big wheel. The "Waltzer" or the "Swirler" was popular with the more daring, or those just wanting to appear fearless. Sadly, in 1937, this ride was to prove fatal for a young 20 year old woman from West Bank who was thrown from one of the carriages and killed.

Following the closure of Gossage's Soap Works, there was widespread concern about the loss of the sports facilities that had been available at their recreational ground. In 1938 the Corporation made arrangements to purchase this ground plus a further two acres of adjoining land. A cash grant of £200 was made available to the Corporation from *The King George's Field Foundation*, an organisation which dispensed grants intended to provide a permanent memorial to the late King. A condition of this grant was that this ground would thenceforth be known as *"King George V Playing Fields"*.

Apart from the numerous leisure facilities now available, there were other traditional ways of spending your time, and the age-old communal way of passing the time was talking. A survey into leisure, carried out in the late 1930s, suggested that "informal talk" accounted for 54% of the time available for leisure[100]. Street corner

---

[100] *"Trends in Leisure 1919-1939"* – A. Howkins & J.Lowerson (Sports Council and Social Science Research Council 1979)

gatherings were common in Widnes among the males – this was an activity enjoyed by both young and old men, and up until the 1960s it was not unusual to see groups of men on street corners in the town, especially around Simms Cross.   In the 1930s this was probably the way the unemployed dragged out their time.   For many of the young men, known as "corner boys", there was no alternative to the streets. Few unemployed had the resources to enjoy other activities[101].

During the Munich crisis of September 1938 the ownership of wireless sets in Widnes increased significantly.   Unlike 1914, the people of the 1930s were able to draw on this additional source of information.   Because the BBC was politically neutral, it was more trusted than the national newspapers.   Locally, *The Widnes Weekly News* gave its readers a concise national news service as well as providing townspeoples' reactions to these events.   It also provided a valuable platform for them to air their opinions.

The consumption of alcohol fell considerably during the wars and there were numerous reasons for this, for example, there were now strict controls on licensing hours and on juvenile drinking. The diversification of social activities such as the cinema and spectator sports also contributed to the fall in alcohol consumption. Amazingly, in 1933 there were only 5 convictions for drunkenness in the Borough.   However, by 1938, this figure had risen again to 63, but this was still a far cry from the early days when drunkenness and drink related crime had been a major problem in the town.   Another important contributory factor was that the alcoholic strength of drinks had been reduced since the early days.

As one form of conviction lessened in this period, we saw the rise of another.   This decade saw an increase in offences against *The Highways Act*.   This largely reflects offences by motorists.   As the motorcar gained in popularity and ownership, we see

---

[101] Additional information given by Mr. Lawrence Rossiter

WIDNES GROUND PURCHASE FUND   ASSOCIATION FOOTBALL MATCH
TOMMY MAGEE'S **WEST BROMWICH ALBION TEAM** *versus* **MERSEY~WIDNES**
Thursday   April 28th 1932

Benefit Match for the Ground Purchase Fund. The team included Widnes players as well as some from the Liverpool & Everton Clubs. Everton's famous Dixie Dean is in the middle row, just behind the referee.

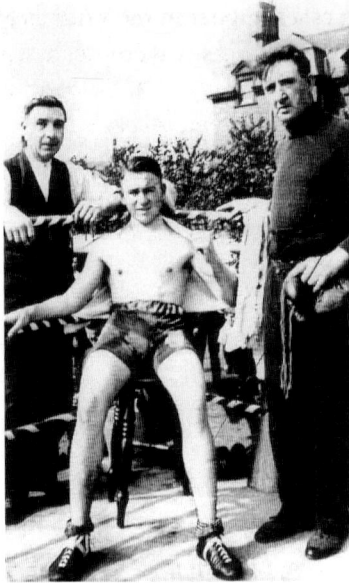

Widnes Boxer, Mick Lucas, with his trainer Hughie Doyle (left).

Widnes Boxer, Martin Miller – Contender for British Cruiserweight Title.

numerous motoring cases appear in the Widnes Magistrates Court. It seems that some of these cases were dealt with quite leniently and people were often sent away with little more than a polite rap on the knuckles. Two cases dealt with by the Widnes magistrates in 1934 demonstrate a considerable degree of understanding by the bench. These cases referred to "speeding". One defendant said that *"it was foggy and his father had told him that if there was any fog about he must get home quickly. It was in obeying his father that he had broken the speed limit, but the road was clear of traffic so there was no danger"*. The bench dismissed the case. On the same morning another driver, who had been driving a heavy lorry while exceeding the speed limit, claimed that *"he could not see the speedometer in the dark and did not realise he was going so fast."* The magistrates decided, in view of his clean record, that this case should also be dismissed. During that same week, the MP for Widnes, Mr. J. Roland Robinson, addressed questions to the Minister of Transport, Mr. Hore Belisha[102], in connection with safety on the roads.

In April 1935 the first local cases came to court in relation to the new speeding restrictions of 30 miles per hour. As in previous motoring offences, these 5 cases were treated quite leniently and only nominal penalties were imposed. However, during that year, the first "driving test" came into being and motorists were faced with a driving aptitude trial. Road signs, particularly "Halt Signs", appear to have caused a great deal of confusion and many motorists considered these signs as just useful suggestions, not commands.

Whilst motorcars were becoming popular, the horse and cart was still the most familiar commercial transportation on our roads. The Widnes Corporation refuse collection service, as well as coalmen and milkmen, all used horse-drawn carts for their work.

---

[102] *Mr.Hore Belisha, as Minister for Transport, was responsible for the introduction of "The Belisha Beacon"*

In the days of "digging for victory", gardeners and allotment holders were regularly to be seen following the carts, shovelling up the horse manure for use on their gardens! It should also be remembered that at this time horses were still used in some works. There was sadness among the workmen at The Gaskell Marsh Works in 1932 when one of their old horses, "Flower", died after 17 years of service in the factory.

Apart from the new motoring offences, another common crime at that time was robbing gas meters. In many cases, this was viewed as a desperate act by poor people. In 1937 two defendants who were appearing before the magistrates claimed that they had "no dole and no relief" and were completely penniless. Because the gas meters were in their own homes, some people did not consider this to be a crime in the true sense. However, court summons for this type of crime were numerous and occurred with a familiar regularity. In one incident, a man stole 5s.6d from the gas meter in his home. He was sent to prison for 3 months. In cases of repeated offence, the culprits could be sentenced to "hard labour" whilst in prison. Some people who were unable to pay for the gas, used discs formed from old "washers" made up to be the same diameter and thickness of a coin. Apart from having to pay back the missing money, people were often prosecuted for this type of "fraud".

The Public Baths, in Waterloo Road, as well as offering swimming facilities, also provided the much-needed use of baths with hot water. Widnes Baths usually closed for the winter months. The exact date of closing was generally left to the engineer, but in 1932 Alderman Millar proposed that the baths should remain open all year round because:

"Ninety per cent of the houses in Widnes had no baths, and men who had families had to chase their families out of the house while they had a bath.

The Widnes baths were a disgrace and a scandal to a town 0f 40,000 inhabitants"[103].

The Baths were indeed a disgrace to the town. Holbrook Gaskell had built them around 1880 for the United Alkali Company. They had subsequently been leased to the Corporation for a nominal rent, which basically only covered the cost of providing steam and water. Despite approaches being made to Councillor Millar by a local firm offering to provide funds towards the provision of a more suitable public baths, nothing was done to provide alternative facilities until the opening of the new Kingsway Centre in 1962[104]. One local resident reflecting on the days of *"The Old Baths"* remembered exciting swimming galas and water polo matches being held there. He also described a typical visit to the old baths when he was a child:

"On entering, your nostrils were immediately invaded with the noxious smell of cleaning chemicals, and your ears subjected to the shatteringly loud shrieking of children's voices. The walkways around the pool were slippery and slimy, and the water was scummy at the edges. All around children were shivering and blue with cold because they had stayed in too long, while others were throwing themselves, or their friends into the water. I suppose it was really unhygienic, but in those days we didn't care too much[105]."

In 1933 Mr. William Smith, the Secretary of The Simms Cross Institute, made a trip to Ireland. Mr. Smith was the guest of Mr. John Carney, a Widnes born journalist who regularly contributed to *The Widnes Weekly News* from various destinations around the world. In the 1920s "Jack" Carney edited *"Labor Unity"* a left-wing newspaper, published in San Francisco. He eventually became

[103] *Minutes of Widnes Town Council* – September 1932
[104] The New Kingsway Centre was officially opened by Councillor John Collins on 18th January 1962.
[105] *Info supplied by Mr. J. Hunt.*

well known as a political activist in America. In 1919 he was sentenced to 2 years in Leavenworth Prison for writing a seditious article. During his time in America, he was involved in workers' rights and various militant left-wing organisations. However, by the early 1930s Jack Carney was back on this side of the Atlantic and was living in Ireland. On this occasion, he had arranged for Mr. Smith to meet the Lord Mayor, Alfred Byrne, T.D[106], at the Mansion House in Dublin. After their meeting, the Lord Mayor escorted Mr. Carney and Mr. Smith to *Dàil Eireann* (The Irish Parliament) where they heard the Irish President, Mr. Eamon De Valera, defending the record of his Government in a debate on unemployment relief in Ireland. On his return to Widnes, Mr. Smith conveyed this greeting to the people of Widnes from The Mayor of Dublin *"The Mayor expressed a hope that the dark clouds of industrial depression will flee before the bright dawn of a prosperous era"*.

In earlier years, many other young men, like Jack Carney, left the town and travelled to foreign climes in the hope of finding a better life. In the previous decade, Canada and Australia had beckoned with promises of employment and a better standard of living. As we know from numerous reports and correspondence, some of these emigrants were bitterly disappointed. In 1936, an ex Widnesian[107] writing from Australia, told of his concerns for would-be emigrants. He hoped to prevent Widnesians becoming victims of immigration schemes and warned all who were considering emigrating to secure a reliable guarantee of employment before leaving England. He said that in Australia at that time thousands were living on relief work and rations. The constant demands on charity organisations to provide assistance had put them under extreme pressure. Soup kitchens and cheap hostels were everywhere and many people were forced to sleep out in the open because they had not got the means to pay for accommodation. Thousands and thousands were unemployed,

---

[106] T.D. *(a member of Dail Eireann – similar to our M.P.)*
[107] *Correspondence – from Mr. J.H. Beecham (1936).*

and the farmers were struggling to survive. However, Australian and Canadian immigration schemes were still in operation and being championed by various politicians. Around this same time, the Mayor of Vancouver, on a visit to London, was reported as saying that:

"Canada needs settlers today as much as ever she did, not only on the farms but in the mines and in trade. Skilled labour is in demand and any boom in the building trade will reveal a shortage. All we want are men who are physically fit, of reasonable intelligence, willing to make sacrifices, and work".

Despite this statement, another ex-Widnesian tells us in a letter to *The Widnes Weekly News*[108] that Canada had, at that time, nearly one million people on direct relief and untold thousands on the verge of it. He also said that there were no real provisions for the unemployed and that thousands of people wander from province to province, like nomads, seeking work. Another emigrant, a Widnes lady living in Saskatchewan, told the readers that:

"For seven or eight years, so many have been on relief that its hard for the Saskatchewan authorities to know what to do. There are thousands of farmers from here right through to the USA who are so hard hit. Many lives have been broken up and many people have been taking their own lives in despair. We hear also that new emigrants are still being allowed to come into the country, adding to more misery when there is room for no more"[109].

In the 1930s the membership of a church or chapel was almost an essential part of life, and no matter which religious persuasion you came from, it created a sense of communal belonging. In those days people did not only visit religious institutions to be baptised, married or buried, or in times of personal crisis or other

---

[108] Widnes Weekly News – January 1937.
[109] Ibid – August 1937.

important moments in life. The church was an integral constituent in most peoples' lives and the parish was usually at the heart of the community. At the start of September 1933 the Methodists of Widnes were celebrating the union of the Primitive Methodists, the Wesleyan, and the United Methodists, which resulted in the forming of a new Methodist Circuit. The new circuit comprised thirteen local churches, ten ex-Wesleyan, two ex-Primitives, and one ex-United. During that year, 400 circuits around England had combined and it was expected another 400 would do so in the following year. At a celebration party in the Lacey Street School, Mr. A.H. Calvert, J.P. had said how pleased he was that Widnes, along with Runcorn and Warrington, had the distinction of being among the first. The formal act of union had taken place the previous year. Deeds were signed, to conform to an Act of Parliament, in a formal ceremony at the Albert Hall in the presence of the Duke and Duchess of York. A local correspondent who witnessed the event described some special moments of the ceremony, *"Dr. Scott Lidgett is handling tenderly a little black oblong of a book – Wesley's Bible. It is a little touch of symbolism that causes a catch at the heart"*. The ceremony was broadcast live from the Albert Hall and a large congregation gathered at the Victoria Road Church in Widnes to participate, from afar, in the service.

"Make the Skyways Britain's Highways" was the slogan of Sir Alan Cobham and his squadron of famous display pilots. Alan Cobham, a WW1 aviator, had flown to Australia and back by seaplane in 1926, and for this feat had received a knighthood. Few believed at this time that flying was, or could be, safe. During the 1920s there had been a series of air disasters, including the London to Manchester Air Express in 1923. However, by the 1930s aeroplanes were becoming more frequent in our skies. In the early years of this decade, Sir Alan Cobham was touring England in an effort to promote interest in civil aviation development. On 14th September 1933 Sir Alan brought his team of aviators, complete with 15 display aircraft, to a field in Hough Green Road. To stimulate interest *The Widnes Weekly News* gave away twelve free

flights to some lucky readers. Members of the Council, including the Mayor, received invitations to the display and were give the opportunity of flying in one of the "air liners" with Sir Alan.

At this time, aviation was becoming more acceptable as a means of travel. The new "local" Aerodrome, at Speke, was creating a lot of interest and commercial air traffic was on the increase. By 1935 there were 30 commercial aircraft arriving and departing daily from this airport and passenger numbers for the month of May of that year were 907. Of course, Widnes already had some interesting associations with aviation. James Valentine, in an attempt to do a circuit of England, landed his monoplane in a field at the Ball O'Ditton in 1911[110]. As one can imagine, in those pioneering days this caused a great deal of excitement. In 1928 Bert Hinckler made a record flight to Australia in a plane designed by the Widnes man, Roy Chadwick, who was at that time the chief engineer for the Avro Aeroplane Company.

Roy Chadwick was born in Farnworth, and went to Simms Cross School before his parents moved to Manchester. His father and grandfather had both worked at the Widnes Alkali Works where his grandfather was a popular foreman. Later on, during the Second World War, Roy Chadwick became famous as the designer of the *"Lancaster Bomber"* and between 1946 and 1947 he was responsible for the design of *"The Vulcan"* which was also manufactured by the A.V. Roe Company (*Avro*). In 1943 he was awarded the C.B.E. and many feel that had he lived he would have been knighted. Unfortunately, Roy Chadwick and three of his crew were killed during take-off, on the test flight of the *"Tudor 11"*, at Woodford in Cheshire, in August 1947.

Another type of transport was under discussion when the Finance Committee of Widnes Town Council met early 1934. The committee was able to report that they had resolved to clear the

---

[110] See Notes: *(James Valentine)*

outstanding debt on *The Transporter Bridge* by the 31ˢᵗ March. The bridge was taken over by the Council in 1910 and at that time it was not a profitable proposition. It had been offered to the Widnes Council and the Urban Council of Runcorn, but the Runcorn Council decided to leave the responsibility to Widnes. The estimated loss at that time was £750 a year. Widnes Council introduced a more economical way of running the bridge and brought in capable engineers to maintain it. Finance Committee member, Councillor Graham said:

"Widnes was reaping the rewards of the courage and foresight of those who decided to accept responsibility for the bridge, which at the end of March would be the property of the people without a penny of debt"[111].

A few months earlier, on the Saturday prior to the August Bank Holiday, *The Transporter* had carried 6357 passengers in just one day. In addition to foot passengers, the figures for vehicles on that day are[112]:

Cycles	537
Motor Cycles	138
Motor Cars	519
Medium Vehicles	159
Heavy Vehicles	61

Around this time there was controversy regarding the need for a new bridge to supplement the two existing modes of crossing the river, *The Old Bridge* and *The Transporter*. Some people feared that these two systems may not be adequate for the future and thought there was a need for a second bridge. The Chambers of Commerce in the twin towns had for some time been exploring the possibility of a new bridge to span the Mersey. Although the Runcorn and Widnes Chambers of Commerce were avidly promoting this

[111] *Minutes of Widnes Council (Finance Committee) January 1934*
[112] *On that same day the bus service carried 16,641 passengers.*

Everyday Life

"dream" the two local councils were reluctant to burden their ratepayers with such a large expenditure. Even if the Ministry of Transport and the Treasury could be induced to make a monetary grant it would still leave the two towns with an enormous debt. At that point in time, the councils were naturally unwilling to take on that responsibility.

In October 1932 Oswald Mosley held his first rally in Trafalgar Square in London. This was an effort to drum up support for his newly formed fascist party, which he named *The British Union of Fascists*. Although not reaping any *significant* membership in Widnes, the B.U.F. did attract a membership of over 10,000 in 6 branches throughout Merseyside. The first fascist rally in this area took place at Liverpool Boxing Stadium in October 1933 and the main speaker at that event was William Joyce, who was later to achieve fame during the Second World War as *"Lord Haw Haw"*. In 1934 it was reported that about a dozen well-attended open air meetings were being held in Liverpool each week. There were two local administration offices in the city, one at Duke Street and another in Catherine Street, for men and women respectively. The Merseyside organisers were Mr. J.A. Collins and Mrs. Peters, both these people had spoken on political platforms in the area.[113] In October 1936 a 300 strong group of "Blackshirts" marched through Liverpool to attend another rally at the Boxing Stadium where their leader, Oswald Mosely, was due to speak. Fighting broke out in the streets and mounted police were sent in. Further violence occurred at the Stadium as protestors tried to disrupt the event. *The Liverpool Daily Post* reported the event with the greatly understated headline *"Lively Street scenes in Liverpool.*[114]*"*

The "Blackshirts" were not the only organisation in what was termed *"shirt politics"* in the 1930s. The adopting of coloured shirts was widespread, both here and in Europe. In England, a

[113] *The Liverpolitan* – March 1934
[114] *The Liverpool Daily Post / The Liverpool Echo* – October 1936

"Black" shirt was the symbol of Mosley's Party. "Brown" shirts were the uniform of the British Fascist Association; "Red" shirts were worn by the Guild of Youth; "Blue" shirts were worn by the Anti-Communists; and "Green" shirts by the Social Credit Association. I suppose, with tongue in cheek, it could be argued that all this was good news for the textile trade! However, for many young men during this era the threat of fascism, and their abhorrence of it, prompted them to travel to Spain to join the International Brigades who were fighting with the left-wing Government against the fascist uprising led by General Franco.

Politics had always been of considerable significance during the period this book deals with. Because of the issues that affected the local population, and the country as a whole, the election of suitable representatives in Parliament were of great importance. In 1935 Mr. J. Roland Robinson was our MP. On 15th April that year, the members of the local Conservative Association were astounded to read in the national press that their MP had found a new constituency for the next election. There was a hastily arranged meeting of the local members in the Lacey Street School to discuss the implications of this announcement. In the election later that year, Mr. Richard Pilkington stood as the new Conservative candidate, against Mr. Alex Cameron. The Conservative candidate won that election but with a greatly reduced majority.

Politics filled the air during the weeks leading up to this election, and as in all elections, the cost of living was an important issue. The Widnes housewife no doubt sought out the most economical way to run her household and was fortunate to have good shopping facilities in the town. A glance at commercial publications for this period shows a wide selection of shops offering a generous range of consumer goods. To those who believed that "milk bars" in Widnes arrived with *"The Penguin"* in the 1950s, it might come as a surprise to hear that *The White Hall Dairy Farm*, of 100 Albert Road, opened the first milk-bar in the north of England on these premises during the 1930s. Also at this time, William Swindells, a coal merchant of 99 Albert Road, was offering not only coal to his customers but also his service as a haulage contractor who could act as a furniture remover for your "flit". "Irwins" promised the housewife the very best groceries at the best prices. Not far away Alex Bromilow advertised his "Christmas Club", so that you could save up for your Christmas wines and spirits. "Unsworth's" and "Calvert's" took care of clothing needs for male and female, while "Linger's" of Waterloo Road offered furniture for cash or on safe easy-pay terms to those on limited budgets.

An event of considerable importance to a little rural part of Widnes took place in January 1935. Although of no great significance to others, nonetheless, I think it worth mentioning for its historical interest and information. The event was the 100th Birthday of Mrs. Emma Swain of Little Heath Farm, Hough Green[115]. Mrs Swain, who appears to have maintained an agile mind and excellent recall of past events, gave an interesting account of the "early days in Widnes". Her memory went back to when the whole area was nothing but a stretch of cultivated fields, pastoral land, and wooded areas. Born in 1835, she was well able to remember the developments that had taken place in the town since the arrival of the chemical industry. She was born and lived all of her life at Little Heath Farm, in Hough Green. Opposite this farm was an old oak which was so sturdy it had to have its branches lopped, or topped, periodically to prevent their weight bringing the tree down. This oak, according to Mrs. Swain, gave its name to the inn, *The Four-Topped Oak*, which was built alongside. Mrs. Swain said that her father went to Warrington with the first licensee of this inn to purchase the licence, which cost 5 shillings. Mrs. Swain also reflected on the old cottage industries of Ditton. These mainly consisted of wrought ironwork and tools produced in smithies attached to the cottages. That district was also famous for its laundry workers – known as *"Ditton Dollies"*

---

[115] Emma Swain died in March 1936 aged 101 years.

and for more than a century the district was known for the whiteness and cleanliness of the bed-linen laundered there. Most of their custom came from affluent households in Liverpool. The dirty washing was collected by cart each week as the clean laundry from the previous week was delivered. The old lady also remembered the manufacture of watch parts and tools in Cronton. She told how upstairs rooms were specially adapted for the artisans, who were so skilled that they could produce sufficient in three days to keep them supplied with food and clothing for a week.[116]

The centenary of Mrs. Swain's birth was indeed a cause for celebration, especially when one considers that the death rate in the Borough, for infant and maternal mortality, had always been high. Like the previous decade, the death rate from tuberculosis was still a cause for concern, the rate for the Waterloo and Victoria wards having increased considerably during 1930-34. Incidents of maternal mortality were exceptionally high in 1936 when the Medical Officer of Health, in his annual report, gave the following figures for Pulmonary Tuberculosis and Maternal Mortality.

Death Rates per 1000 of the population for years 1935-36

	Deaths from T.B.	Maternal Mortality
1935	0.61	1.12
1936	0.49	7.76

It was accepted by the Medical Officer that the remarkably high figure for maternal mortality in 1936 could have been prevented by more careful ante-natal supervision. The Maternity Home at that time had accommodation for only 10 patients and during the year 1936-37, the total admissions amounted to 189. Cited among the main causes of maternal mortality was thrombosis within 3 weeks of confinement; gastro-enteritis; hydramnios; and eclampsia.

---

[116] See Notes: *(Appleton Village)*

When the Medical Officer of Health published his report for 1937 the death rate for the town was slightly down on the previous year, being 11.9 compared with 12.9. The maternal mortality rate and the death rate from pulmonary tuberculosis, although still high, were both below the averages for the previous five years. However, infant mortality rate was 92 compared to 82 the previous year. The subject of housing, with particular emphasis on overcrowding, was again a feature of the report. While the instances of more than one family sharing a single dwelling had been slightly reduced, the overcrowding produced by large families occupying small houses was still a major problem[117].

King George V died on 20th January 1936 after a brief illness. The news of the King's death was received with genuine sadness in Widnes. Special services were said at all the churches in the town. On the day of the funeral, the Town Hall entrance was draped in black and purple, and flags flew at half-mast on all the public buildings and business premises in the Victoria Square area. Earlier in the day, St. Paul's and other churches had been open to the public for a relayed broadcast of the funeral service. Afterwards, a civic procession including the Mayor, aldermen and councillors, representatives of the police and military, as well as local charities and educational establishments, moved across the Square from the Town Hall building to St. Paul's Church for a special memorial service. The vicar, the Rev. J.G. Tiarks, paid tribute to the new King at the end of the service. He said:

"He knows more closely perhaps than any of his predecessors the daily lot of the people of his empire. He has personally made it his business to understand the needs of the poorest of his subjects. He has been with them on the field of battle, in the mills, in the mines, in the fields, and not least in their homes. He has made it his special task to understand what the grim reality of unemployment means to so many and to give the lead in all hopeful ways of alleviating it".

---

[117] Widnes Council Minutes 1938 – *Report of the Medical Officer of Health*

There is no doubt that the new King, Edward VIII, had built up a stock of popularity during his time as the Prince of Wales, especially as he had visited many depressed areas and made outspoken public remarks about slums and unemployment. Many of his remarks were based on observations made during his tour of the depressed areas of the northwest in November 1932. He made a brief visit to Widnes at that time and saw at first hand the dire effects of unemployment on this town. Although his visit did little, or nothing, to alleviate the problems of unemployment, it appears to have had a more beneficial effect on morale and certainly enhanced his own reputation as a *"man of the people"*.

When he ascended to the throne he was 41 years of age. He was still a bachelor, although he had had numerous liaisons with several married women. The new King's lifestyle, and his affair with Mrs. Simpson, was common knowledge in Fleet Street although the national press refrained from making this public. Foreign newspapers *did* report on this matter, but the wholesalers censored all imported newspapers before they reached the British public. Because of this, the general population were unaware of the drama that was about to be played out.

On 27th October that year Mrs. Simpson's divorce case was heard far away from London, in Ipswich, where she had established a fictitious residence. She was granted a *decree nisi* from her husband, Ernest, who had gallantly agreed to act as the "guilty party" in order that her reputation would not be tarnished. It was only a matter of time before the newspapers would break their silence. During that week, the King spent time at his private house, Fort Belvedere, in Windsor Great Park, where he received the Prime Minister, Mr. Baldwin. Baldwin advised the King against marrying Mrs. Simpson and threatened that the cabinet would resign if the King did not follow this advice. The King suggested some form of compromise, hoping that a morganatic marriage would be acceptable, whereby he would be King but Mrs.

Simpson, as his wife, would not be Queen.   The Government stood firm and the King made his own decision.

On 11th December, the King abdicated and was succeeded by his brother, Albert the Duke of York, who took the title of George VI. The abdication was given legal effect by an Act of Parliament, which, curiously, passed through all its stages in a single day. Edward left England immediately, consoled by a large sum of money, said to be £25,000 a year, which George VI paid to him by a private arrangement.

The news of the abdication reached Merseyside less than a half hour after the formal notice was handed to the speaker in the House of Commons.   Most people listened to the special broadcast by the BBC but special editions of the local newspapers were printed and distributed quickly.   The Mayor of Widnes, Pat Hanley, said that the national press that morning had prepared them for the King's decision.   He said:

"That after the first shock has passed the people of Widnes will face it in a calm and dignified manner. In the unprecedented and anxious situations from which we have emerged I feel sure the sympathy of everybody will be extended to Queen Mary and to members of the Royal family and to the Prime Minister".

Some modern observers have said that as the monarchy has no political power, the Abdication of 1936 had no contemporary or historic importance.   However, there *were* implications for the relationship between the Church and the State.   The President of *The Widnes Council of Christian Witness*, the vicar of St. Paul's, The Rev. J. G. Tiarks, was less compliant than Councillor Hanley. The Rev. Gentleman was quoted thus:

"It seems incredible that King Edward VIII, who acceded to the throne with such magnificent gifts and high hopes last January, should, in eleven short months tell his people that it is best "for the stability of the Throne

and the Empire and the happiness of his people" that he should abdicate. Let us be deeply thankful for his practical sympathy in everything that concerned the welfare of his people.

The manner of his going is inexpressively sad. In truth, the decision which the King announced today was inevitable when he allowed himself a course of action which, if persisted in, could only have one conclusion. This is not the time for judgement, but let every man ponder in his own heart the plain lessons that this unhappy crisis teaches".

On leaving England, Edward VIII was created Duke of Windsor. Prior to the war, the Duke and Duchess were photographed socialising with Adolph Hitler and members of the Nazi establishment. Subsequent documents and writings suggest that his behaviour throughout the war was far from commendable. By the summer of 1937 Britain had a new King. It also had a new Prime Minister as Stanley Baldwin was replaced after a troubled three years in office. Neville Chamberlain, previously Chancellor of the Exchequer, took over the reigns of office. The people of Widnes had only a short while to wait before they had the opportunity of seeing their new King and Queen close up The following year, in May 1938, the royal couple undertook a tour of industrial Lancashire, and made their first visit to Widnes.

Commercially, Widnes had come a long way since the early days when Ann Street and Waterloo Road had been the main commercial areas. By the 1930s Victoria Road, Widnes Road, and Albert Road had firmly established themselves as the prime shopping locations. Apart from "The Co-op", there were other grocery stores like "Quinn's" and "Irwin's"; confectioners such as "Eaton's" and "Kirkham's"; and numerous butchers, fishmongers, and greengrocers ready to provide the housewife with value and choice. For countless years "Calvert's" offered Widnesians quality and service with their extensive choice of clothing for all the family. Their large premises were unequalled in the town. However, in March 1935 "Burton's" came to Widnes and presented the male population with a vast range of styles and fabrics, as well as low cost "off the peg" options. The following year, on 27th November, another establishment opened its doors for the first time in Simms Cross. This new shop, "Abrahamson's", known to all as *"Abie's"*, offered an extensive array of clothing and furnishing for those with a leaner budget. The local Chamber of Commerce heralded the arrival of these new shops as a sign of the town's enterprising spirit.

It is hard to imagine now how diverse our population was such a relatively short time ago. Of course, integration is a fundamental factor in creating a harmonious society. Nevertheless, the loss of a cultural identity which defines our heritage is to be regretted. Once there were numerous ethnic orientated societies in this town, Welsh Societies and Church groups, Irish Clubs and Associations, and a Lithuanian Society. The passing of time has dimmed the light of this ethnicity and sometimes only surnames serve to remind us where many of us came from. In the late 1930s, in many sections of the community, there was still a desire to maintain a strong cultural character. The Welsh had a *"Cymrodorion Society"* and many of the churches still performed their services entirely in Welsh. In January 1939 the BBC North Regional Station broadcast a unique concert from St. John's Presbyterian Church in Runcorn. *The Widnes and Runcorn Welsh Society* had organised the service, which was conducted entirely in Welsh. This was the first time a broadcast of that kind had been attempted outside of Wales.

In this decade, the Lithuanians of Widnes were still a significant group. In February 1938 the Lithuanian communities of Lancashire were celebrating the 20th anniversary of Lithuania's independence. Crowds of Lithuanians from Manchester, Liverpool, and surrounding districts, came to Widnes by coach to join Widnes Lithuanians for a special service of remembrance at the War Memorial in Victoria Park. After a solemn ceremony, in which pledges of loyalty to the crown of their adopted country were given, a representative of the local Lithuanian community laid a wreath of yellow and red roses, the national colours of Lithuania. Two youths, one bearing the British flag, the other the Lithuanian flag, stood to attention during the ceremony. Then the National Anthem was sung, followed by the anthem of the Lithuanian Republic and *"Faith of our Fathers"*. After this solemn ceremony, coaches took the parties to St. Patrick's Church in West Bank where Mass was celebrated by Father Hayes, with a sermon given by Father Slavinas. Later, after speeches of welcome in Lithuanian, by Mr. S. Karalius, President of *The Widnes Lithuanians* and Mr. F. Williams, Secretary, the group were entertained in St. Patrick's Hall by a musical concert. Among the local performers was Miss Jessie Stakauches, who played a selection of music by Dvorak and Hayden on the violin.

A few months after this event, another section of our society was celebrating their "special day". Members of the Widnes and Garston branches of *The Loyal Orange Lodges* took part in the provincial celebrations of their *"glorious twelfth"*. The members of the Widnes Lodge had a group of around 50 people conveyed by coach to Southport where they joined the Liverpool contingent. There were more than 3000 people at the Southport rally and six special trains were chartered from Liverpool to take them there. Apart from the 12th July celebrations, the Widnes Lodge held an annual "Orange Lodge Ball" in the Conservative Club at the beginning of November each year.

Politics and the Labour Party in particular, was a hot topic in Widnes during the spring of 1938. A serious rift occurred among local members, causing a split in the party. The result was that the *Widnes Divisional Labour Party* was disaffiliated from The National Labour Party by order of the National Executive. The cause of this discord was the selection, by the Widnes Divisional Labour Party, of a Mrs. Van der Elst as the prospective parliamentary candidate for the Borough. The National Executive had vehemently refused to endorse her candidature. Many local members also refused to back her.

Mrs. Van der Elst, at that time, had been a member of the Labour Party for less than two years. In March 1936 she started a campaign for the "Abolition of Capital Punishment". From this campaign, she began to nurture parliamentary ambitions. She was extremely wealthy, having made a huge fortune out of manufacturing beauty lotions, face creams and soaps. Before her foray into politics she had been known as a successful, if somewhat eccentric, businesswoman who dabbled in the occult. But to claim that Mrs. Van der Elst was merely eccentric would be paying her a great compliment. In November 1935 she had stood as an Independent Conservative candidate for the Putney division of Wandsworth. The result of that election was that the Unionist candidate polled 22,288, the Labour man 10,895, whilst Mrs. Van der Elst had forfeited her deposit with a poll of only 1,021. In April the following year, she decided to try her hand at Labour and joined the Labour Party. Within a short space of time, she had made overtures to members of the *Widnes Divisional Labour Party*, with her eye to the coming elections.

There can be little doubt that this woman was simply using Widnes as a means to an end. She wanted to get into Parliament at any cost, under any banner. Whilst the protracted internal wrangling continued in Widnes, a by-election was called in Central Southwark due to the death of the sitting Labour member. Mrs. Van der Elst immediately withdrew her nomination as prospective parliamentary candidate for the unofficial Widnes Labour Group and presented herself as an Independent National candidate in Southwark. This left the disaffiliated group in Widnes looking more than a little foolish for having placed their confidence in her. Unfortunately, for Mrs. Van der Elst, once more she was unsuccessful in her attempt to enter Parliament. The author of her biography, Charles Neilson Gattey, describes the visits to her home of two of her Widnes supporters.

" — the phone rang. It was Holroyd, a Labour Party member from Widnes, calling her from there to discuss what she could do for the town

211

to make her popular. She suggests a brass band good enough to win the national championship at Crystal Palace. He prefers the idea of a football club that will win the Cup. She says she will do anything for the town"

On another occasion: "— *Mrs. Van der Elst had invited two members of the Widnes Labour Party to visit her for the weekend. She did not let them sleep in the house, but paid for their accommodation in a Brighton hotel. When Holford and Punter* arrived, she quickly hid her diamond and sapphire necklace inside her dress and pinned her brooches on the back of the sofa. The following day, after dinner and an obligatory séance, the two Labour men left at two o'clock with a cheque for their expenses"*[118].

During the following months, numerous public and private "Labour" meetings were held in Widnes. Later, a new "official" local Labour Party, loyal to the National Executive, with support from local trade unions, was established. Among the members of this new "official" Labour group were Alderman Dan Garghan, Councillor Pat Hanley, Mrs. E. Hanley, and Councillors Hesketh and O'Garra. In September that year, their officially endorsed candidate, Mr. Louis Anderson Fenn, (whose wife was from Widnes) was welcomed at a huge meeting in The Regal Cinema. Also on the platform that evening, was the legendary MP for Jarrow, Miss Ellen Wilkinson. However, because of the war, the next General Election did not take place until 1945. By this time, another candidate, Commander C. N. Shawcross, was representing the Party.

In previous pages, I have documented some of the numerous marine disasters involving residents and vessels from this town and its surrounding areas. From time to time, the Mersey took its

---

* *I presume Holford was the same man referred to previously as Holroyd – the names are taken from the quoted text.*

[118] The Incredible Mrs. Van der Elst – *Charles Nielson Gattey* *(Leslie Frewin, London 1972).*

toll in human life.   History's pages have been marked by the sorrowful record of men, women and children who have gone to their deaths in this river, when engaged either in commerce or pleasure.   Although all of these tragic events brought dismay and heartbreak to our citizens, I suppose the events of June 1938 surpassed any, for a widespread outpouring of genuine public grief and sympathy.   A seemingly innocent pleasure trip on the river had barely got underway when in only a few brief minutes six members of the happy group of nineteen passengers had lost their lives. Among the six were five young children, and a 36 year old man from Davies Street, who left a widow and six young children.   As the tragic events of that sunny Sunday afternoon were described at the inquest, the town was stricken by the horror of the incident.

It was around 4.00 p.m. on a warm Sunday afternoon when *The Britannia* took on its passengers from the promenade slipway with the intention of sailing as far as Fidler's Ferry. The promenade and gardens were full of local residents enjoying the June sunshine and the sands below were well populated with children and adults making the most of the fine weather.   Some people watched with vague interest as the small boat pushed out into the channel. Sadly, it was not more than 150 yards from the promenade when a strong gust of wind caused the vessel to capsize, throwing the occupants into the river.   Not only were there screams from the occupants of the boat, but also from the spectators on the riverside who watched in horror as they saw the boat overturn.   People began to wade out into the river in an attempt to help, small motorboats and yachts in the vicinity responded quickly.   Some people made valiant efforts to rescue those who had been swept beneath the waves.   A man from James Street dived in and brought a child out from the submerged cabin, then dived in again and brought another two children out. The distraught father of some of the children, although injured, managed to bring two of his own children to safety, as well as his wife and sister.   He made a further attempt to rescue two more children but was unsuccessful, losing his own life in the process. At the end of that beautiful June day, a man and five small children had lost their lives. The children ages ranged from just two to six years.

At the inquest into the disaster, the boat's owner, a man from Beaumont Street, said that the boat was positively seaworthy and in good order. Ironically, it had formerly been a ship's open lifeboat, having come from the liner *"Architect"* which had been shipwrecked in the Mersey some years previously. The Widnes owner said he had improved the boat and installed a new petrol engine. Shortly after the Widnes tragedy, questions were raised in The House of Commons. It was suggested that the Board of Trade should take action to ensure that all passenger boats used in tidal rivers were seaworthy, that they should be subjected to an annual inspection, and issued with a certificate to confirm their reliability.

By a bizarre coincidence, the man who lost his life in this awful calamity had been involved in a gallant rescue attempt the previous year, and had been honoured by *The Royal Humane Society* for his bravery. That incident, in which a youth had got into difficulty in the strong ebb tide, resulted in the deceased man and three others rescuing the semi-conscious youth and managing to bring him ashore. That incident happened at almost the same spot where he lost his own life a year later.

The West Bank district was plunged into grief as all the victims were residents of that small area. Although this region of the town had a diverse ethnic and religious mix, such was the interaction between these groups, that just to be a *"West Banker"* made you part of a unique extended family that acted as a single community in times of trouble. As in previous tragic events, this community, as a whole, shared in the loss and grief of their neighbours.

One of the town's finest ecclesiastical treasures, *St. Luke's Church,* in Farnworth, was the subject of some discussion in 1938 when a local correspondent raised the subject of the ancient sundial which had once graced this building. He wrote:

"I should like to draw the attention of your readers to the fact of an ancient sundial that was lost to the public eye some twenty years or so ago, at Farnworth Church. It was situated immediately above the Cuerdley Chapel window so that all and sundry coming up Farnworth Street could observe it. In the wisdom of those who wished to preserve the stonework or structure just after the War the dial, which had lost its gnomon or style, was cemented over.

The cement has now dried out and been weathered so much that on a dry sunny day one can discern still the dial and see some of the hour marks. As no doubt this dial was contemporary with the building of the Chapel, it takes us back to the good Bishop Smyth and pre-Reformation times and is a relic, which should be treasured and if possible restored. According to Poole's "History of Widnes" there was a telling Latin sentence painted on it, giving lesson well worth remembering at all times, which ran "Tempus vitae Monitor" (Time is the monitor to life)".[119]

As that commentator was reflecting on past architecture, Widnesians were admiring a new architectural offering, The Health Centre on Kingsway, which was officially opened in August 1939. The estimated building costs were £18,000, a large sum in those days, but a good and worthwhile investment for the people of Widnes. The Borough Engineer, Mr. James Holt, and the Chief Architect, Mr. Austin T. Parrott, were responsible for the design and planning of the building, and the principal contractor was The Atlas Building and Construction Company. Whilst paying tribute to these men, who were actively involved in providing the finished building, we should remember that the inspiration for this Health Centre was the vision of the late David Lewis. David Lewis had devoted much of his public life to the health service in Widnes. In his plans for the development of

[119] *Widnes Weekly News*

Widnes, he had envisaged a civic centre with a place that would provide health service, child welfare, and school medical services for the population. Unfortunately, David Lewis did not live long enough to see his visions take form.

The 1940s

The 1940s was a period of shortages of almost everything, particularly food. The food shortages necessitated rationing which made it especially hard to provide a decent and nourishing meal for the family. One lady told me that: *"shortages and rationing made almost every meal a test of culinary ingenuity"*. Despite this, many people would argue that the diet was healthier and, unlike today, there were no Government directives needed to deal with problems of obesity. In an attempt to relieve shortages, campaigns were started in 1942 to persuade people to *"Dig for Victory"* which encouraged the cultivation of gardens and allotments to increase food production.

Prior to the war, for the vast majority of people national concerns were remote from daily life. However, the onset of war brought the nation together. People whose social horizons were normally enclosed by the street or the neighbourhood became more aware of being part of a larger picture, the sense of sharing a collective trauma brought people together. In Widnes, like everywhere else, for those who had suffered unemployment the war became a great leveller. Whilst unemployment had only blighted some, war affected everyone. It would appear that in wartime Widnes, class or ethnic solidarity became somewhat diluted by preoccupations with survival.

Once war had been declared, all political parties agreed an electoral truce. In May 1940 Neville Chamberlain resigned as Prime Minister and Winston Churchill succeeded him. Churchill agreed to form a new Coalition Government and, in consultation with Clement Attlee, the major posts were distributed between the parties.   Despite the demands of war, the new Government was able to pass some important social legislation. The "means test" was ended and pensions were raised. The Government also introduced other new measures that brought about lasting changes. Among these was a new system for payment of income tax. Pay as you Earn (PAYE) was initiated on 10th February 1944.

Both local and national Governments voiced plans for social rebuilding after the war, and *The Widnes Weekly News* became a platform locally for those wishing to air their views or share their own ideas on how the country should recover.   In London, the Coalition Government, in planning for reconstruction, charged Sir William Beverage with the task of preparing a report into the basis of a post-war Welfare State. *The Beveridge Report of 1942* changed social attitudes and laid the foundations for our modern Welfare State.   After this report, a movement for social reform gained momentum.

Apart from the far reaching plans for social reform outlined in *The Beveridge Report*, there were also sweeping changes planned for the education of our children. In 1944 the President of The Board of Education, Mr. R.A. Butler, in his *Education Act of 1944*, raised the Board's status to that of a Ministry. "Rab" Butler also set in motion plans to raise the school leaving age to 15, the introduction of the 11+ exam, and the compulsory inclusion of religious education in all schools.

During the war, Winston Churchill's leadership was vigorous and rousing.   His speeches promised little but sacrifice, nevertheless they inspired patriotism.   However, as Prime Minister, in the years from 1942, he showed little enthusiasm for the social security and allied services plan outlined by Sir William Beveridge.   Despite this, his defeat in the elections of 1945 came as a surprise.   It seems that while the electorate remembered his personal leadership skills during the war, the country rejected the

Conservative Party's domestic policies and opted for Labour's more progressive image.

In line with *The Beveridge Plan*, the Labour Government brought in *The National Insurance Act* in 1946. This provided for all to be compulsorily insured against both sickness and unemployment. The old age pension was also raised again and the Ministry of National Insurance established a *National Health Act* providing for the setting up of a national health system. The Minister for Health and Housing, Aneurin Bevan, proposed the nationalisation of the existing system of voluntary and municipal hospitals as well as the Poor Law infirmaries. The Labour Party's maxim was that they wished to give security to all, *"from the cradle to the grave"*. After the war, the new Labour Government as well as providing social security for all also carried out a programme of nationalisation which included the coal industry, electricity, gas, railways and road transport.

Naturally, all these new welfare arrangements were of benefit to the population but the main thing in everybody's mind in 1945 was demobilisation. "Getting back to normal" was what everyone wanted. However, it would be some time before this happened. Rationing continued for a number of years after the war, and here in Widnes the urgent problem of housing still needed to be tackled.

While Britain was endeavouring to deal with the aftermath of the war on both national and local levels, elsewhere in the world dramatic changes and events were also afoot. In 1945 an International Military Tribunal was sitting in Nuremberg to judge those accused of crimes against peace and humanity. In the following years of this decade, Juan Peron was elected President of Argentina; a new State was set up in Israel; Mahatma Gandhi was assassinated in New Delhi; and Ireland was formally proclaimed a Republic. The world was a changed and changing place, as this island and this town struggled to regain its normality.

War and its needs

In Widnes, and throughout the entire country, there was widespread fear of war, dating back to the 1914-18 conflict. There was also a persistent and increasing fear of aerial bombing, and of the use of poison gas as a military weapon. As early as 1935 the Government was sending circulars to Local Authorities about the dangers of air raid attacks. The Town Clerk of Widnes brought the matter to the notice of the Town Council in July, outlining factors that had a bearing on the protection of the civilian population. Local Authorities were instructed to bear these in mind when preparing schemes for town planning. It was stressed that despite the need for such measures, this in no way implied a risk of war in the near future! The proposals sent to Widnes, by The Home Office, included the establishment of a civilian gas school for instructors who would give anti-gas training in their own districts. Protective clothing and respirators were to be issued by the Government to the local police, fire brigade, and first aid organisations.

Obviously, at this time the subject of national defence was already to the fore in many minds. There was much talk about the possibility of some form of compulsory national service being introduced. However, the Government had previously pledged to rely on a voluntary system during peace times and enrolment in "The Territorial Army" was steadily growing. In Widnes, the local TA branch were hoping that additional expenditure, proposed by the Government to improve conditions for "Territorials", would mean that they might get a share of this money for a much needed extension to the Drill Hall (Barracks) in Peelhouse Lane.

Long before the war, in January 1937, the Widnes Town Council had discussed the question of "local defence" in the event of a war breaking out.   Lancashire County Council held a series of conferences for the 110 administrative Local Authorities in the county. The purpose of the conferences was to try and arrange a scheme for air raid precautions. It was later agreed that Widnes Council would co-operate fully in this scheme.   Earlier, the Government sent out a circular to all Local Authorities intimating that some scheme of precautions would need to evolve. After a substantial period of intensive training of local police and officials, the public were made aware of the dangers posed by the possibility of air attacks. Newspapers were given press releases that highlighted the increased dangers faced because of new technological developments in warfare. Civilians were warned of the dangers of high explosive incendiary bombs, possibly weighing up to 250 lbs per bomb, and also of poison gas attacks.

Despite national newspapers warning the public of this growing danger, it was interesting and reassuring to readers of *The Widnes Weekly News*, in March 1938, to be told that there was probably no threat to Merseyside:

The probability of Merseyside being the target of an enemy attack is indeed very remote. There is no possibility of an invasion by land reaching this area and an air attack would have to battle through many obstacles. Yet, there is the million to one chance that air bombs might be dropped and the district must be prepared. If an attack came while children were in school, it is computed that at least thirty minutes warning will be given and, in that time, children could be dispersed to their homes or places of safety. For the adults of the population, air wardens will have given instructions as to the measures to be taken.[120]

Regardless of these reassurances, in Widnes, defence preparation was gathering pace. As well as police, firemen, and

---

[120] *Widnes Weekly News* – March 18th 1938.

The St. John Ambulance Brigade, local civic officials and industrial managers were also being given a certain amount of training in a scheme of home defence. The "Territorials" were being brought up to full strength and were to be equipped with weapons to meet any situation. Some of the local factories had started training groups in first aid and gas precautions, as well as in the use of protective clothing. The Everite was among the first of the firms in the district to provide practical instruction and information in "Air Raid Precautions". Inspector Hodgson of Widnes Police, who had received special Home Office training in gas warfare, held classes at The Everite Works. Employees of Southerns Ltd., timber merchants, who had premises nearby also attended classes at The Everite.

Mr. Chamberlain returned from Munich in 1938, displaying a piece of paper carrying Adolph Hitler's signature guaranteeing peace. Although there was initial relief, there was still a sense that trouble was looming. At the Albright & Wilson Works, in Ann Street, the management ordered that office windows should be painted over with blackout paint and procedures were laid down to deal with the glare from the furnaces and slag pit if necessary. In September, respirators were issued to all Widnesians and an appeal was made for Civil Defence workers. By February 1939 over 500 men were enrolled and assigned to 86 posts (afterwards reduced to 29 posts). The Government also introduced *The Military Training Act*, which required that every British male subject, between the age of 20 and 21 years, should register for military training. Radio broadcasts and public notices informed members of the public that this registration was to take place on June 3rd 1939. Any person who failed to register would be fined £5. Conscientious Objectors were also required to register at the same time and place. The first prosecution in the country, under this regulation, took place in Widnes, when a young man was fined for falsifying his birth certificate in order to evade military training.

Barely one month before the outbreak of war, Merseyside had been reflecting upon the indelible mark that had been left upon local life and history by the events of 25 years ago. At the end of that First War, in a celebration of peace, the Vice Principal of our local Secondary School, Mr. C.R. Lewis, had composed the following verse entitled *"Well Done!"*

> *And is the whole thing over?*
> *Sing hey, sing hey, 'tis done!*
> *Old England lies in clover.*
> *And lays aside her gun.*
> *We've turned his wrath to wailing*
> *Our gallant men prevailing*
> *And there, his woes exhaling,*
> *All vanquished lies the Hun.*

In the first week of September 1939 Widnesians were enjoying the varied entertainment on offer at our local cinemas. The Plaza was showing Anna Neagle in *"Sixty Glorious Years"*; The Empire was offering humour in the form of *"Climbing High"* with Jessie Matthews; The Regal was running the latest *"Bulldog Drummond"* adventure; The Premier was screening Gene Autry in *"Prairie Moon"*. While those with a preference for live performances were able to see *"Vaudeville Parade"* at The Alex. This show promised a cast of eight "star acts" including vocalists, comedians and a piano accordionist. In a few days, all these places of entertainment were closed by order of the Government. However, their closure was short-lived and within a few weeks the local population were once again able to divert themselves for a little while from the tensions of war.

The home defences on Merseyside were seemingly well prepared for the event of war. Barrage balloons were erected, and when the fateful day dawned, mothers and children from Widnes, Runcorn, and Garston were swiftly evacuated and orders were given to commence the blackout. An official announcement was issued advising parents that all schools would be closed until further notice. The Borough Engineer's Department set about equipping public shelters with seating and lights, and additional new shelters were being built. The air-raid shelters would be available to the public night and day. The registration of aliens became a matter of urgency. Directives issued by the Secretary of State, stating that all aliens (other than persons under 16 and British born women not being enemy aliens) must register at once with the local police. All aliens of German nationality, whether previously registered or not, were required to report to the district registration officer immediately, taking their passports and documents of identity with them. Citizens were advised to remain indoors during the hours of darkness.

On Friday September 1ˢᵗ 1939, twelve trains and six motor coaches, which had been requisitioned by the Minister of Transport from Warrington and other Lancashire districts, transported 7,400 people from Widnes to Blackpool – among them were 5,649 children. The adults included mothers of children under 5, expectant mothers, some local schoolteachers, and blind people. Children of school age were grouped with their own school under the care of a schoolteacher. Every child was "labelled" and on reaching Blackpool, they were each issued with a carrier bag containing *"iron rations"* before being billeted. The rations included two large tins of milk (one sweetened and one unsweetened); two packets of biscuits; a tin of corned beef and two slabs of chocolate[121]. Unfortunately, schools were divided and it was not always possible to keep families together. One can only imagine the trauma experienced by these small children finding themselves in strange surroundings, separated from their parents and siblings. For some parents back home in Widnes it was no less traumatic.

---

[121] Information: Mrs. P. Hughes

It appears that on the whole the evacuation operation worked smoothly and efficiently, although the billeting process was not without a few minor hitches. When the expected air raids failed to happen, parents were given permission to visit their children at Blackpool. These visits unsettled both children and parents and by the end of the month it was estimated that almost two thousand children had been brought back home.

It seemed in the early days that education was likely to be one of the casualties of war. The Home Office and Board of Education had previously decided that all schools in the town must close, so this meant that there was no educational provision for the thousands of children who had returned home from Blackpool. One of the reasons for the closure of the schools was that they did not have adequate shelter accommodation for the children. As so many children had returned from the evacuation programme, there were serious concerns locally about the lack of educational or supervision facilities. The Council, in order to try and solve the situation, proposed a truncated scheme to bring a modicum of education to groups of about 20 children with organised recreation facilities. However, the Government refused to let the schools reopen and thousands of children lost precious months of schooling. It was not until February the following year that the President of the Board of Education announced that all children, wherever, would be provided with an education.

On Friday 17th November 1939 the air raid sirens sounded in Widnes for the first time. On the home defence front, there were, in addition to other volunteers, 770 Air Raid wardens trained for duty in the Widnes Police Division. There was also an auxiliary fire service and a fire brigade reserve, rescue parties and decontamination squads, ambulance drivers and messengers, all ready to play their part in protecting the local community. By the 15th September, the lists of Air Raid wardens and their posts were circulated to the population. The public was informed that the Air Raid posts would be manned night and day. Apart from the town posts, posts were also established in the outer townships of Bold, Clock Face, Tarbock, Cronton, Halewood and Hale. The Head Wardens had a number of posts under their control and each post had approximately 25 wardens. The Head Wardens were named as:

Wilfred Hough, 132 Mersey Road (Posts 26, 27, 28 and 29)
William Green, Derby Arms Hotel (Posts 22, 23 and 24)
John Moran, 82 Mottershead Road (Posts 17, 18 and 21)
George A. Crewe, Deirdre Avenue (Posts 19, 20 and 15)
Norman Brewer, Mayfield Road, Birchfield Rd (Posts 8, 9, 10)
George Purnell, 5 Appleton Road, (Posts 11, 13 and 14)
James Ashton, 100 Derby Road (Posts 1, 2 and 4)
Stanley Halfpenny, 118 Warrington Road, (Posts 5, 12 and 16)
T. David Gibbs, 418 Liverpool Road (Posts 3, 6, 7 and 25)

In response to an appeal by Mr. Anthony Eden in May 1940, for the formation of a *Local Defence Volunteer Force*, two thousand volunteers registered at Widnes Police Station. The job of these part-time "soldiers" was to spot and report the whereabouts of any enemy parachutists who happened to land in the district. To start the ball rolling in the way of armaments, 25 rifles were issued to the LVF by the local police station. They were mostly "Canadian Ross" rifles, and the idea of 25 rifles to equip 2000 volunteers didn't go down too well. This would appear to have had distinct echoes of "Dad's Army"! However, by July, more rifles began to arrive from America, and the total increased to 650 weapons including "American Brownings". By October 1944 their stock of equipment included anti-tank rifles, two-pounder artillery, a dozen different types of grenade and even the latest flame-throwers. It is interesting to note that Widnes was the first battalion to produce its own "Molotov Cocktails". These weapons were made by Messrs. Peter Spence & Sons Ltd. and, for some time, were placed on the list of "priority work" at that factory.

Obviously, most of the volunteers had little or no experience of handling guns, so a course of marksmanship training was carried out at Pex Hill Quarry. A room above the electrolytic plant at The Pilkington Sullivan Works was also used for this purpose. A meeting, supervised by Brigadier General Sole, was held at Widnes Library to draw up the Widnes defence plan. Lt. Colonel Allenby Brown was the first Battalion Commander before responsibility was handed over to Major Edwards. The LVF later became known as *The Home Guard* and subsequently some of the local firms took over sections of the battalion. Although our local *Home Guard* started off merely as a group of inexperienced men with just 25 rifles, they became a highly efficient and skilled battalion. Although they were never called upon to ward off German invaders, they were nevertheless an important link in our chain of defence.

Official indications of war were obvious with the arrival of troops into the town. The troops were billeted near some local factories and Lewis guns were put in place along the riverbank to defend the bridges. Anti-aircraft guns were sited in strategic places around the town. The blackout came into operation, and all homes were issued with their dark green "blackout blinds" or curtain material. Street lamps were put out of operation and even bicycle lamps had to be blacked out. All road signs, railway station signs, and Post Office names were painted out. Metal was in short supply so iron railings from the park and the cemetery were removed with oxy-acetylene torches, and melted down. Later, all private residences were required to relinquish their ornamental gates and railings, as well as old pots and pans, in order to help with the war effort.

Conscription had started straight away. After *The Munich Crisis* most people had already mentally prepared for the inevitability of war. However, preparation did not make it any easier to say goodbye to husbands, sons or brothers as they headed off to play their part. Tangible reminders of the previous war were still strong and had left an enduring mark on our community. Those who had suffered loss in that conflict had hoped never again to go through the experience.

The first reports of casualties began to surface in Widnes in 1940. Thereafter, a continuing roll of honour appeared in the pages of *The Widnes Weekly News* alongside names of local men who had been taken prisoner or had been reported missing. By 1943 the list of men who had made the supreme sacrifice was sickeningly long. The lists of those missing, or who were prisoners of war, were also distressingly lengthy. The names on these lists came from all sections of our society. Conscription had meant that wealth, religion, or class did not determine the boundaries of citizenship. In February 1943 the Mayor held a civic reception for the relatives of the dead, missing, or captive men. The Mayor, Councillor Harvey, said that the gathering was intended to: *"Bring them together to get to know each other better and share experiences. He assured them that Widnes remembered gratefully all the loyal service rendered in so many ways"*. Sadly, this conflict added 289 names to our War Memorial.

A few months after this reception the Hon. Secretary of the Widnes Division of the Joint War Organisation of *The British Red Cross* wrote to the Town Clerk stating that he had been asked to have the two "German graves" in plot 12c in the Borough Cemetery photographed. The photographs were to be forwarded to relatives in Germany. Permission was also sought to place flowers or evergreens on these graves. Permission was granted for both these requests. I think most local people hoped that maybe someone would do the same for local lads who had been killed in other countries.

The graves in question were of two crewmen from a German "Heinkel 111" which was shot down by an anti-aircraft gun on a night in March 1941. The bomber came down in flames near to the I.C.I. Recreational Club in Liverpool Road. Three of the occupants, who baled out, were taken prisoner. One of them came down in Ash Lane in Hough Green where he immediately surrendered to a local farmer. All three prisoners were taken to the police station where the R.A.F. Intelligence Service interrogated them. The two young men who lost their lives were given a ceremonial funeral at Widnes Borough Cemetery.

In early 1940 over 300,000 British and French forces were trapped in Northeast France. Between 26th March and 2nd June a spectacular evacuation plan was put into operation. The epic stories of Dunkirk and the rescue of thousands of troops from the bomb-shelled beaches were brought into our homes by radio and newspapers. One story was of two Widnes lads, who were born in the same area of Simms Cross, attended the same school, and joined the same regiment (*The South Lancs*) before the outbreak of war. Although in the same regiment, their paths had not crossed during the war. During the evacuation of Dunkirk, one of these boys had reached the temporary security of a rowing boat, which was packed to capacity; the other not so lucky, had waded out to sea with thousands of others. Heavily burdened with rifle, pack, and 50 rounds of ammunition, and being very tired, he soon found himself in difficulty and with no hope of being picked up. As night approached, it looked hopeless. As a crowded rowing boat passed him, he thought he heard his name called out. In a flash, a rifle barrel appeared under his nose and someone shouted, *"Grab it Paddy!"* At the other end of the rifle was his old school friend, whose quick action saved his life. Later, both boys were hauled aboard a trawler where they were bombed. The crew of the trawler had earlier been under heavy fire and had run out of ammunition. The 50 rounds of ammunition that "Paddy" had carried was swiftly put to use and helped to beat off the Luftwaffe as the trawler made its way back to the English shore. This is an amazing story of a fortuitous reunion of two school pals. The rescued soldier was Pte. Patrick Sinnott, of Timperley Street, and his rescuer was Pte. Frank McKiernan[122].

Some Widnes men had the dubious honour of being "first" such as the Widnes man who was the first paratrooper to land by parachute into North Africa. Private Joseph Bate wrote home to describe his "first landing" in the North African Campaign. He also spoke of meeting other Widnes lads in North Africa. He assured his family and friends that they would all *"give Gerry an extra clout for Widnes"*.

Throughout this period, Widnes men were serving in various theatres of war on land and on sea. Some wrote letters home from El Alamein where the foundations of victory in Africa were laid; others wrote from Italy and Sicily where some were part of the attempt to break the German Gustav Line at Montecassino. Some, serving in the Navy, sent messages from the Pacific and various other places. We should remember also the many local men who were taken prisoner and spent long periods in "Prisoner of War" camps. We can be justly proud of all those local men who played an important part in this conflict.

Of course, not all conscripts were fighting the battle on foreign fields. Some young soldiers were defending the country on the home front. In July 1945 a young Widnes soldier was killed whilst transporting an unexploded bomb. At the time, our erstwhile correspondent, the incomparable Jack Carney, wrote a moving article about this incident. An extract is written below:

When I recently read about a Widnes boy I little thought he was the tiny baby I saw at his mother's breast so many years ago. And now he is dead. He did not die the romantic death of the soldier slain on the battlefield. No drums rolled at his funeral and no rifles were fired over his grave. Alone his mother and father and a few relatives gently handed him

---

[122] Oral History *(Sinnott Family)* and *Widnes Weekly News*

back to mother earth, knowing that at last he would find comfort and friendship in the cool earth.

Maybe you would like to hear the story of this Widnes lad. He was killed on the home front. This week a Polish airman received the D.F.M for a deed no less heroic than that performed by this son of Widnes. The enemy had dropped a few unexploded bombs on a West country city. All around were fine buildings and the homes of simple folk. If the bomb was left undisturbed it would eventually explode and destroy buildings and people within an immediate radius of two or three hundred yards. The son of Widnes, who had only been in the army for six weeks, along with a few other boys, was given the job of removing the bomb. They laboured for hours and finally extracted the bomb from the deep earth. Proudly they bore the bomb away to be exploded on a dump. As they were riding along with it, they collided with another lorry and when the smoke had died away and the road made clear, two boys lay dead – the son of Widnes and a Liverpool lad.

The father, just a chemical worker, with never any more money than would carry him through to the next pay day, rushed to see, as he thought, the last of his son. The journey in this respect was a fruitless one. The authorities in charge of the hospital were kind and bade the father rest for the night. They knew the shock that waited him. The father did not see the dead body of his son. Cruel, maybe, father of the son of Widnes, but in this cruelty there was overwhelming kindness. I have seen too many bomb victims not to appreciate the reason for not allowing him to see his son.

The son of Widnes returned to Widnes – in a coffin. His regiment was too busy, so the captain in charge wrote, "to send an escort or maybe a firing party". But then the boy was returning home to the town that first heard the patter of his tiny feet. Here he would be among his own people. Here he would find in death so much that had been denied him in life. People would watch his coffin wend its weary way along that road whence no traveller returns. The Union Jack would be wrapped around his coffin. People would pay a dual tribute to the flag and to the boy who had died

that Widnes and Britain and the Empire – and the world – might live.
Someone had blundered. But then, a poor chemical worker and his wife
were left alone with their grief. Through the mist of tears, they gazed for
a flag, but the flag never came. Someone had blundered.

Son of Widnes died no less a death than those who die in the Middle East.
Widnes forgot him. His death was without that essential touch of drama
that throws up in high relief the glory of his dying.

The Victoria Cross is a nation's grateful acknowledgement of
heroic deeds performed on its behalf. To deserve this medal the
recipient must have performed an action of such conspicuous
character as to clearly distinguish this person for gallantry and
intrepidity. Often this action involves jeopardy of life or the
performance of hazardous duty. On 14th February 1942, a local
man, Thomas Wilkinson of Oakland Street, performed such an
action.

Lieutenant Thomas Wilkinson was a member of *The Royal Naval*
Reserve and was at that time the Commanding Officer on board
H.M. Ship *"Li Wo"* a patrol vessel of 1000 tons which had formerly
been a passenger steamer on the Upper Yangtse River. On 14th
February 1942 this ship was on passage from Singapore to Batavia
with a ships company of 84 officers and men. Her armament was
one 4 inch gun and two machine guns. Since leaving Singapore the
previous day, the ship had beaten off four air attacks and suffered
considerable damage. Late in the afternoon two enemy convoys
were sighted, escorted by Japanese naval units including a heavy
cruiser and some destroyers. Lieutenant Wilkinson told his men
that rather than try to escape they should engage the convoy and
fight to the bitter end, in the hope that they might inflict some
damage on the enemy. Within an hour, *"Li Wo"* had been
critically damaged and was sinking. Lieutenant Wilkinson then
decided to ram his principal target, the large transport ship that
had by then been abandoned by her crew. When Thomas
Wilkinson finally ordered that the *"Li Wo"* be abandoned, he

himself remained on board and went down with her. There were only about ten survivors, who were subsequently taken prisoner by the Japanese. *The Victoria Cross* was posthumously bestowed upon Lieutenant Thomas Wilkinson, in recognition of his own heroism and that of all who fought and died with him.

There is no doubt that the exploits and heroics of local men during wartime could fill an entire book. Each man's war a story in itself, each making his own important contribution to our national freedom. Unfortunately, it would be nigh on impossible to name and pay tribute to every local man who lived through the ordeal of prison camp, armed combat, aerial bombardment and numerous other appalling activities of war. However, there are a few notable and well-documented incidents I would like to include here. One incident involved a Widnes sergeant serving in *The Royal Artillery*. This man was awarded *The Distinguished Conduct Medal* (DCM) for displaying great bravery at Tebourba in November 1942. The sergeant, John Eustace, was in charge of a gun when tanks attacked his battery. During this action, he was left the sole survivor of his detachment. Despite being alone, under heavy machine-gun fire, and surrounded by enemy tanks, he loaded, layed and fired his gun. In all he fired 22 rounds, destroyed two tanks and hit others. He remained in action until the enemy withdrew and his was the only gun saved from that day's action.

The following summer a Widnes airman was awarded *The Distinguished Flying Medal* (DFM) for his "promptness, courage and presence of mind". 23 year old Sergeant John McCreadie was attached to 106 Squadron and had flown in many operations against enemy targets, including the Rhur Valley. One night in January 1943 while returning from a sortie, the aircraft in which he was flying was unable to locate base because of poor visibility. As the petrol supply was running low, an order was given to abandon the aircraft. Four members of the crew did so, but the navigator's parachute opened in the aircraft and became entangled, leaving the navigator suspended outside the aircraft in mid air. With commendable courage, Sergeant McCreadie managed to pull the navigator back into the plane and he also assisted the pilot in making a successful forced landing.

The George Medal, personally awarded by the King, and normally awarded to civilians, was presented to Sergeant Frank Faulkner of *The Royal Artillery* for rescuing several people from a bombed hotel after an air-raid in East Anglia. He entered the building minutes after the bomb had hit it. Despite warnings from police and rescue squads, who said the building was unsafe and could collapse at any time; Sergeant Faulkner rescued several people, then crawled under the debris to the basement of the hotel to rescue a woman who was trapped under two metal girders and tons of debris. He sang to the woman to keep her spirits up, and for almost six hours he eased the girders with his back, but after ten hours he was forced to amputate both of the woman's legs.

Space does not permit me to document the countless acts of bravery and the official citations of the many Widnes men who fought with outstanding courage during this war. A Widnes pilot, Warrant Officer Alan Charlesworth, gave his life trying to save members of his crew. Another Widnes pilot, Squadron Leader Edward Gordon Jones, received numerous honours for gallantry and devotion to duty. The list of our brave townsmen is long and impressive and I sincerely apologise for not being able to give proper and deserving credit in these pages.

Whilst, of course, there should be emphasis on the loss of life sustained during this time, there were also little snatches of brighter news filtering through from our troops abroad. In India, in 1943, a group of Widnes lads formed a rugby team and were successful in winning *The Calcutta Rugby Football Tournament* without having had their line crossed. The surnames of the members of that team were: *Halfpenny, Davies, Donegan,*

McConnell, Colebrook, Leedham, Fenlon, Woods, Grady, Egerton, Shaw, Saxon, O'Donoghue, Budworth and Newton.

A young man called Eric Wilkinson wrote to Jack Carney from Northern Italy[123]. In his letter, he described how a group of local lads spent one evening shortly before Christmas 1944. *"The lads were gathered round the table eating rock cakes and drinking tea, waiting for their turn to read "The Weekly News", while at the same time we were thinking of how a bowl of "corndog scouse" would go down"*.   Back home people were dreaming of a turkey for Christmas, while others might think themselves lucky if they got a rabbit — the Widnes lads in Italy were dreaming of a bowl of "scouse"!

The First bombing incident in Widnes happened on 29th August 1940 when a bomb fell in Lunt's Heath Road. Although there were no fatalities, a man was seriously injured when an incendiary bomb exploded under his foot. The following week, on September 4th, some houses in the town were struck by a salvo of bombs. One house in Hale Road was totally demolished and its four inhabitants killed.   By an amazing fluke, the next-door house remained standing with not a window broken! In the summer, a large bomb fell on The Everite Works but nobody was hurt.

The New Year started badly. In January 1941 some houses in Milton Road were damaged and there were a number of injured at various locations in the town although, thankfully, there were no fatalities. As mentioned earlier, in March 1941 a German aircraft was shot down over Widnes and fell on the I.C.I. Recreational Club's sports field. The pilot and another crewman were burned to death, but three members of the crew who baled out were captured and taken to the Police Station for interrogation.   An anti-aircraft shell hit the plane first, and this caused loss of height and speed. Then a night-fighter picked it up and fired from point blank range.   Finally, when the fall had become "a scream of

---

[123] Jack Carney (correspondence)

punctured engines" it struck a barrage balloon cable.   Shortly afterwards, during the heavy blitz on Merseyside, a number of bombs were dropped in the vicinity of Moss Bank.   One fell in a field near Tanhouse Lane, another fell on the railway lines between the site of Bowmans Chemical Works and The Pilkington Sullivan Works, a third one fell on Cuerdley Marsh.   All three exploded. Rumour has it that a fourth unexploded bomb fell on The Pilkington Sullivan Works tip where it was left, until a bomb disposal squad was brought in to deal with it during the 1960s.

In May 1941 Merseyside experienced one of the worst periods, as Liverpool was heavily blitzed.   The skies in Widnes were lit-up as residents witnessed sustained attacks on the port of Liverpool for four consecutive nights.   Enemy planes passed in regular waves over a widespread area for several hours each night, dropping load after load of incendiaries. The residents of Widnes could see searchlights continually tracing their pattern across the night sky and the flicker of bursting anti-aircraft shells.   The mornings brought the full horror to the residents of Liverpool as they surveyed the damage and the large lists of civilian casualties. The following Sunday, the parishioners at St. Marie's Church, in Lugsdale, offered prayers for the Rev. Canon Martin Coady, a Roman Catholic Canon of the Liverpool chapter.   Canon Coady was killed in the air raid on 3rd May, whilst administering the last rites to a dying man near his church in the Kirkdale area of the city. The congregation offered their sympathy to the Lucas family of Market Street, who were close relatives of the late Canon Coady.

For several months, Merseyside was free from enemy night raiders.   On 20th October 1941 the spell was broken.   Nine people were killed in Widnes that night and twenty people, including five children, seriously injured.   In addition to these casualties, many other people received less severe injuries and there was considerable damage to properties.   A number of small formations had passed over the town dropping several bombs.   These formations were met with devastating fire from anti-aircraft guns.

It was a bad couple of hours, but by midnight the raid was over. A parachute mine fell in Farnworth, causing widespread damage and casualties were found under the debris of houses. The fatalities were in Windermere Avenue and Marsh Hall Road. In Windermere Avenue, four members of one family were killed. Those hospitalised included other people from these roads and the surrounding areas of Windermere Street and Claremont Drive.

There was a great deal of fear and agitation in Halton View in November 1941 when a huge "parachute mine" fell to earth in a field at the back of Warrington Road School. The houses in the immediate vicinity were quickly evacuated and a police guard was put on the unexploded bomb until it could be rendered harmless. During the night, a reckless daredevil[124] gained access to the bomb and removed parts from its mechanism. He also cut away some of the silk cord which suspended the weight to the parachute. The following day he was giving away pieces of the cord to the locals as "souvenirs". The man in question was a Royal Navy Petty Officer, from nearby French Street, who was home on leave.

The last recorded enemy visit to the town was on 10th August 1942 when a bomb damaged the I.C.I. Central Laboratory in Waterloo Road. The adjoining railway line was put out of action. A nearby lodging house was also hit by fragments, which penetrated into the building, slightly injuring an elderly man. This was the last raid on Merseyside. Despite Widnes being a prime target for aerial bombing, because of the chemical works, only one enemy bomb found its way to an important industrial target. This was the bomb that struck the Central Laboratory.

During the war, Widnes Borough Council made a number of special requisitions of land and buildings to deal with the emergencies of war. A garage in Thomas Street, owned by Messrs. Garlick, Burrell & Edwards Ltd., was requisitioned to

---

[124] Identified as Mr. Vincent Connor

serve as an emergency mortuary for civilian casualties. A number
of sites around the town were selected for the erection of static
water tanks, for fire prevention, and these too were duly
requisitioned from their owners. The Ministry of Supply also
brought in special laws relating to salvage. These regulations
made it an offence to destroy, throw away or put into a bin, any
rag, rope or string. The same rule applied to waste paper and
rubber. Kitchen waste collection and disposal schemes were also
in operation. Arrangements were made for kitchen waste to be
distributed to, or collected by, smallholders who kept pigs or small
livestock.

Because of the food shortage, people were urged to grow
vegetables on their allotments. They were also encouraged to keep
pigs, chickens, hens, and rabbits. *The Widnes Rabbit Club* had over
80 members who claimed to be doing a war service in the
production of fur and flesh! However, the unauthorised slaughter
of animals was a crime, and there were heavy fines imposed by
The Ministry of Food.   Licences to slaughter an animal were
granted to pig owners on the assumption that the meat was to be
consumed by the owner and his household. Supplying meat to
others was viewed as *"black marketeering"* and the person
unlawfully buying or receiving meat was also fined.   In 1941 the
people named below were granted an official licence to slaughter
animals:

Mr. W.H. Hewitt,	*72 Birchfield Road*
Mr. T.P. Owens,	*40 Bower Street*
Mr. E. Albiston,	*11 Muspratt Street*
Mr. H. Chatterton,	*25 St. Anne's Road*
Mr. S. Hill,	*11 Birch Road*
Mr. W.Jackson,	*27 Dickson Street*
Mr. James Duggan,	*22 Ann Street*
Mr.J.Purnell,	*28 Rock Lane*
Mr. W.S. Purnell,	*144 Albert Road*

The question of Irish neutrality during the war was hotly debated in Widnes. Many admired The Irish Free State for their stance, while others thought differently. Despite the Irish Minister, Mr. Eamon De Valera, wishing to protect his country from involvement, Ireland did not escape unscathed and in 1941 Dublin was bombed. During that bombing 27 people were killed and over 40 people were seriously injured. 25 houses were destroyed and more than 300 other properties were badly damaged. A protest was made to the German Government claiming *"an intentional attack on the territory of The Irish Free State"*. Political circles in Berlin expressed the opinion that the bombing of Dublin was a provocative act by the British, but the British Government vehemently denied this[125].

In view of the large Irish descended population in Widnes, there was a lot of discussion locally regarding the Irish attitude to the war. However, it should be noted that during this period a sizeable number of Irish citizens travelled from Ireland to enrol in the British Forces. These Irishmen fought alongside their British neighbours in all theatres of this war. They believed that Hitler was as much a threat to their own country as he was to England.

The Papal attitude to the war was also brought into question by some members of the local population. *"Where does the Pope stand?"* was the theme of numerous letters and discussions. In fact, the Pope, while maintaining strict neutrality in temporal issues, had never ceased to condemn the practice of the Axis powers. During the first nine months of the war he had worked to prevent the conflict from spreading. The British Government had made a point of paying tribute to his efforts. Despite this, in 1944, The Rev. R. Townsend wrote to *The Widnes Weekly News* giving his opinion that *The Lateran treaty of 1929* had made Fascism in Italy and the *See of Rome* mutually dependent. This article, naturally,

---

[125] *Liverpool Daily Post* (June 6th 1941)

provoked a lot of adverse feeling locally, especially among the Catholic population of the town.

The evacuation of children from danger areas took on a new slant in 1944. After the initial evacuation of Widnes children at the beginning of the war, and the subsequent return of most of them shortly afterwards, Widnes was now considered a "safe area" and children were brought into this town from other places. One evening at the beginning of August 1944, a train rolled into Ditton Junction carrying 314 evacuees. As the train came to a standstill, young mothers and bewildered children stared curiously from the carriage windows at the reception party on the platform. The Mayor and Mayoress, together with assorted members of the Council, and representatives of various charitable organisations and schools, were waiting to greet them and allocate their accommodation. The evacuees were mainly from the Dagenham area. The Mayor, in his welcome address, told the adults in the party that they should: *"just imagine you are Widnesians until the peace bells toll and you are able to return to your homes again!"* The evacuees finally went home in June 1945, less than a year after their arrival.

The news of *"Victory in Europe"* came on 8th May 1945 with the unconditional surrender of Germany. The official announcement came over the wireless and appears to have taken most people by surprise. Needless to say there was great jubilation throughout the country and here in Widnes people partied well into the early hours. It was noted that the following morning American jeeps were much in evidence in the town, to pick up their own "stragglers" from the night before. Despite the celebrations, it was not until 14th August that Japan's Emperor finally accepted the Allies terms for ending the war completely.

American Servicemen were a familiar sight in Widnes during the war years. Nearby, Burtonwood was the maintenance and supply base for all the US Airforce in Europe, so as one can imagine it was an important and very busy place. As well as providing new bombers and fighters to the US squadrons, technicians and mechanics at the base modified and repaired a huge number of aircraft. Because of this, many people referred to it as *"Lancashire's Detroit"*. Naturally, American servicemen became part of the local social scene and consequently there were numerous romantic liaisons with local girls. At the end of the war there was an official recognition of the number of English girls who had married American GIs. *The War Brides Act of 1945* enabled the brides of GIs and their children to enter the United States as non-quota immigrants. In June 1945, the first group of "Widnes War Brides" left the town on their journey to America.

With peace came a number of fascinating revelations hitherto unknown to the local public. One interesting fact to emerge was that a local radio engineer had been recruited to work on highly secretive work relating to radar developments. Mr. W. A. Prince, a local radio shop owner, was part of a team of six civilians, three from Warrington and two from Manchester, who were selected by the Government to work for two years on a secret project at Burtonwood Air Base. The six men were called away from their businesses in 1941 at a time when bombing was at a height. They were not told what their work would be until they were actually on site. Aerial interception was a special branch of radar and, until then, night bombers were raiding England with a certain amount of ease. The ground control team were able to detect Nazi bombers as they left their aerodromes, but the night fighters had not yet attained the skill they afterwards developed. The six radio engineers spent considerable months making a study of the problems and came up with a complete unit that would fit into the cockpit of the night fighter plane. With this unit, the exact position of the enemy aircraft could be located. The "Aircraft Interception Unit" developed by this team, caused such a heavy toll on enemy aircraft that night raids were gradually eliminated. At the end of the war, Bill Prince[126] returned to his radio repair business in Albert Road, and it was only then could he divulge his individual role in the development of this special radar equipment. His work at Burtonwood had been dangerous. He was required to make test flights with the fighter planes on their missions and also salvage apparatus from wrecked planes. No doubt his normal business would have seemed extremely tame after these very dangerous, but exciting, experiences.

One Monday morning in September 1945 the Exchange Telegraph tape machines announced the arrival into Southampton of the giant transatlantic liner *"Aquitania"*. The following morning a BBC news bulletin reported that among the passengers disembarking from this ship were a number of important scientists. These men had spent the previous 15 months in America where they had been involved in the development of the atom bomb. Among the members of that elite team disembarking from the *"Aquitania"* was Dr. J.P. Baxter, Research Manager of the Widnes I.C.I. Central Laboratory, who was also a member of Widnes Town Council. Dr. Baxter, along with two other research chemists from the Widnes Laboratory, Arthur Jones and Harold Evans, had been sent to America to participate in the final stages of research into splitting the atom. The previous explorations into atomic energy done by these three men, at Widnes, had made them valuable contributors to the final research, which resulted in the development of the atomic bomb. The bomb was subsequently used with such terrible devastation on Hiroshima and Nagasaki. The part played by I.C.I.`s Widnes Laboratory, and Gaskell's Works, in the development of atomic energy is now well known. Uranium extraction and metal production processes were developed here. This research led to the production, at I.C.I.'s Rocksavage Works, of the uranium rods charged into the first atomic plant at Harwell.

---

[126] *W.A. Prince was the father of the local folk-singer and musician, Bill Prince.*

Industry

The onset of war had a marked effect on the Widnes and Runcorn chemical industries.   Apart from normal production, special operations under the control of the Government were put into action and chemical work became a reserved occupation.   The war also upset industrial markets by restricting their ability to trade. This kept their prices high and uncompetitive.

Some of our local factories were manufacturing essential chemicals for the war effort.   In Runcorn, The Randle Factory, which was situated on Runcorn Salt Marshes, was producing deadly mustard gas as well as various acids and ammonia. This was "top secret" work and all employees at this factory were made to sign the "Official Secrets Act". Because of the nature of the work carried out there, it became known locally as *"The hush hush"*. The factory was built especially for war production although the gases made there were never used. They were stored under the Welsh mountains for safety. After the war, the gases were supposedly dumped into the Mediterranean Sea. As one can imagine the security was very tight and guards patrolled 24 hours a day. The working conditions were strictly monitored and employees, after taking a bath at the end of their shift, were examined by medical staff for mustard burns.

We are aware now, that at that time many chemical processes and ingredients used in them were extremely hazardous to health. In December 1941 an inquest into a workman's death in a Widnes factory was held in camera. The circumstances surrounding the man's death were not divulged, because it was thought that it was *"not in the national interest"* for the details to be made public.   It was known that the cause of death was due to nephritis, as a result of the work on which he was employed.

The only factory in Widnes to have armed troops on guard was Albright & Wilson, who produced phosphorous and other essential chemicals for the war effort. There were resident soldiers on duty in the works during 1939 and 1940. The troops lived nearby in wooden huts, although prior to this they had been billeted in tents inside the works. After 1940, when the soldiers left, the site was protected by the Home Guard who did a good job and took their duties very seriously. During 1941 a large number of incendiary bombs fell on the Albright & Wilson Works, but the defence team dealt them with quickly and efficiently.

Like Albright & Wilson, who produced amongst other things, flares for ships, other factories in Widnes also manufactured essential chemicals and equipment, some of which were given to the Government for free. Orr's Zinc White Ltd. (The Vine Chemical Works) manufactured pure zinc oxide which was donated to the Government. In Widnes, Thomas Bolton & Sons Ltd. and McKechnie Brothers Ltd. were both producing armaments during the war. Scrap metal, and sometimes even recycled shells, helped to keep available copper at a steady level. The firm of J. H. Dennis Ltd. was also able to supply the rising demand for copper sulphate at this time.

Peter Spence & Sons were also manufacturing important products for the war effort, as were the men at The Widnes Foundry who were producing vital components for war equipment. Chemicals of course were in heavy demand during the war, so there was also a continuous demand for chemical plant equipment. The Widnes Foundry's expertise in this sphere meant that their productive power was extended to the full to provide this equipment. The list of items they produced during this time is interesting, and illustrates the extent to which the wartime industries depended on the engineering resources of this country.

The items are far too numerous to list in full but they included TNT nitrators and separators; sulphuric acid stills and coolers; portable slipways and roller tracks for launching craft cradles; vessels and plant for the production of penicillin, synthetic rubber, and magnesium.

As we know, the work in chemical factories was extremely arduous. The wartime needs exacerbated these conditions. There was an unremitting demand for maximum production and workers were urged to *"keep at it"* to help win the war. Most chemical factories operated a continuous process during this period and many men were required to work a 48-hour week. In almost all factories, workers were issued with glucose, orange juice, and salt tablets to help sustain them through the long and gruelling hours of work. Shift workers ate their meals on site and often slept in the works air raid shelters. Most of these factory shelters were ill equipped and unpleasant – one was even dug into a waste tip!

Almost everyone smoked at this time. Because of this, the scarcity of matches at the beginning of the war became a real problem. At that time the majority of lighter flints were being imported and, unfortunately, the main supplier had been Germany! One evening the chairman of I.C.I., Lord McGowan, was seated near a member of the Government at a social event. The man grumbled about the lack of matches and the shortage of lighter flints. A suggestion was made that I.C.I. might come to the rescue. As I.C.I. had already experimented with the manufacture of flints in the Widnes Laboratory, an idea was formed to set up a means of production. On 15th September 1941 a new plant was assembled at The Pilkington Sullivan Works for the production of high quality flints. Afterwards, the manufacture of cylindrical flints for use in gas appliances and cigarette lighters was to become a successful commercial venture for I.C.I.

The year 1941 marked the centenary of the opening of Thomas Robinson's and John Cook's engineering foundry in St. Helens, although they did not establish "The Widnes Foundry" until some twenty years later. Despite the fact that Widnes Foundry was now under new ownership, the management felt that this auspicious event should be celebrated in some way. The directors announced that a grant of one week's wages would be given to each man who had been in the company's employment for 12 months on the 30th June 1941. For those with less than 12 months service, the grant would be proportionate. In addition to this generous gift, those with over 20 years service would also receive Savings Certificates of varying amounts depending on service. In 1941, although the company had passed into the hands of Thomas W. Ward Ltd., Miss Robinson, a descendant of the founder, was still employed at the Widnes works as a member of the clerical staff.

A *"De-Rating Act"* had come into force in 1929. This Act exempted industries from paying three quarters of its rates, so that in the years from 1930 to 1937 British industries were saved £170,000,000.[127] The I.C.I. alone, saved £200,000 a year as a result of this Act. The exemption was designed to help industry through the years of depression. Whilst it helped industry, it put great pressure on Local Authorities despite the provision of block grants from the Government (which were actually funded through indirect taxation). In Widnes, the de-rating of industry hit badly as it came at a time when the rationalisation of local industry threw many out of work. Some questioned the wisdom of this Act during the war years, as many were concerned about post-war development in the town and how to fund it.

During the war, if one were employed in a factory where production was deemed to be of national importance, you were not allowed to leave your job or fail to turn up for work without good reason. The penalties for negligence of duty under the conditions

---

[127] *Jack Carney.*– (Correspondence, June 1943)

of the "Essential Works Order" were severe, and prison sentences were often the result. The National Service Officer at the local Labour Exchange allocated some jobs in local factories. If you missed work, you were required to report not only to your employer but also to the Labour Exchange with an explanation! One young woman, who did not like her job, was fined £5 for every day that she stayed away from work. Another person was told to either *"go to work or go to prison"*. A 19 year old, employed as a packer at the I.C.I., was charged with *"absenting herself from work of national importance without having a reasonable excuse"*. Having been away from work for a total of 5 days in a 6 month period, she was summoned to appear before the magistrates. It appeared that the girl's absences were mostly concerned with the early morning shift. The reason she gave was that she overslept because there was no alarm clock in the house and she could not get one. Today, this would be a feeble excuse, but it should be remembered that during the war it was not easy to buy an alarm clock or a watch. For this reason, the man who travelled from street to street *"knocking people up"* was very much in evidence during the war years.

During the First War, women had taken the place of absent men in many occupations. Now, during this war, women were once again returning to factories and working in occupations that had previously been the sole province of the male worker. In normal times, it would have been unthinkable to see women doing heavy industrial work. Nonetheless, in the 1940s women worked in most of the factories in Widnes and showed a willingness and energy in all the jobs they were allocated. An employment table of workers employed at the I.C.I. Pilkington Sullivan Works during the period from 1943 to 1945 shows the number of women workers were as follows:[128]

---

[128] *Catalyst Museum* - (courtesy of Paul Meara)

> 1943 *Women replacing men (Adult & Junior)*   259
> 1944 *Women replacing men (Adult & Junior)*   279
> 1945 *Women replacing men (Adult & Junior)*   260

Not surprisingly, by 1947 the numbers were reduced to 107 and there were no junior female workers. However, even though men returning after the war replaced most of the women workers, women continued to be employed in this factory and most of the other local factories from that time onward.

Despite women stepping into the breach to replace absent male workers, there was still a shortage of labour for Britain's wartime industry. At the beginning of 1940 employment agents from England travelled to Ireland to recruit labour for essential industries. There was a good response to this country wide recruitment drive, especially in areas where there was high unemployment. It is evident that substantial numbers of men from all over Ireland responded to this call, and travelled to England to provide labour for essential war work.

During the war, most local firms paid an allowance to their employees who were serving with the armed forces. Employees of J. H. Dennis's Cornubia Copper Works were given a payment of 10 shillings a week for a single man and £1 for a married man. This was a generous amount when it is compared to the 2s.6d given by The Everite Works to its absent servicemen.

At a meeting of the Widnes Trades Union Council in 1945, one of their members raised the question of air pollution in the town. He made particular mention of the pollution caused by dust from the I.C.I. Powerhouse in West Bank. Some days the dust, which looked like black sand, lay inches thick on windowsills and gutters. On one occasion, it was so bad that it was being swept up in shovels from back yards. The matter had been referred to the Town Council and representations had been made to I.C.I. Their excuse was that it was caused by bad fuel. In London, Battersea

Power Station had remedied a similar problem by installing new equipment. It was suggested that this was unlikely to happen in Widnes *"as it was a question of spending money and there was no return on those things"*.

Unfit for Human Habitation

When war came, Widnes had been well on the way to rectifying the problem of bad housing. In the 6 year period between 1933 and 1939, nearly 3300 new houses had been built in the Borough. The Council had built almost 1300 of these, the rest were the result of private enterprise. In 1939 as the country was plunged into war, the actual position in Widnes was that there were 225 people living in slum housing and over 1000 in overcrowded conditions. The Town Council had already acquired land and had plans in place ready to proceed as soon as labour and materials could be released. At the end of 1943, it was estimated that the town needed 550 additional new houses in order to solve the immediate housing problems. This figure was broken down as: 50 to replace slum housing, 200 for overcrowding, and 300 to meet the needs of newly married couples forced to live in lodgings[129].

Apart from the duty to deal with the problem of substandard housing, the Council were also mindful at this time of the potential need to accommodate families who may be made homeless by enemy action. With this in mind, in November 1940 the Housing Committee made a resolution that any houses that might become vacant on any of the Corporation housing estates should not be re-let, other than to families rendered homeless by enemy action. It was planned to collate a pool of twelve houses. These houses would be kept in readiness for any such emergency. The Medical Officer of Health was put in charge of maintaining the pool at a level of 12 houses.

---

[129] *Capt. R. Pilkington, M.P.* (December 1943)

Earlier, the Council had acquired the power to requisition houses which were empty, providing due notice was given to the owner. This had removed some of the congestion. They were also given the power to compulsorily billet families in houses where there were two or three bedrooms and only one occupant. People were also encouraged to move into smaller houses if their own houses were larger than they needed. In April 1941 the Council made a compulsory possession order on the following premises: 54 Victoria Road, 8 Albert Road, "Westmeria" Mill Brow, 175/177 Liverpool Road and 31 Derby Road. It was said that these premises were requisitioned for the purpose of storing furniture and/or housing persons rendered homeless by enemy action.

For those living in privately owned rented houses there was still the problem of exploitation. There were countless decent landlords who did repairs and charged a reasonable rent for their houses. But, there were also the unscrupulous landlords who preyed on the hapless tenants' ignorance of the law. There had been various *Rent Restriction Acts* between 1919 and 1944, designed to provide both the tenant and landlord with important legal protection. One of the requirements of The Act was that tenants should be provided with a rent book and a certain security of tenure. During the 1940s there were numerous prosecutions and heavy penalties were imposed on a number of local landlords for contravention of *The Rent Act*.

The Waterloo ward was a continual focus of concern. Although a section of this area had been cleared, and its inhabitants re-housed in Corporation owned houses, the onset of war had brought the Corporation building programme to a halt. The result of this was that a substantial number of privately owned rented properties, which were really unfit for habitation, were still being occupied in this area. Despite the unwholesome condition of these old rundown houses, most landlords made no attempt to improve or repair them. Some landlords actually sought to instigate rent rises when in fact the tenants should have been seeking reductions.   These landlords were justifiably called "bloodsuckers" by the clergy at St. Patrick's who had been asked to take up the cause of the tenants.

In January 1945, the clergy from St. Patrick's Church asked a young man from Wellington Street to address a public meeting to discuss the appalling conditions of the houses in the Waterloo ward.   The meeting was held in St. Patrick's Boys' School and was presided over by the Rev. Father Hayes.   It was emphasised that the meeting was in no way political in character, but had been called to highlight the condition of houses in the area.   The young man had already approached some landlords, on the tenants' behalf, and had also been to the Town Hall but there had been no satisfactory results.   For that reason, a public meeting was called to highlight the plight of the Waterloo residents.   The young man pointed out to the audience that the housing problem was a national one as well as a local one, but he maintained that Widnes was perhaps the worst town in the north of England regarding housing conditions.   In the true spirit of other remarkable local men like Dr. John O'Keeffe, David Lewis and Dan Garghan, this young man decided to "take on" the landlords who wanted to raise rents. He told the tenants they should endeavour to get their rents reduced by reporting the matter to the Sanitary Inspector.

A month later, after a plea to the local Medical Officer again failed to produce any result, a further meeting was called.   The clergy from St. Patrick's, Father Hayes and Father Whitty, told of their visits to houses in the Waterloo ward and the abysmal conditions they found there. Father Hayes said:

"This state of affairs is not becoming to the dignity of human beings. They have the right to live and the right to work, and the right to a living wage. A human being has the right to a decent house, and it is only when there is a decent house and a living wage that a human being can carry out the end for which he was created and put on this earth. Under the conditions prevailing in parts of the town, what man, or woman or child

has an opportunity of attaining the destiny for which they were made? It was not an exaggeration to say that some of the people were being treated as if they were not human beings. That condition of affairs ought not to be allowed to continue, and they were met that night because they realised the dignity of the human being, and that the working man and the working woman were entitled to live in conditions which gave them the chance of moral development".

Father Whitty told the meeting that he had spent over 2 hours that morning going from house to house to see these conditions for himself so that he could form his own judgement. He believed that these houses were not fit to live in. The first thing he had noticed was the dampness, the humidity, and the appalling condition of the walls in most of the houses he visited. The said the plaster was falling off the walls and the dampness was due to the fact that there was no damp course. Walls and floors were unsafe and *"the footboards and stairs were almost an invitation to suicide."* The next thing he noticed was that washing facilities were primitive; he said *"a savage in the middle of Africa had almost as good washing facilities as the mothers and families had in those houses".* He said that the sanitation was also primitive; the lavatories did not flush and were without seats, the yards were unpaved and were full of water puddles; there were collections of refuse in the corners as there were no dustbins. The slates on the roofs were loose or missing and in two of the houses, one half of the back bedroom windows had fallen out. It appeared that there had been no attempt at repairing them for a good number of years and the position had now become desperate.

Some members of the audience voiced their serious concerns about rubbish accumulating in backyards because of the lack of dustbins. There was now a serious problem with rats and mice owing to the mounting piles of rubbish. Bins had not been provided for years, and the lack of them had become a threat to the

health of the inhabitants and to the whole district[130].   This issue
was of particular concern to the young man. He had been to the
Town Hall on numerous occasions and asked that dustbins be
provided for each house. He had explained the appalling situation,
but was told that it was impossible to provide bins because there
was a shortage, due to the war.

At the end of the meeting it was decided that this young man,
together with The Rev. Fathers Hayes and Whitty, be appointed a
deputation to meet the Minister of Health to raise this matter. The
young man was happy to embark on this mission to help his fellow
residents of Waterloo.   Over the coming months he led a
demanding campaign to improve the lot of the community.
Because of his perseverance, many families found that apart from
rent reductions, some landlords even starting doing minor repairs.
The remarkable young man in question was 22 year old Jack
Ashley, a defender of the underdog, and in later life the champion
of the disabled population of this country.

The dustbin saga gained new heights when Jack Ashley went
down to London as a member of a Trades Union delegation.
While he was there, he went around the city searching for a
supplier of dustbins. On finding a suitable trader, he immediately
ordered bins for the tenants of Waterloo and told the shopkeeper
that he should send the bill to Widnes Corporation.
Unsurprisingly, the Corporation refused to foot the bill. The
following week, our *Weekly News* correspondent in London, Jack
Carney, wrote:

"I am not trying to make political propaganda, but I would rather be
young Ashley, the knight errant of the dustbins, than any other man in

---

[130] *Under the terms of The Public Health Act of 1936, landlords were required to*
provide dustbins for household refuse. In the event of a failure to do so, the
Council had the power to provide dustbins, and recover expenses from the
landlord.

Widnes. *There is the story of a real social service attempted, and although it had no immediate success, it may yet become the symbol of social service in Widnes. I do not, as people know, decry social ideals, but the first place to start is in your own back street. Young Ashley was wise in his generation".*

The condition of the houses in the Waterloo area continued to dominate the news. Two other visitors to the area sent letters to *The Widnes Weekly News* describing the appalling conditions they had seen there:

"One family, including three small children, are compelled to live and sleep in the kitchen owing to the falling in of the bedroom; hardly any windows at the rear of the house; the children ill at present through dampness and draughts; mother recently confined in the same kitchen; owing to absolute lack of space one child now has to sleep at grandmother's.

Another family, father and daughter; rain dripping onto beds; overrun with mice; floor of scullery just earth; walls wet with damp; fireplace so bad that smoke and soot fill the kitchen, which does no good to the father who suffers from chest trouble; boiler cannot be used for washing; back windows boarded up, no panes.

A family in which there are eight children with only one bedroom, which, regardless of overcrowding, is in an unhealthy state – the walls crumbling with damp; a house with two panes at the back and three at the front. The whole house is in a shocking state, just falling down and verminous through decay. In another house, there are six children and the same conditions prevail. They have tried to put windows in but owing to the frames being rotten, this is impossible".

The visitors also extracted comments from some of the tenants who said: *"the houses not fit to live in; ought to be pulled down; been in the house forty years and never had a repair done; twenty years without repair; bedroom floors not strong enough to hold beds; the bedroom ceiling has to be held up with props; I put my three weeks old baby to bed one night and next morning it was dead – pneumonia owing to the damp room".*

In October 1945 Commander Christopher Shawcross, the newly elected Labour MP for Widnes, made his maiden speech in The House of Commons.   Commander Shawcross referred to the housing conditions in parts of his constituency and said that they were worse than in any other part of the Kingdom. Speaking of a case that had occurred at the end of January, he said:

"A small child in one of these slum cottages died of pneumonia. The mother told me that within minutes the corpse was alive with cockroaches and vermin, which infest these hovels. The father of the dead child was at that time overseas in the Forces".

Commander Shawcross suggested that it should be made illegal for landlords to draw rent for properties that had, in many cases, been unfit for habitation for 25 or 30 years. Immediately following Commander Shawcross's speech, the Government Minister of Health, Mr. Willink, said that *"if the things which the honourable and gallant member described are exactly as he described them in Widnes, then the Local Authority cannot have been fulfilling its statutory duties"*[131]. Although our new MP's speech was reported verbatim in the local press, together with the remarks of Mr. Willink, the Minister of Health's criticism of the Local Council went unchallenged.

Since that initial "Waterloo Housing" meeting, called by the clergy of St. Patrick's in January 1945, there had been some amazing developments in the Waterloo ward. 22 year old Jack Ashley stood as a candidate in the local election in October of that year. He stood as an Independent Labour candidate and he topped the poll, with the official Labour candidate coming in

---

[131] Hansard – October 1945.

Princes Amateur Boxing Club, Runcorn – c.1931
(Includes both Runcorn and Widnes boxers).
Names: Back row from left: George Massey; Harry Clarke; Jim Redmond;
Frank Ashley; Jack Redmond (trainer)
Front from left: Jim McConnell; Larry Harrolds; Ned Lucas; Jack Riley and
Mick Lucas

The Widnes Star Novelty Band

V.E. Day Celebrations in Kent Street – May 1945

second. Within a month of being elected, he was leading a deputation to interview the Town Clerk and other officials on the matter of rents, house repairs, and the provision of dustbins. Attending that meeting were the Medical Officer of Health, the Borough Engineer, and the Sanitary Inspector, as well as the Town Clerk and other members of the Council. Councillor Ashley took with him between eighty and ninety rent books, which the Town Clerk undertook to look into. The meeting was a satisfactory one and resulted in the Town Clerk calling a further meeting to which the landlords were invited. Dustbins were also to be provided for all who needed them!

In mid November of that same year, our local MP, Commander Christopher N. Shawcross, tabled a question in the House of Commons, addressed to the Minister of Health, Mr. Aneurin Bevan. Commander Shawcross asked the Minister if he *"proposed to introduce legislation to make illegal the collection or payment of rent for dwellings which are unfit for human habitation.* Mr. Bevan said that there were already provisions in place, under the terms of *The Rent Restrictions Act*, enabling part of the rent to be withheld where the house is not in a reasonable state of repair. He did not think any further action was necessary. Owing to the unsatisfactory nature of the reply, Commander Shawcross gave notice that he would raise the matter on the Adjournment.

Later in the month, the Senior Regional Officer, Ministry of Health, intimated to the Council that they could now proceed with the planned 166 houses on the Lowerhouse Lane site. The Housing Committee was also making arrangements for the erection of temporary housing, in the form of 150 prefabricated bungalows, which had been allocated to Widnes Council. The Ministry of Health had authorised the use of 23 acres of land in Hale Road for this purpose. It was suggested at the time that German prisoner of war labour should be used to erect them.

As in earlier decades, the acute need for housing caused some people to improvise. A group of homeless squatters took over *The Heath Road Prisoner of War Camp* immediately after the war ended in 1945. By the end of the year there were 2000 people on the waiting list for houses. Some applicants had been on the list for as long as 13 years! Among the applicants waiting to be housed in decent accommodation were approximately 1000 serving and ex-servicemen and, on top of that, there were munitions workers to be considered. Some of the people on the list were living in lodgings and others in grossly overcrowded conditions and, as we have seen, some were living in accommodation unfit for human habitation.

Education

One of the early casualties of the war seems to have been the education system. The evacuation of children and the subsequent closing of schools threw national and local education arrangements into chaos. Some people suggested that the Board of Education should have provided some kind of correspondence course, enlisting the aid of local teachers. Fortunately, after the initial panic, it was not too long before a workable educational system was put back into operation. Compulsory education was able to resume in Widnes in April 1940.

In January 1940 it was proposed that additional school shelter accommodation be provided for non-evacuated children. It was estimated that there was a need for shelter accommodation for a total of 1350 children in the following schools: St. Bede's (200) Farnworth (100) St. Marie's (400) St. Patrick's (100) Simms Cross (200) Warrington Road (100) West Bank (200) and Kingway Centre (50). These were to supplement existing shelters at Ditton, Farnworth and Simms Cross.

There were obviously numerous disruptions to schoolwork during wartime. During night raids children would lose precious hours of sleep, this meant that they were allowed to start school later in the morning. When the air raid warnings sounded during the day, they would have to leave their lessons and head for the shelters. In September 1940 the headmaster of Warrington Road School voiced concerns about some children wandering to school unaware that a warning had been sounded and that explosions had been heard not far away. He discovered that several parents had their wireless sets too loud and did not always hear the air raid warnings[132]. He asked the children to warn their parents to *"subdue their wireless sets"*.

The attendance table below, for November 1940, shows that at this time many children were only in receipt of part-time education. It was hoped that the provision of additional shelter accommodation would mean that more children would be able to resume full-time education. The table also shows that at that time there were only a small number of children remaining in the evacuation programme in Blackpool.

School	Full-time	Part-time	Blackpool
St. Bede's	*276*	*590*	*23*
Farnworth		*522*	
St. Marie's	*966*		*20*
Widnes C. of E.		*94*	
St. Patrick's	*415*		
Simms Cross		*1282*	*31*
Warrington Rd.	*606*		*17*
West Bank	*349*		*2*
Ditton C. of E.	*136*		
Ditton C.	*117*		
St Mary's, Ditton		*248*	
Halebank	*232*		
Central	*398*		*1*
Fairfield			*4*
Open Air			*7*
TOTAL[133]	**3837**	**2394**	**105**

---

[132] *Ref: SL565/4917/Cheshire Records*
[133] By September 1942, there were only 76 children in the Evacuation Programme. 37 of these were in Blackpool and 39 elsewhere.

In March 1941 an opening ceremony was performed at the new Fairfield Senior Girls' School. Although the building was not quite complete the Council decided to proceed with the opening ceremony. School accommodation was urgently needed because First Aid posts and ARP posts had occupied many of the local school buildings. This meant that many of the local schoolchildren were still only receiving a part-time education. All building programmes were held up because of the war, but Widnes Council protested to the Board of Education and was allowed to continue with the building of this school.

Although the new school was built for girls, it was decided that from the 1st April 1941, when the school was ready for occupation, that boys would also be admitted so that for a time it would be a mixed school. One pleasing feature of the new school was that it stood in its own playing fields of 20 acres and it was envisaged that it would also provide playing fields for other schoolchildren in that part of the town. The final cost of Fairfield Senior Girls School amounted to £25,523.14s.6d. Today this would only buy you a nice car!

In July 1941, at a meeting of the School Management Sub-Committee, a number of local scholarship awards and renewals were announced. The following places and renewals were given for "The Wade Deacon Grammar School".

Timmis Scholarship - (value £10 per annum)
First Year   *Harry Heesom, West Bank C. School*
Second Year   *Harry Snape, Gordon Collier,*
                   William D.Hunt
Third Year   *W.A. Smith, S.G. Munslow*
Fourth Year   *Dennis J. Roche*

Farnworth Foundation - (value £10 per annum)
First Year   *Norman S. Worrall, Warrington Road*

	B.P. Hardman, Farnworth E. School
	D.C. Bates, Farnworth C.E. School
Second Year	*Robert Lygo, Joseph Plumpton,*
	Kenneth B. Hankinson,
	Thomas Stevens
Third Year	*Eric Miller*
Fourth Year	*Albert L. Davey, John Coates*
Fifth Year	*J.W. Foden, K. Lomax*
Sixth Year	*Philip H. Starmer*

The Ada Squires - (value £10 per annum)

Second Year	*Joan Martin*
Third Year	*Vera Antrobus*

In October of that year, Charles Vowles, a promising student at the Widnes Technical College, was awarded the *"Sir William Mather Scholarship in Mechanical Engineering"*. The value of this particular scholarship was the generous sum of £55 for 3 years.

Of course, in some cases, the awarding of scholarships to Grammar Schools often put economic pressure on a family. The cost of a uniform and books was sometimes prohibitive and meant that some children were unable to take up offers of places. Some parents were inclined to think that it would be better for their sons or daughters to finish school as early as possible in order that they could bring in a wage. This attitude was fuelled entirely by economics, and did not mean that they were indifferent in matters relating to educating their offspring.

In December 1941 Widnes Education Committee submitted a programme to provide a system of nurseries for an estimated number of 700 children aged between 2 and 5 years. The nurseries would be open from 7.00 a.m. to 6.30 p.m. By June 1943 there were sixteen nurseries in the town. The first one opened on February 2nd 1942 at Fairfield Infant School. The cost to parents of a nursery place for their child was 6d a day, which covered day care, dinner, and milk morning and afternoon. The local Medical Officer intimated that no child would be accepted at a nursery unless it had been immunised against diphtheria.

The nurseries were, initially, a wartime provision and few people expected that they would be required when women had returned to their peacetime roles as mothers and homemakers. This view was reinforced just after the war when, in March 1946, the Parish Priest at St. Marie's said in his Sunday sermon:

"As a wartime measure the Nursery was a necessity, but now it is not necessary for mothers who are not working. The Catholic ideal is for mothers who are not working to look after and care for and feed their own children, and every good Catholic mother is glad to do these things"[134].

Technically, the wartime nurseries were managed by the Maternity and Child Welfare Department of the Ministry of Health. Although some wartime classes were under the supervision of the Education Committee they were still financed by the Ministry of Health.

In the summer of 1942 The Board of Education sent a circular to all Local Authorities in England saying that leave of absence could be granted to schoolchildren for employment in agriculture. In Widnes, the Education Committee passed a resolution sanctioning leave of absence for children to be away from school to help in "the war effort". In normal times, some children took time off, without permission, to go "potato picking" or "pea picking" on local farms. The new official legislation meant that there would be stricter regulations on the employment of children in agricultural occupations. The new rules stated that the hours worked by a child should not be more than seven in any one day or thirty-six in a week!

---

[134] *St. Marie`s Parish Records* – March 1946

There was great interest taken by the public of Widnes in the appointment of the Headmaster of Simms Cross School in 1944. The Education Sub-Committee recommended the candidate, but the Council refused to confirm his appointment without further debate. The matter dragged on for some weeks until eventually the matter was voted on at a special meeting of the Town Council. The appointment was eventually confirmed by twelve votes to eleven. Because council and committee minutes which by their very nature omit some details of debate, it has been necessary to utilise press reports as supplementary material. It would appear that a member of the committee, Fr. Hayes, made a number of provocative statements regarding the appointment of a new headmaster. The matter bewildered most of the general population. However, among letters written to *The Widnes Weekly News* one man said:

"Why for instance, should parsons who have sole power over their own Church schools have any say at all in the Council school appointments? The Council schools are provided by the State, and are non-denominational and they should be free from anything tainted with dogma"

In 1943 the School Attendance records were published and the following schools were named as the "best"

St. Mary's School, Ditton	*91.8%*
Warrington Road School	*90.8%*
Widnes C. E. School	*87.1%*

Everyday Life

As we know, during the previous decades, large numbers of Widnesians left the town and headed for foreign climes. Offers of employment and a range of attractive incentives had persuaded many to try their luck in other Commonwealth countries. For some the reality did not live up to their expectations, but for others a new start led to better and more rewarding lives. A few made amazing progress in their adopted country. One man who did so was William Edward Dickson, a past pupil of Farnworth School, who migrated to Australia in 1913. Prior to emigrating, William Dickson was employed as a clerk at Gossages Soap Works. After his arrival in Australia he joined the Australian Labour Party. By the age of 31 he had been appointed to the Legislative Council of New South Wales and, in 1941, William Dickson was selected to be a member of the re-constructed war-time cabinet for Australia, under the newly appointed Premier, Mr. A. W. Fadden.

"Careless talk costs lives" and *"Tittle tattle lost the battle"* were memorable slogans from wartime Britain. The subject of "rumour mongering" became a serious business and a number of prosecutions were brought for spreading false stories. One local woman circulated a fictitious story claiming that nine German spies had been caught near her house. The summons against her was worded thus: *"that by certain false statements she had endeavoured to influence public opinion in a manner likely to be prejudicial to the defence of the realm"*. The woman was fined 2 shillings. This was not an isolated case. Gossip, in peacetime known as "jangling", was a harmless pastime for many women; however in wartime it could be a crime.

At the start of the war people had been issued with blackout material or blinds. It was important for security reasons that no light be visible during the hours of darkness. Most people were mindful not only of their legal obligations to maintain the blackout, but also for their own safety during aerial bombardment. Factories working continuous shifts faced great difficulties operating their furnaces during hours of darkness as the flames could act as a beacon in the night sky. Some works tried to restrict operations to daylight hours but this proved to be impractical. Other factories, like Albright & Wilson, found solutions that enabled them to obscure light. They solved the problem by burning waste gases under the boilers and in the calciners. Steam also masked the operations, so water was sprayed on the slag pit.

Such was the public concern at the dangers of displaying light, that a large group of people smashed thirty windows at The Widnes Foundry one night in 1940. The windows in part of the factory had not been blacked out because the area was not normally in use at night. That particular night an electrical fault caused the lights to come on. A crowd of local people, and the local Air Raid Warden, Mr. Patrick Finnegan, were soon on the scene. Whilst the warden tried calm the crowd, a Special Constable arrived on the scene, but he was unable to prevent the crowd from smashing the windows in order to put out the lights. The timekeeper claimed that a man with a fixed bayonet had threatened him. However, the man was simply preventing the angry crowd from getting into the time office. The firm was fined £5 for permitting light to be visible, and the warden was praised for his prompt response. The blackout also made travel at night quite hazardous. Car headlights and even bicycle lamps were blacked out, so visibility was limited. It was particularly perilous for pedestrians. Head on collisions were common in the blackout, as they were in the smog!

In 1941 Widnes was celebrating a half-century as a Borough. Councillor Thomas Smith was unanimously elected as the chief citizen of Widnes in its "Golden Jubilee" year. During the fifty years since it became a "Borough" Widnes had changed almost beyond recognition. At its incorporation, the town had no park, no Transporter Bridge, no promenade gardens and no buses. There had been no responsibility for municipal housing and no secondary education. To our modern eye, Widnes of 1941 was a place lacking in many necessities, but to the inhabitants of that time, Widnes was a place to be proud of. Not least because of the progress that had been made in health and education provisions during its fifty years of incorporation. Social and industrial conditions had improved greatly and the layout of the town had developed in a way that men of vision, like David Lewis, had previously only dreamed of. Tellingly, in his address to the citizens of Widnes during its Golden Jubilee year, the Mayor, Councillor Smith, said *"there is a bond of friendship and good fellowship in the town which has never been so strong before, and we should not let it die"*.

Apart from the many social and welfare improvements activated by the Local Council, there were also benefits being introduced by the Government around this time. The *Vitamin Welfare Scheme* was brought in at the end of 1941. This scheme provided all children under two years of age with free supplies of cod liver oil compound and blackcurrant juice and, when available, orange juice. In 1942 the scheme was extended to include pregnant women and children under five. Free school milk was also introduced. In Widnes, a scheme providing free immunisation against Diphtheria was put into operation during 1941. That year there had been 160 cases of Diphtheria, and 9 deaths had occurred from this disease during the year. Scarlet Fever was also a serious problem in the town.

During the summer of 1941, 13 cases of Para-Typhoid were reported in the town, chiefly among children. The cause was found to be a synthetic cream used in the manufacture of cream cakes. Fortunately, only one wholesale confectioner, whose premises were in Liverpool, used this cream.   Thankfully, there were no deaths from this outbreak and the responsibility for dealing with the source of the infection was placed upon the Liverpool Authorities.

The inaugural meeting of the *Widnes Air Training Cadets* (A.T.C.) took place in February 1941. The Widnes group was to be named 310 Squadron and its first Commanding Officer was Mr. Ibeson.   The welfare of the cadets was to be looked after by the Widnes Higher Education sub-Committee under the chairmanship of Alderman Edwardson.   All cadets would receive drill instruction, physical training and armaments.   Named among the first Widnes cadets were:

L. Twigg, W. Brassington, F. Leigh, A. Harding, A. Timmis, J. Hill, D. Hogkins, A. Richards, A. Stevens, D. Carmichael, L. Lockett, A. Whittle, C. Robertshaw, R. Snape, H. Basnett, J. Neild, D. McCafferty, R. Gough, K. Mildren, H. Morris, D. Hartles, G. Briscoe, D. Fox, G. Pickston, C. Pedlar, A. Davies, T. Boardman, H. Bissett, K. Rawson, H. Whitfield, G. Smith, F. Jefferson, J. Moran, W. Reid, J. Yarwood, J. Hornby, and W.Kidd.

The Air Ministry had initially set up these squadrons as a preliminary training for the Royal Air Force, although it was stressed that cadets were not compelled to join the RAF.   It was expected that membership of the squadron would encourage young boys to attain a degree of education which would be of benefit to them in any of the forces.

Another institution established because of wartime requirements was *The Citizen's Advice Bureau*.   It was originally formed to cater for the needs of those in the Services, as well as civilian citizens.   It was proposed that the Bureau should act as a pathfinder and advisor to those who had little knowledge of the provisions the State could offer.   The Widnes branch was set up at 28 Widnes Road in the summer of 1942.   During the first six months it dealt with more than 1200 clients, proving that there had been a serious need for such a service.

In the 1940s many towns set up their own "Brains Trust" or debating forum. The first meeting of *The Widnes Brains Trust* took place at St. Paul's Parochial Hall in June 1942. In the chair on that evening, acting as question master, was Professor Raleigh Batt of Liverpool. The members of "The Trust" were: *the Vicar of St. Paul's, (The Rev. Parry-Williams), Dr. Thelwall Jones, Mr. W.E. Hartles, Councillor T. Swale, Commander J.E. Pallant, and Mr. Hector Ireland.* The questions covered a wide range of subjects ranging from *"Why were there no lady councillors in Widnes?"* and *"Why was there an absence of humour in the Welsh people?"* A question about how the empty ground behind St. Paul's Church should be developed, brought forth a good deal of amusement especially when Hector Ireland suggested that all the spare land in the town should be filled up with cricket pitches! The evening was well attended and the proceeds from the sale of tickets was donated to the Mayor's *"Aid to Russia"* fund.

Whilst those attending the first meeting of *"The Brains Trust"* had done their bit in contributing to an important cause; in another part of town, around the same time, money was being raised in the backyard of 17 Davies Street, West Bank, for an alternative cause. A "Children's Concert" was organised by three local ladies, Mrs. Shaw, Mrs. Francis and Mrs. Ashton. The admission charge was a nominal one-penny, and in addition to the concert, the neighbours provided the children with a tea-party. Mrs. Carter, of Davies Street, donated a prize for a raffle, and the total proceeds from the event was £5, which was donated to *The Red Cross Fund*. Among the children taking part in the concert were:

Girls: *W.Ashton, D. Ashton, J. Higgins, M. Lomax, B. Francis, M. Francis, G. Churms, D. Andrews, D. Weir, P. Twigg, A. Snelson, F. Pickering, D. Bains.* The boys included: *B. Woods, J. Churms, R. Bates, A. Snelson.*

This venture proved to be a popular success and the organisers were spurred on to produce further fundraising events. By the end of the year the resourceful Mrs. Ashton had arranged other things, including a concert at St. Mary's Parochial Hall, which played to a capacity audience. This time the proceeds were in excess of £11, which was forwarded to the Chancellor of the Exchequer to go towards the cost of a *"Churchill Tank"*.

One of the developments of the war years was *"The British Restaurant"* these establishments were primarily proposed by the Government, but run by Local Authorities. Initially, they were opened for the benefit of industrial workers, but later they were used by many sections of the local community. 1942 saw the opening of two *"British Restaurants"* in Widnes. The first one, in Victoria Road, opened in June and was, initially, exclusively for workers. It proved to be a huge success.

In November, a second restaurant was opened in New Street above the Montague Burton Shop. This time the general public were invited to make full use of the facilities on offer. The restaurants proved to be very popular as the meals were cheap and you did not have to use your ration coupons. However, as sugar was withdrawn from all catering establishments in an attempt to effect economical consumption, customers were required to bring their own sugar to restaurants and cafes. Originally, the meals for the British Restaurants were cooked at a "cooking depot" in Barrows Green and transported to the restaurants in insulated containers. Later, the meals were cooked on site. Two full-time restaurant supervisors were employed, each receiving a salary of £130 per annum. Both establishments employed a part-time cashier who received a wage of £1.7s.6d per week. Mrs. L. Booth and Mrs. M.A. Heron were the supervisor and cashier at the Victoria Road establishment and Mrs. C. Evans and Mrs. M. Gerrard were employed as supervisor and cashier at Widnes Road.

By September 1942 the restaurants were serving an average of 300 meals a day. The provision of these restaurants was a way of alleviating the hardships caused by food rationing. It had been necessary to introduce rationing to deal with food shortages and there was a great deal of panic regarding the availability of supplies. Meat, butter, and sugar were rationed from early 1940, other foodstuffs, including tea, were added later on. Fruit, vegetables, fish, bread and coffee were never rationed although apart from the problem of availability, choice was often limited. Bananas were not seen for years. When they eventually became plentiful again, after the war, young children didn't know how to eat them and most tried to eat the skin as well!

Food rationing loomed large in most peoples' lives. Because you had to register your ration book with your chosen grocer or butcher, this system effectively tied households to one shop. Most people found it advantageous to stay on good terms with their grocer or butcher, as favoured customers were usually the first to benefit from any extra provisions that arrived. Of course, there are always people willing and able to make money through illicit means, so at this time racketeering through the black-market was rife. There were numerous prosecutions locally, and some people were prosecuted on more than one occasion.

Early in the war, for people with relatives living in Eire, where there was no rationing, the possibility of having food smuggled over was very tempting. As travel between these two countries was monitored and custom and excise procedures were strict, some people used the post as a means of sending food to relatives here. However, the authorities often intercepted parcels containing presents of food such as sugar and tea. The receipt of such a parcel constituted a contravention of The Rationing Order and carried heavy penalties. In Widnes, there were a number of prosecutions for breaking the law in this manner. The penalty was usually a fine of £5. Later on, Ireland also experienced shortages because, like Britain, they were dependant upon merchant ships for much of their supplies.   During the war many merchant ships were lost because of submarine warfare. This meant that Ireland was also forced to impose rationing on goods such as tea, butter, petrol and clothing.

For the housewife, apart from the problem of providing decent meals for the family, the very act of shopping took a long time, as there were often lengthy queues due to people having ration coupons checked and cancelled. Time was also taken up because the shop assistant would be serving little bits of this and that, and the rations also needed careful weighing.   Food rationing was strictly regulated and monitored by inspectors. In April 1941 the proprietors of "The Home and Colonial Stores", in Albert Road, were fined £7 with costs of 2 guineas for a breach of the rationing laws. The manager of the store was also fined a sum of £5 for "aiding and abetting".

Clothes rationing was particularly difficult especially for young women wishing to get married. There were numerous stories about people making wedding dresses from captured parachutes and other improvised materials.   "Calvert's" sold blanketing material by the yard. This material was not rationed, so people dyed it and made jackets and coats. Coupons were also needed for furniture, which was all of "utility quality" which meant that it was basic, but of a serviceable standard. "Sextons", in Alforde Street, proved to be a boon to young people setting up home as they sold old second-hand furniture which was exempt from rationing.

The residents of Widnes, whilst optimistically geared up for coping with enemy air attack or other hazards of war, were totally unprepared for dealing with unforeseen freak weather conditions. In October 1943 a whirlwind wreaked havoc on the town, killing one person and injuring several others. Serious damage to buildings caused further mayhem. The path of the whirlwind came up from the river and through the industrial area, causing damage at The Thomas Vickers Works, Thos. Bolton & Sons, Richard White & Sons, and also to Central Station. The storm then travelled through the Kingsway Estate and up as far as Farnworth Station. There was considerable damage in all these locations. However, the most serious damage occurred around the Moor Lane and Ellis Street area. Two women returning to work after dinner were caught up in the storm and thrown into the air. It is believed a garage door that had been ripped from its frame struck them. One young woman was badly injured and was pronounced dead on arrival at the Accident Hospital. A number of other people were also hospitalised but fortunately, there were no other fatalities. The structural damage was considerable. Ellis Street caught the full force of the wind. The small street was ravaged, with the majority of window frames being blown in, doors ripped off, and chimneystacks collapsed into the bedrooms below. Remarkably, none of the terrified residents were injured. Nearby, the roof of the Welsh Congregational Chapel and adjoining houses in Moor Lane were badly damaged. Across the road, the Corporation Bus Garage was also hit. The wind swept around the building and crashed through the gable end causing some of the brickwork to fall inwards. Massive steel girders supporting the roof gave way under the heavy strain and the roof collapsed. Fortunately, as it was dinnertime, there was only one man in the garage at the time and he managed to escape without a scratch. The storm caused £3000 worth of damage to the bus garage, a considerable amount in 1943!

Strangely, this whirlwind was similar to an occurrence which had happened thirty years earlier, almost to the day, in October 1913. On that occasion the wind wrecked buildings at Gossages Works, took the roof off The Empire Rink and did extensive damage to the fabric of the building. The storm happened around 9.00 p.m. when the Empire Rink was full. The terrified skaters ran from the building as the gable end of the building buckled. There was also widespread damage in the Simms Cross area of the town, where roofs and chimneys were blown off houses. Although there were reports of people being swept off their feet, miraculously there did not appear to be any serious injuries.

For countless years the remarkable Mr. Gar Kiddie had dominated the entertainment and theatrical life of Widnes. He will forever be associated with the old Alex Theatre, which he ran with his brother, Jim Kiddie, who predeceased him. "Doctor" Gerrard, Jim Kiddie and Mr. Frank Bray had joined together in a business venture to build The Alex in 1887. The new theatre was built to replace Mr. Preston's old wooden building in Wellington Street, which had been known as "The New Alexandra". Frank Bray was the brother-in-law of the Kiddie's, so the ownership of the new theatre was a real "family concern." There was genuine sadness throughout the town when Gar Kiddie died at his home in Lacey Street in 1943. He had been a monumental figure in all aspects of theatrical and musical entertainment in the town for generations.

Of course, Gar Kiddie had relinquished control of The Alex long before his death in 1943. By 1940 The Alexandra Theatre was under the management of William Connah, but by December 1941 Basil Lamb Thompson had assumed the role of manager. The people of Widnes had supported this theatre for generations, and The Alex had treated them to some of the best entertainment of the day. Numerous "big stars" appeared here in the early days of their careers. However, some stars, who were already household names, came to town to entertain the theatregoers of Widnes. In 1944 the well-known radio star, Wilfred Pickles, appeared here. At that time, he was already famous as a radio star and had previously appeared in a number of British films. Two years after his visit to Widnes he launched the programme that he was most famously associated with, *"Have a Go"*, this ran on BBC radio from 1946 to 1967. Before the days when television was part of everyday life, the radio was the main form of entertainment in the home. Wilfred Pickles' popular money winning quiz was a favourite. The live audience and radio listeners liked his self-effacing style and his catch phrases such as –*"How are yer?"* *"Are yer courting?"* and *"Give him the money, Mabel"*. This was typical of the sort of simple entertainment that could be enjoyed by all the family during the long winter nights around the fireside.

Over a long period of time, the chemical industry had attracted countless workers into the town. Many of these were single men, so there were numerous lodging houses in the south end of the town near to industrial locations.   In 1939 the average cost for accommodation in one of these establishments was 8d a night or 4 shillings a week.   Owners of lodging houses had to be registered with the Council, and the premises needed to be inspected and approved by the Medical Officer of Health.   Lodging House owners faced strict regulations and they were required to keep an up to date register of all their lodgers. Owners who failed to comply with these regulations received heavy penalties.   In 1940 the following premises were approved, and their owners' given permission to operate as a "Lodging House Keepers":

Mr & Mrs Forde	*27 Caroline Street*
Mrs. M. Jones	*53 Ann Street*
Mrs. R.A. Geraghty	*1 Water Street*
Mrs. R.A. Geraghty	*2 Wellington Street*
Mr. A. Goulding	*1 Victoria Road*

"The Alien Registration" regulations were strictly administered during the war years. To many, in a town with an established and sizeable population from the Baltic States, most of who had by this time been in the town for many decades and had married and raised families here, these regulations might have seemed offensive.   The older members of these communities (those not born here) were required to report to the local Police Station at regular intervals. This seemed all the more grating when one recognises the fact that most of these families had sons or brothers away at war doing their "bit" for England, the country of their birth. Some other local residents, who were foreign nationals,

were registered as "enemy aliens" and their movements were strictly regulated. They were not permitted to travel more than five miles from their place of residence without a travel permit. They were also not allowed to leave their place of residence between the hours of 10.30 p.m. and 6.00 a.m. One man, a Finnish national, who lived in Ditton, was interned for breaking these regulations.

The ethnic origins of some of our townspeople were again highlighted in 1944 during an evening lecture at The Widnes Technical College. The theme of the lecture was *"The Baltic State of Lithuania"* and the speaker was Miss D. Alexander, an England based Lithuanian who had escaped from Lithuania just before the outbreak of war. The speaker told the audience about her country's long struggle for independence and its current struggle against German Nazism. The lecture was extremely well attended and many of the questions and comments from the floor were from local Lithuanians who spoke to Miss Alexander in their native language. One lady, from Brunner Road, expressed concern about her brother and other members of her family who were still in Lithuania. She said she had had no word from them since the country was occupied. Another Widnes lady was thrilled when Miss Alexander mentioned a famous Lithuanian sculptor, Peter Rinsha, who was living in South America. Peter Rinsha was this lady's uncle. Miss Alexander spoke frequently of the Lithuanian town of Kaunas. For many of our Widnes Lithuanians this evoked special and poignant memories, as Kaunas was their "home area".

The arrival of the American servicemen in town was greeted with mixed feelings. It seems that generally, adults and males disliked them, while children and girls loved them! One local man described them as *"jeep driving, gum chewing, and arrogant!"* Widnes was also "host" to prisoners of war. There were two camps in the town, one in Barrows Green and another in Heath Road. The prisoners, who initially were mainly Italians, were put to work in local industries and on farms. They were marched under supervision to their place of employment and marched back again at the end of their working day. Despite this, it seems that they had a fair amount of freedom and were even able to attend local dances. Some mixed reasonably well with the English workers, who admired their artistic abilities. One prisoner, who worked at Orr's Zinc White, was proficient in the art of copper etching. He made a number of beautiful religious engravings for his English workmates. Naturally, in view of the fact that they had relatives fighting in Italy, the majority of people did not feel very affable towards them. *The Liberal Club* (The Lib), in Widnes Road, was a popular venue for the Italian prisoners, and there were many angry letters to *The Widnes Weekly News*, from local men, complaining about local girls dancing with *"Wops"*. Such was the animosity that numerous fights broke out among the prisoners and local men, so the prisoners were eventually banned from attending. Later on, there were German prisoners in the town who were equally, if not more unwelcome. It appears that the German prisoners were kept under far stricter control than the Italians had been.

One of the most outstanding personalities to have lived in Widnes died in May 1944. For more than half a century Dan Garghan had championed the cause of the poor, the unemployed, and all who were socially disadvantaged in our communities. He came to Widnes when he was just four or five months old, and lived in the same house in Cromwell Street until his death over eighty years later. He was born in Oldbury, near Birmingham, and was brought to Widnes when his father came here to work at Muspratt's. His father later became a foreman in the salt-cake plant at the Golding-Davis Works. As a young man, Dan Garghan was to the fore in a campaign for "free speech" in Victoria Square that became a national as well as a local issue. At that time, he crossed swords with the authorities and elected to go to prison rather than pay the fine imposed upon him. His early working life, and his experiences in the local chemical industry, gave him the drive and ambition to try and bring about improvements in working conditions and pay. Dan Garghan's deepest concerns were always for the welfare of others. All of his adult life was spent strenuously fighting on behalf of those in need. To the West Bank community he was something akin to a God, and his death brought a distinct shroud of sadness to the community, especially around the Waterloo area where he spent most of his life.

In January 1945 Widnes was experiencing another marine tragedy. A sand hopper owned by William Cooper & Sons went down in the Mersey and a crew of five lost their lives. The vessel, loaded with sand, was on a journey from Garston Bank to Widnes, but it never reached its destination. The vessel completely disappeared and was not found until three days later when it was discovered totally submerged in a channel opposite Eastham. The crew of five were missing. At a later inquiry, it was suggested that an unexploded bomb, a relic of the 1941 blitz, which may have lain there for some time covered with silt, had sunk the hopper. All members of the crew were from West Bank. Some of the bodies were never recovered.

It came as some surprise to the residents of Widnes and Runcorn to learn, in the spring of 1945, that their respective councils had been having secret talks into the possibility of amalgamating the towns. Provisional proposals for the reform of Local Government were first made known in July 1942, but it was some three years later that the two councils began to make some movement in the matter. Captain Pilkington, then the local MP, did not think that the idea was practical but others were of the opinion that, in view of the proposals from the Government on the reorganisation of Local Governments, the amalgamation was bound to happen.

The main argument against the question of amalgamation appears to have been the River Mersey. Jack Carney, our frequent correspondent, could not take this argument seriously because, he said:

"With another bridge between Runcorn and Widnes the Mersey could be spanned and continuous transport made possible. Here is an opportunity for a progressive councillor to bring his proposals to the fore regarding a new bridge over the Mersey".

Public houses have always played a large part in the social life of this, and other industrial towns. In the early days, there was a pub on almost every street corner in the south end of Widnes. Drunkenness had once been a serious problem here. However, in 1944 it was reported by the local Police Superintendent that less than one person each week was convicted of drunkenness during that year. Despite this, some people were critical about the provision of *"singing-rooms"* in pubs, claiming that they were encouraging people to become drunkards. These critics suggested that if people wanted to sing they should attend good musical concerts. One correspondent in response to this criticism said:

Those who lecture the men and women of Widnes live in comfortable homes with radios, pianos and other forms of entertainment. Each year they take a holiday in the place they select. What of the men and women who sing? Have you visited their homes and sat beside their fireplaces with the week's washing dripping on you? Have you seen children forced to stand up because there are not enough chairs for all? I know mothers in Widnes even at this late day and age, who have never been inside a cinema. These women spend most of their waking hours in the kitchen, either cooking or sweating over a boiler. Before the next licensing sessions come round, I hope the authorities will learn something of the social side of Widnes. When the homes in the Waterloo ward rank in beauty with some of the new public-houses in Widnes then we shall have in some way prepared the ground for a change in the social tastes of men and women. How many critics of the poor, if they were compelled to live in those derelict houses of Waterloo ward could show a social record of less than one drunk each week?

On 14th August 1945 the war finally ended when Japan accepted the terms set out by the Allies for ending hostilities. The surrender of Japan came less than a week after American planes had dropped atomic bombs on Hiroshima and Nagasaki. The news that the war was finally over was a cause for great celebration throughout the country. The residents of Merseyside celebrated the return of peace to the world in their own inimitable style. Searchlights swept the sky, huge bonfires were lit and bells and bands sounded throughout Widnes. Albright & Wilson Ltd. placed a 40 gallon drum, half full with phosphorus, on top of their number one tower. This beacon burned for days.

At midnight, on the 14th, a statement by the Prime Minister was broadcast on the BBC. Within minutes of the broadcast the bells of St. Paul's Church were ringing out. Eric Devlin, the bellringer, hurried from his home in Fairfield Road as soon as he heard the news. People flooded into the streets and makeshift bands of whistles, harmonicas and melodeons were to be heard everywhere. Two bonfires had been started in no time, one on spare land in Lugsdale Road and another in Clarke Gardens. In the Waterloo area, the people of Milton Street quickly lit their bonfire on a nearby field. In Simms Cross, in addition to the bonfires, hundreds of people assembled at Gerrard Street corner. Music was plentiful, so they danced and sang till the early hours of the morning. Nearly every area of the Borough had a bonfire blazing away within a short time. Pianos were dragged out of houses into some of the streets to accompany the impromptu singing and dancing. The sudden pulling back of curtains and blinds in lighted houses seemed almost like flashes of lightening in the night sky, as people were unused to seeing so much light after six years of blackout. Within a few days the street lighting returned to normal and the townspeople were able once again to travel safely through the streets of Widnes at night. The word "safely" is used only in the context of being able to see traffic and other pedestrians, as there were no real fears of muggings in those days!

The celebrations continued for almost a month. Street parties were held throughout the town and children were given a memorable time. Dance bands enlivened the evenings in Victoria Park and the Promenade Gardens in West Bank. *The Widnes Subscription Band* and *Nazareth House Band* opened their programmes with renditions of *"Happy Days are here again!"* After the initial euphoria, people began to settle back into some form of normality. However, it was only when the cinema going public watched *"Pathe Newsreels"* that the full horrors of war began to unfold. The newsreels showed for the first time the shocking scenes from inside the "Concentration Camps". Shock, disbelief, and revulsion were felt, as emaciated creatures in ragged clothing were shown staring out from the screen. Some people were unable to watch and had to leave the cinema; those who stayed were haunted by the awful graphic evidence of these systematic crimes against humanity.

Some of the popular spectator sports were suspended during the war years. *Widnes Football Club* closed for the duration, although some of its players made guest appearances for other teams, notably Halifax, where the triumvirate of Tommy Shannon, Tommy McCue and Harry Millington all made "guest" appearances. In fact, Tommy McCue actually won a Yorkshire Cup Final medal during this period[135]. After the war, Naughton Park re-opened at the end of August 1945 for a Widnes Trial Match. Some of the players were only home on leave, or had other commitments which prevented them from making themselves permanently available, so the Widnes committee were envisaging some real problems in fielding a team. *Widnes Cricket Club* had continued to play during wartime, despite disruptions due to players being absent and the shortage of leather cricket balls. Many of their wartime matches were for charity, but with the return of

---

[135] Information kindly supplied by Tom Fleet *(from his unpublished history of the Club).*

players in 1945 things were getting back to normal and the first team won the championship that season.

Other things were also returning to normal. The ending of "the blackout" meant that the town was once more illuminated, and the population were able to dispense with the use of torches when they went out for the evening. Cinema foyers and dancehall entrances were once again bright and welcoming. Other traditions like the Sunday evening *"monkey run"* were also re-instated. I am informed[136] that the Widnes *"monkey run"* stretched from Peelhouse Lane to Hutchinson Street, or along the Cut Bank. Most northern towns had a similar tradition known by other names. Some called it a *"monkey parade"*. This old custom involved young men and women, dressed in their best clothes, parading up and down the town with their friends on a Sunday evening.

By late September, people were raising concerns about the demobilisation process. The war had been over for some weeks and families were anxious to see their loved ones back home now that the war had ended. Six years was a long time to be away, and some of the Widnes boys who had been just emerging into manhood when they left were now grown men. Parents were anxiously waiting for their sons to come home. There were many complaints about "red tape" holding up demobilisation. However, with hindsight, it is easy to see that if the servicemen were released en masse it would have meant a sudden an unsustainable influx into the labour market. The Americans had been demobilised in large numbers as soon as the war ended, but by the end of the year there were almost ten million unemployed workers in the United States.

In October, the first repatriated prisoners of war arrived home in Widnes. Most of them were unwilling to talk of their experiences. However, some told horrific stories of their time in

---

[136] Re: Mr. J.C. Lewis

prison camps, especially the camp at *Songkurai,* in Siam (Thailand), where only about 250 prisoners of the 1680 who were imprisoned there survived. To reach the camp, the prisoners were forced to march for 17 weary nights through the sweltering jungles of Siam. At the camp, they were put to work piling earth and stones onto railway embankments. Each day they laboured, from 5 o'clock in the morning till 9 o'clock at night, before returning to their accommodation which consisted of bamboo huts without roofs. They were exhausted and starved. There were several cholera epidemics and many men died, those that survived became emaciated skeletons. However, some of the returning prisoners said that the mental tortures were worse than the physical suffering. They were forced to live without the common decencies of life, such as washing and wearing clothes. Furthermore, thousands of letters from those at home in Widnes were withheld from them. It seems incredible now, when we are all aware of the ongoing effects of post-traumatic stress, that these men were ever able to resume a normal life again.

The year 1945 saw the end of the war and the coming of peace. It also saw a surprise election of a new Socialist Government. Many had thought the electorate would support Winston Churchill, if only for the great part he played in leading the country through the war.   In Widnes, political changes were also afoot.   The Labour Party gained the seat in Widnes, and Commander Christopher Shawcross replaced Captain Richard Pilkington as our Member of Parliament.   Richard Pilkington had represented the Widnes Division for ten years and his defeat came as a surprise.

Our new representative, Christopher Shawcross, had an interesting pedigree. He was the great nephew of John Bright, the legendary radical leader, famed as a parliamentarian and orator. He was also the brother of Hartley Shawcross, who was elected to represent our neighbouring town, St. Helens, in that same election. In fact, the two brothers had fought a colourful joint campaign in the area, and both were elected with healthy majorities. Both Shawcross brothers were barristers, although Hartley was the more famous, having appeared in a number of high profile cases including the trials of John George Haigh, the acid bath murderer, and Klaus Fuchs, the atom bomb spy. On his election to Parliament, Hartley Shawcross was immediately offered the position of Attorney General in the new Labour Government. In this role, he led the British prosecution at the Nuremberg trials. In September 1945, he also prosecuted William Joyce, the infamous *"Lord Haw-Haw"*, for treason. Joyce was found guilty and executed.

In Widnes, later that year, the local elections caused a considerable stir of excitement. These elections were unusual in that for the first time in the history of the Borough, municipal elections were taking place in all seven wards. Previously, only in October 1892, in the first elections under the Charter of Incorporation, had every ward had been fought at once. However, in that year there were only six wards, as Ditton did not come into the electoral equation until 1920. Our new MP, Commander Shawcross, visited the town prior to the election to drum up support for the Labour candidates. At a Sunday night meeting near the market in Alforde Street he told the assembled crowd:

"I would like to remind you that Widnes as a town has got a very bad name among all those who have ever been in it or even heard about it, or smelt it – because believe me it stinks. It does not stink now perhaps as strongly in the physical sense as it did not so very long ago, but it still stinks metaphorically speaking by reason of the appalling conditions of housing and by the arrangements in which you have to live".

Continuing, he alluded to some of Labour's opponents in the forthcoming election and to Dr. J.P. Baxter in particular, who was a Conservative candidate, he said:

"Dr. Baxter had something to do with the atomic bomb. He did not suppose Dr. Baxter had ever seen the result of his work in those cities on which that bomb was used in Japan, but he had only to walk down the streets in Widnes to see all around him destruction and devastation and misery which his party had produced and maintained over the years".

He followed this up with numerous charges against local employers. He concluded his speech by reminding the audience:

"That there was one thing for which Widnes was famed throughout the United Kingdom and indeed in many distant places in the world, and that was its football team. That is the one good thing which has been produced by the ordinary people of Widnes, in spite of the dreadful conditions in which many of them have been born and reared".

On the day of the election a dense fog shrouded the town and, apart from a few early morning workers, polling was slow. However, in the afternoon a steady flow of voters began to appear. The West Bank and Waterloo area appeared to be the busiest. One of the unusual features of this election was the large number of cars being provided for Labour voters, which were for the first time in excess of those for Conservatives. That night when the results were declared, there were some surprising gains and defeats. Labour gained three more seats but the Mayor-elect was defeated in his "home" ward of Victoria. In Waterloo, the Independent Labour candidate, 22 year old Jack Ashley, topped the poll beating the official Labour candidate who came in second.

Perhaps it is not surprising that this young man went on to greater things. The signs were there even then. Despite his youth, he had the heart of a lion. The abysmal conditions which were prevalent in the Waterloo ward at that time had been accepted with a certain degree of resignation by the inhabitants. Few people were able or courageous enough to deal with "figures of authority" and so an atmosphere of passive acceptance existed. Landlords ignored complaints, refused to repair or maintain houses, and yet continued to collect extortionate rents for properties which were, in some cases, unfit for human habitation. Growing up in these conditions, young Jack Ashley recognised the need for change. Once he had established that it was the right of a tenant to have a rent reduction for any property in bad repair, he went to the Town Hall and collected dozens of "rent reduction forms". Then, he issued a form to every house in the neighbourhood. From then on, people started coming to him for advice if they had problems. It was no surprise that he topped the poll at his first ever election!

Prior to that election, Jack Ashley had become involved in trade unionism. At that time, relations between workers and management in many factories were not good. Some factories were run by autocratic managers who had little or no concern for the welfare of their workers. Conditions and processes in some of these factories were outdated and there was scant regard for safety. Several companies discouraged union activity, or else refused to recognise some trade unions. At the age of just 20 years, Jack Ashley organised a union at Thomas Bolton & Sons and strenuously fought for its recognition. Although very young, he recognised that there should be reciprocal responsibilities between worker and employer, to set out the jobs which the workforce were to fulfil, and the services which the management were to provide. As a union representative, he successfully initiated a new form of relationship and moral framework that was equally beneficial to the workers and the management.

In October 1946 Jack Ashley was awarded a scholarship at Ruskin College Oxford. Two years later, he won a 2 year extra-mural scholarship to Cambridge where he became The President of *The Cambridge Union*. He returned to Widnes in 1951 with an Oxford diploma and a Cambridge degree. Afterwards he joined the BBC working as the Producer of high profile programmes such as *Panorama, Monitor* and *Gallery*.[137] His acute social conscience,

---

[137] *Journey into Silence* – Jack Ashley M.P. (Bodley Head Ltd., London 1973)

and sense of fair play and justice, meant that Parliament was a natural draw to him. Despite his own adversities, over the years he has worked tirelessly for the disabled and disadvantaged. Many of his *Parliamentary Bills* have led to the provision of numerous "disabled facilities" which we all so easily take for granted today. Today, Jack Ashley sits on the benches of *The House of Lords*, as Lord Ashley of Stoke, Companion of Honour. Despite his elevation to the peerage, this remarkable son of Waterloo has never forgotten or ceased to be proud of where he came from.

Towards the end of this decade, Widnes and the rest of the country were to see great changes in the way poverty was tackled. *The Welfare State* was founded in 1948. Although this was built on many services that were already in place prior to the war, it was seen as a sweeping departure from *"The Poor Law System"* that had come before it. The new Welfare State promised social protection for everyone, as a right of citizenship. It would not be just for poor people but for everyone. In a town like Widnes, where high unemployment had gone hand in hand with bad housing and poverty, the new Welfare State heralded a new dawn for our population. Although this system promised much, as we now know, over the years the scheme was found to have serious inadequacies. It did not respond to many of the needs it was supposed to deal with. It failed to take into account things like disability, long-term unemployment, and divorce. Nevertheless, at the end of the 1940s the population of Widnes were able to benefit from many of the new and improved welfare benefits that *The Beveridge Report* had helped to bring about.

Epilogue

While researching for this book I was struck by the fact that different parts of our society seemed to have had different kinds of experiences and aspirations. The value of oral history in drawing these threads together into a general, though admittedly incomplete, picture has been inestimable. I am extremely grateful to the many people who shared their memories with me

Both wars raised expectations and lifted the horizons of the working class people who made up the greater section of our local population. In the aftermath of the first war, protest and complaint seemed to be the main theme of peoples' lives. But, from these statements of protest, we can gain an insight into what people feared. The struggle to create a decent standard of living for themselves and their families lay at the very heart of this protest. Unemployment, bad housing, poverty and malnutrition were no strangers to homes in many parts of our town.

However, we should not entirely view the two decades between the end of the wars as wasted years of gloom and doom. During that period many genuine achievements occurred both nationally and locally. Widnes made considerable advancement in housing and education. It was only the onset of the second war that halted progress for six years. However, despite the improvements made prior to the war, everyone knew that much more needed to be done, especially with regard to slum clearance.

It is now over sixty years since the end of the Second World War. Death has removed thousands of pre-war memories and birth has replaced them with others whose adult experiences will be of the 21st century.   The slums of Waterloo have long since vanished, and new private housing estates have been developed on many of the green fields that once surrounded the town. Most of the old established industries have closed their doors and been replaced by new service industries and small businesses.   It would seem that industrially, socially, and politically, Widnes of the inter-war years is another land.

Notes

Downer Fyldes

William Fyldes, known as *"Downer"*, was a notable Widnes character.   He met his death tragically in the Mersey, off Hale Head, on 16th February 1916.   He and another man, Thomas McDermott, of Pear Street, were returning to Widnes on board *"The Weaver"* a "sand flat" belonging to William Cooper & Sons, when it capsized during a gale.   *"Downer"* was rescued by a tug,*"The Aviator"*,captained by Mr. William Bushell of Runcorn. Alas, *"Downer"* was dead before they reached shore and his body was brought to West Bank.

"Downer" was something of a local celebrity and a well-loved character in West Bank.   He was known for his outrageous clothing. One day it might be a uniform, another it might be a shooting suit or top hat, tailcoat, and gloves.   It is said that he possessed a ready wit and would entertain passers-by with broad puns and amusing repartee.

Two years before his death, he was in Prescot Infirmary suffering from a serious illness. During this time, a rumour that he was dead circulated throughout the town and people were mourning his loss. When he heard of this he sent a message to the local community saying: *"Like Mark Twain, rumours of my death have been greatly exaggerated"*.

Preston's Theatre

The actor, J. B. Preston, arrived in Widnes in 1870 and immediately recognised that there was a need for a theatre in the town. He had a large wooden building erected adjacent to the Wellington Hotel in Wellington Street, where he put on a varied entertainment programme. A resident company of actors, actresses and comics, performed Shakespearean plays and Victorian melodramas. From time to time, travelling players were engaged for special appearances. Among those who appeared at this theatre was the legendary Dan Leno.

The theatre was well patronised. On special nights the audience included the leading shopkeepers, publicans, managers and clerks of the town. These reasonably affluent people would occupy the front seats and orchestra stalls. The working-class had to be content with the gallery.

When J. B. Preston retired, the building was taken over by Mr. George Mellon, who was well known as a sporting promoter. George Mellon put up the stake money of £50 for the famous "1 mile running race" between the Widnesian, J. Concannon, and Glaswegian, J. McGowan. The race took place at the old "*Star Inn Ground*" in St. Helens. The Widnes man was the winner.

Marine disasters

There is an interesting Widnes connection with another famous maritime disaster. One of the survivors of *The Tayleur,* which was wrecked in fog off the Irish coast in 1854, was a Widnes man. In that disaster, 380 people were drowned. Althanasius Cowley, the son of Mr. James Cowley who was at that time the owner of Widnes House, was one of the survivors. Among the passengers who perished were the wife and daughter of Patrick Hayes who had owned an oil works in Lugsdale.

Patrick Hayes was already operating his *"Oil Works"* in Widnes prior to the arrival of John Hutchinson. He had a row of 24 cottages built in Dog Lane (Milton Road) for his workmen. He also had a splendid house built for himself in Highfield Road. Later, this house, Highfield House, was to become the home of John McClellan and in later years became Widnes Maternity Home. A report on the original interior of this house claimed that there was an ornamental relief in the tiled flooring. This was said to include the name of the original owner, Patrick Hayes.

Some time prior to 1854 Patrick Hayes left Widnes for Australia to establish a business there, leaving his wife and daughter in Widnes until he had made suitable provisions for their arrival. When the time was right for them to follow him, they embarked for the long voyage on *The Tayleur*. Shortly after leaving Liverpool the ship was wrecked off Lambay Island. Mrs. Hayes and her daughter were among those who perished. Incidentally, the cottages built for Mr. Hayes' workers survived until 1939 when they were demolished, having been described at that time as *"a blot on the landscape"*.

Mr. J.W. Barkla (Furniture Store)

When excavations were done for the Manchester Ship Canal, which was opened in 1894, a number of "centuries old" oak trees were removed. These trees were purchased by a firm of cabinet makers from Warrington who used the oak to construct furniture. One of the apprentices who worked on this old oak was a young man called J.W. Barkla from Widnes. In later years this young craftsman opened his own business in Victoria Road where he sold quality items of furniture, some of which was handmade.

John Laveric

John Laveric was a larger than life character. He was a familiar figure with his long white hair and beard, and was usually seen on horseback riding through the town. In later life he was known mainly for his eccentricity, but in his youth he was a well-known and popular local sportsman. In view of his background, it is not surprising that he was a proficient swimmer and boxer. His father, also John Laveric, who was a native of Reading in Berkshire, was one of the most prominent swimmers of his day. John Laveric senior, played polo for *The Widnes Swimming Club* and was responsible for the Widnes club winning many prizes. As a committee member of *The Widnes Swimming Club*, he promoted and trained most of the outstanding young local swimmers of those times.

John Laveric (Junior) died in 1978 aged 68 years. In his youth he was described as *"the best dressed man in Widnes"*. He drove a Rolls Royce and was a very successful businessman and entrepreneur. However, in his latter years he led an ascetic life, without the modern conveniences most of us find necessary for our day to day comfort. He drank water, and ate only fresh vegetables because the thought of animals being slaughtered upset him. He always believed that no one would do him harm, because he would not harm anybody. He spent most of his days at The Black Cat Billiard Hall (which he then owned), chopping up wood which he delivered free of charge to needy pensioners, for fuel.

He was well known for his personal kindness and charitable deeds, all of which were done unselfishly and without publicity. During his lifetime he gave away a fortune to charity. He was the last owner of Ditchfield Hall. When he sold this estate he gave the entire proceeds to charity, mainly to Cancer Research. This donation led to a much publicised and very bitter dispute with the Inland Revenue. Despite his naturally quiet nature, such was his frustration with the Tax Office that he smashed numerous windows at their premises in Broseley House. This incident was witnessed by a crowd of onlookers who cheered and applauded in support. However, John soon found himself before the magistrates and was ordered to pay for the damage.

It would be possible for me to write extensively about John Laveric, but I will let the formal words of his "Will" speak for themselves: *"This is the Last Will and Testament of John Laveric, of Hanging Birches Farm, Norlands Lane, Widnes, in the County of Lancaster, Gentleman"*. The title "Gentleman" was true in every sense.

James Valentine

The first aeroplane to land in Merseyside was piloted by James Valentine and came down in a field near to The Ball O'Ditton in 1911. The pilot was taking part in air-race sponsored by *The Daily Mail*, to promote the development of aviation in Britain. A £10,000 prize was offered to the winner. The race was really a time trial, with the plane completing the circuit in the fastest time declared the winner. It has been claimed that this race was the inspiration for the 1960s film *"Those Magnificent Men in their Flying Machines"*.

The race started at Brooklands, in Surrey, on 22nd July 1911. Competitors were required to fly to Edinburgh before returning to Brooklands, via Exeter and Brighton. Of the 17 participants, 9 were British. There were to be 11 compulsory stops for the pilots, who navigated using a strip map that was wound around two drums in the cockpit. Very soon, competitors started to drop out because of mechanical problems – or because they got lost!

James Valentine was piloting a French built *Depurdussin* monoplane when he made a forced landing in farmland belonging to Mr. Kelly of Upper House. Apart from the problem that had caused him to make a landing at Widnes, his machine received a further mishap when a reaper who was cutting corn in the field accidentally ventured too near the plane and pierced the tyres with his scythe. Whilst he awaited the arrival of his French mechanic, Mr. Boisselet, who was travelling by motorcar from Manchester, the aviator was taken to Upper House where he enjoyed the hospitality of Mr. Kelly. It is said that he was very interested in the history of Upper House and enthusiastically admired its handsome oak staircase and decorated ceilings. He said that when he was next in South Lancashire he would like to bring an architect friend to look at the house.

Shortly after his mechanic arrived, James Valentine left Widnes by car to spend the night with his brother at Alderley Edge. During the night hundreds of curious Widnesians made their way to the field to see this strange machine. Valentine returned at 10.00 a.m. the following morning, and as he donned his overalls and headgear there were cheers from the crowds of onlookers who were waiting to give him an enthusiastic send-off.

The race was won by Lieutenant Conneau who was flying under the name "Beaumont" with a flying time of 22hours and 29minutes. Emile Vedrines came in second and James Valentine took third place.

Old Appleton

Whilst Emma Swain had recorded her recollections of the area around Hough Green, Ditton, and Cronton, there are also interesting recollections of Appleton by an old "Appletonian" which I feel should be recorded here. During the 1930s, an elderly man wrote of his memories of Appleton during the 1870s. I quote an extract below:

In those days there stood at the top of the street two houses. In one of these houses, groceries were sold, though nothing was displayed in the window to show that it was a shop. In the yard behind the house was an interesting object – a stone capped draw well, the bucket raised and lowered by a handle at the side. From this well, the villagers got their supplies of drinking water. For other purposes, they relied on supplies of rainwater collected in rain-tubs standing by the walls of the cottages.

At the back of many of the houses in Appleton Village and in Appleton Lane (now Birchfield Road), there were workshops in which men were employed in making tools used by the watchmakers, and in making different parts of watches, these watches were put together by "the movement makers". In one of these shops, a clever craftsman, with a small but wonderful machine called a "wheel cutting engine" cut the teeth in the watch wheels. He also cleaned and repaired all the watches and clocks in the district.

Another important industry was wire drawing. The wire drawn was pinion wire, the grooved wire used for the pinions of clocks and watches. In those days, no steam or electricity was used for drawing the grooved wire. This was accomplished by means of large wheels with handles on the rims resembling the steering wheels of ships. These wheels were pulled around by the "wire drawers" who found it no easy task. After this, the softened wire was hardened and packed into strong wooden boxes made by the wheelwright in his shop on the other side of the street. Most of the wire was sent to Coventry, the great watch-making centre, or to Switzerland.

Many men also found employment in the wide, deep, stone quarry that occupied a considerable area at the far end of the village. A blacksmith was also engaged in the quarry smithy, sharpening and repairing the tools and implements of the quarry men.

Let me turn to another industry. Through an opening in the street called "The Weint" was the village smithy, where children coming home from school looked in at the open door. They loved to see the flaming forge, and hear the bellows roar.   Here the horseshoes were fashioned and horses shod.   The blacksmith also made the iron parts for the carts made by the wheelwright in his shop on the opposite side of the street.

On the brow in front of this shop lay piles of tree trunks waiting to be sawn into planks and beams in the deep sawpit by the side of the shop.   It was a pleasing sight to see the wheelwright at work making the parts for carts, wheelbarrows and ladders and to see them when finished, standing on the brow in front of the shop, gaily painted, waiting for the owners names to be inscribed on them.

Another industry carried on – not exactly in the village, but only a short distance away, was the brewing of old English ale at Widnes House.

No threshing mills then!   The farmer with his jointed flail threshed out the corn from the sheaves lying on the floor of his barn.   It was then taken to be ground at the mills of Bold[1], Ditton or Woolton.   These were windmills.   A goodly number of men found work on the farmland belonging to Appleton House, St. Bede's Rectory and the Leigh Estate.

The shoemaker and the tailor, who plied their trade in shops by their home must not be forgotten, nor the postman who began his journey at Hale, bringing his bag of letters to the Appleton Post Office to be called for by The Royal Mail gig with the Widnes letters, which were taken on to the Warrington head office.

Though the village was small, the variety of industries carried on in it made it a place of note in those days.

Other documented memories of old Appleton came from Miss Foster, a retired schoolteacher, who was born in Appleton in 1852. She reminisced as she approached her 90th birthday:

---

[1] This mill was located in Mill Lane, Bold Heath.

She and her sister had attended Appleton School where two nuns taught them. Miss Foster was a promising scholar and on May 3rd 1866, began a five-year apprenticeship as a pupil teacher. On February 2nd 1872, she entered Mount Pleasant Training College, where in December 1873 she passed her exams with distinction. On her return home, she travelled for the first time on the railway, which had just been completed to Widnes. After a few years at a school in Warrington, she returned to St. Bede's school in Appleton, where she remained until her retirement in 1917.

At this time, Miss Foster still lived in the house she was born in, at 103 Birchfield Road. She recalled the Appleton of her childhood, which nestled at the top of "the hill" in a cluster of tiny cottages; the busy workshops; the beautiful views across the fields and the personalities of the community. Like the previous writer, she remembered the postman, who walked from Hale, sounding his horn to announce his arrival, and the people running out of the cottages to receive their letters.

Bibliography and Sources

Modern Britain – T.K. Derry and T.L. Jarman
(John Murray 1979)

A Social History of England – Asa Briggs
(Penguin Books 1987)

A Social History of England – Francois Bedarida
(Methuen & Co. 1979)

English History 1914-1945 –A.J.P. Taylor
(Oxford University Press 1965)

Industrialisation and Society – Eric Hopkins
(Routledge, London 2000)

On History – Eric Hobsbawn
(Abacus– 1997)

Contemporary Britain 1914-1979 - Robert Pearce
(Longman Advanced History)

Post Victorian Britain 1902-1951 – L.C.B. Seaman
(Methuan 1970)

The People's War – Britain 1939-1945 – A.Calder
(Cape 1969)

Ramsey MacDonald – D. Marquand
(Cape 1977)

The First Industrial Society – Chris Aspin
(Carnegie Publishing 1995)

The Chemical Industry 1900-1930 – L.F. Haber
(Oxford, Clarendon 1971)

Trends in British Society since 1900 – A.H. Halsey
(Macmillan 1972)

Change in British Society – A.H. Halsey
(Oxford University Press 1983)

The Coming of the Welfare State – M. Bruce
(Batsford, 1968)

Parliamentary Reform 1785-1928 - Sean Lang
(Routledge 1999)

Educational Reform 1900-1950 – M.J. Hoskins
(Oxford, Thesis 1976)

The Evolution of the British Welfare State – Derek Fraser
(Macmillan 1984)

Housing and the State 1919-1944 – M. Bowley
(Allen & Unwin 1945)

The Home Front – E. Sylvia Pankhurst
(The Cresset Library 1987)

British Population in the 20th Century – N.L. Tranter
(MacMillan Press 1996)

Trends in Leisure 1919-1939 - A. Howkins & J. Lowerson
(Sports Council & Social Science Research Council 1979)

Britain 1900-1945 - Roy Stapley
(Hodder & Stoughton 1992)

Homes fit for Heroes – Mark Swenarton
(Heinemann 1981)

Poverty and Progress – B.S. Rowntree
(Longman Green 1941)

The White Slaves of England – Robert Sherard
(Pearson's Magazine, London 1896)

The General Strike – Julian Symons
(Cresset Press 1957)

King George V – Harold Nicholson
(Constable 1952)

Twenty Centuries of British History – Hugh Bodey
David & Charles, London 1975)

The Incredible Mrs. Van der Elst – Charles Nielson Gattey
(Leslie Frewin, London 1972)

Into the Crucible – Jean M. Morris
(Countyvise 2005)

Journey into Silence – Jack Ashley M.P.
(Bodley Head, London 1973)

The History of the Chemical Industry in Widnes
 D.W.F. Hardie   (Imperial Chemical Industries 1950)

A History of Widnes – George E. Diggle
(Corporation of Widnes. 1961)

Publications & Journals.

Widnes Weekly News
Liverpool Daily Post
Liverpool Echo
The Liverpolitan
St. Helens Reporter
Widnes Town Council Minutes of proceedings
Widnes Medical Officer of Health – Annual Reports
Widnes Education Committee - Minutes
Lancashire and Cheshire Historical Society
Chemical Industry Journal
Imperial Chemical Industry – Company Journals
Trades Union Congress Archives
Hansard
Salvation Army Records
St. Marie's Parish Records

Source Locations

The National Archives, Kew, Richmond, Surrey.
Merseyside Public Record Office, Liverpool
Lancashire Public Record Office, Preston
Cheshire Public Record Office, Chester
Manchester Central Record Office
National Archives, Dublin
National Library, Dublin
Liverpool University Library
Press Association Library
Widnes Public Library
Liverpool Central Library
Warrington Public Library
St. Helens Central Library
Catalyst Museum, Widnes

Index

W

Wade Deacon Grammar School ·
164, 261
Wage reductions · 47
Walker, Col.Hall · 13, 71
War Brides · 241
War Memorial · 15, 19, 21, 209,
228
Warrington Road School · 79, 80,
81, 168, 237, 259, 264
Waterloo · 47, 93, 110, 111, 119,
133, 136, 145, 147, 148, 149,
155, 156, 158, 161, 169, 170,
174, 180, 181, 194, 203, 204,
208, 237, 251, 252, 254, 255,
256, 278, 279, 280, 285, 287,
289
Waterloo Social Club · 149, 180
Welsh · 87, 88, 89, 140, 184, 209,
243, 269, 273
Wesleyan Chapel in Moss Bank ·
112
West Bank · 37, 38, 41, 56, 72, 75,
81, 87, 89, 101, 102, 108, 114,
119, 133, 136, 147, 161, 169,
170, 176, 180, 190, 191, 210,
214, 248, 259, 260, 261, 269,
278, 281, 285, 290

Whirlwind · 15, 272, 273
Whiston Institute · 42, 117, 126,
153
Whitty, Rev. Fr. · 252, 253, 254
Widnes Battery · 15, 16
Widnes Coal Field · 40
Widnes Cricket Club · 69, 95,
187, 188, 281
Widnes Extension Bill · 83, 90
Widnes Football Club · 69, 184,
281
Widnes Foundry · 28, 31, 60, 137,
244, 246, 266
Widnes Free Church · 55
Widnes House · 70, 291, 297
Widnes Labour Exchange · 40,
114
Widnes Medical Relief and
Distress Fund · 47
Widnes Queens Nurses
Association · 24
Widnes Rugby Club · 95
Widnes Soap Company Ltd · 133
Widnes Yacht Club · 92
Wilkinson · 29, 90, 110, 124, 181,
212, 232, 235
Windermere Avenue · 237
Wireless · 28, 29, 50, 51, 104, 105,
192, 240, 259